"The Catholic sacrament of confirmatio[n]
navigate. In order to find their way thr[ough, they can]
receive help from studies of its origin, its historical development, and
sacramental theology. Denysenko proves his adroitness with each of
these, but the uniqueness of this book comes from him offering a different,
and surprisingly fruitful, source of help: Orthodox Christianity. He
offers Catholics a primer on Byzantine chrismation, in order to set up a
conversation between East and West. First, he gleans a liturgical theology
from the rite's *lex orandi*, including its use for the reception of converts.
Then he presents the perspective of numerous Orthodox theologians. And
all this he can then bring to the table for an honest dialogue, since he is
also well-versed in contemporary Catholic discussion about confirmation.
The result is what he calls 'a gift exchange,' pointing out riches the East
and West can share with each other. Being happily grounded in his own
Orthodox tradition, yet ecumenically hospitable, he gives us a work
that will cross-fertilize the Catholic understanding of confirmation and
Orthodox understanding of chrismation. The superb result is a study that
bridges the academic and the pastoral so as to regenerate our appreciation
of this venerable liturgical celebration."

—David W. Fagerberg
University of Notre Dame

"Few fields of theology are as confusing as that of the sacrament of
confirmation. Many of those who grasp the complexities of the Roman
Rite do not fully appreciate the practices of Eastern Rites. When Nicholas
Denysenko takes you on a careful, clear, and informed tour of Orthodox
chrismation, he opens doors that you probably didn't even know were
there. *Chrismation: A Primer for Catholics* makes a much-needed and
invaluable contribution to a hitherto neglected area in the study of
confirmation. Denysenko's creative conclusions will enlighten ministers,
catechists, and the faithful of churches East and West."

—Paul Turner
Pastor, St. Anthony Parish, Kansas City, Missouri
Facilitator, International Commission on English
in the Liturgy

"In this book on chrismation, Denysenko exemplifies the best in ecumenical liturgical scholarship. Drawing on both Eastern and Western sources, ancient and modern, he uncovers for the reader the richness and diversity of both traditions. Catholics and Orthodox alike will benefit from reading this work."

—Paul Meyendorff
The Alexander Schmemann Professor
  of Liturgical Theology
St. Vladimir's Orthodox Theological Seminary

Nicholas E. Denysenko

Chrismation

A Primer for Catholics

A PUEBLO BOOK

Liturgical Press   Collegeville, Minnesota
www.litpress.org

A Pueblo Book published by Liturgical Press

Excerpts from the English translation of *Rite of Confirmation (Second Edition)* © 1975, International Commission on English in the Liturgy Corporation (ICEL); excerpts from the English translation of *Rites of Ordination of a Bishop, of Priests, and of Deacons* © 2000, 2002, ICEL. All rights reserved.

Excerpts from Nicholas Cabasilas, *The Life in Christ*, translated by Carmino J. deCatanzaro, introduction by Boris Bobrinskoy (Crestwood, NY: St. Vladimir's Seminary Press, 1974). Used by permission.

Excerpts from *The Great Book of Needs*, expanded and supplemented, vol. 1: *The Holy Mysteries*, trans. St. Tikhon's Monastery (South Canaan, PA: St. Tikhon's Seminary Press, 1998), 62–95. Used by permission.

Excerpts from documents of the Second Vatican Council are taken from the Vatican website, www.vatican.va.

Scripture texts in this work are taken from the *New Revised Standard Version Bible* © 1989, Division of Christian Education of the National Council of the Churches of Christ in the United States of America. Used by permission. All rights reserved.

© 2014 by Order of Saint Benedict, Collegeville, Minnesota. All rights reserved. No part of this book may be reproduced in any form, by print, microfilm, microfiche, mechanical recording, photocopying, translation, or by any other means, known or yet unknown, for any purpose except brief quotations in reviews, without the previous written permission of Liturgical Press, Saint John's Abbey, PO Box 7500, Collegeville, Minnesota 56321-7500. Printed in the United States of America.

1 2 3 4 5 6 7 8 9

Library of Congress Cataloging-in-Publication Data

Denysenko, Nicholas E.
    Chrismation : a primer for Catholics / Nicholas E. Denysenko.
      pages cm
    "A Pueblo book."
    Includes bibliographical references and index.
    ISBN 978-0-8146-6273-1 — ISBN 978-0-8146-6298-4 (ebook)
    1. Chrismation. I. Title.

BX378.C47D46 2014
265'.2—dc23   2014001603

To Michael Plekon,
friend and mentor,
for steadfast encouragement

Contents

List of Tables and Figures   ix

Preface   xi

Acknowledgments   xiii

List of Abbreviations   xv

Introduction   xvii

Chapter 1: Chrismation in the Byzantine Rites of Initiation   1

Chapter 2: Chrismation and the Reception of Converts   40

Chapter 3: Orthodox Theologians on Chrismation   90

Chapter 4: Chrismation and Catholic Confirmation   140

Conclusion   189

Index   203

Tables and Figures

Table 1.1: Epicleses in BAR: Consecration of Chrism   11

Table 1.2: Epicletic Blessings in the Consecration of Chrism   13

Table 1.3: The Order of Baptism in BAR nos. 113–26   16

Table 1.4: Variant Formulas of Anointing with Chrism   25

Table 1.5: Postbaptismal Chrism Anointing Formulas   26

Table 1.6: Comparison of Chrismation Blessings between Prayer and Anointing Formulas   29

Table 1.7: Comparison of Blessings: Consecration of Chrism and Anointing with Chrism   31

Table 2.1: Ancient Constantinopolitan Rite for Receiving Converts (Eighth Century)   44

Table 2.2: Text of Prayer at the Laying-on-of-Hands   52

Table 2.3: Preliminary Rites of Chrismation   57

Table 2.4: Comparison of Prayers of Chrismation   60

Table 2.5: Rite of Anointing with Chrism in the Reception of Converts   65

Table 4:1: Sequence of Initiation Rites Compared   153

Figure 1.1: The Eucharist as Source of the Consecration of Chrism   35

Figure 4.1: Chrism Mass and Chrism   167

Figure 4.2: Oils, Chrism, and Confirmation Reconfigured   170

Preface

In 1994, I graduated from the Carlson School of Management at the University of Minnesota with a bachelor of science degree in business with a marketing emphasis. I assumed that I would get my first postcollege job as an entry-level marketing professional. The closest I came to achieving this initial goal was landing a second interview with Target, which was searching for team leaders. Alas, I did not get the position and had to look for work elsewhere. I do not know if this was a missed opportunity or an act of divine providence, but I am grateful for what transpired afterward. Instead of working in business, I took a job as a full-time music director at St. Mary's Orthodox Cathedral in Minneapolis, a large parish community of the Orthodox Church in America.

Working as a music director in an Orthodox parish involves a variety of tasks. Besides preparing rehearsals and leading the singing at worship, I also sang the responses at numerous services by myself. Our community was large and had a broad range of ages, so each year ushered in dozens of memorials, funerals, and baptisms. St. Mary's also received numerous Christians who had been baptized in other traditions, so I also sang the responses for numerous chrismations. My active service at baptisms and the reception of converts exposed me to the diverse ways in which Orthodox Christians anointed people with Chrism. In addition to singing the responses at these services, I also heard the presider explain the meaning of the rites to the people and families who had gathered, a pastoral initiative directed especially to people who weren't familiar with the Byzantine Rite used by the Orthodox Church.

My service at St. Mary's concluded in 1997 when I enrolled at St. Vladimir's Orthodox Theological Seminary and began to engage Orthodox theology from an academic perspective. During the course of my studies, I spent a great deal of time in the seminary chapel and participated in even more baptisms and chrismations.[1] The experience of participating in chrismations climaxed during the baptisms of my two nieces and daughter. I recall the privilege of explaining the meaning of chrismation to those gathered at the baptism of my younger niece. There were many children present, and I recall telling them that baptism was kind of like a "church tubby," where God gives the child a bath that really cleans her. And the anointing with chrism left an "invisible tattoo," one we couldn't see, but that was eternally visible to all the angels, archangels, and our fathers and mothers who departed this life before us but are alive in Christ. These experiences, beginning with the numerous chrismations at St. Mary's, were gatherings exuding meaning, hope, belonging, and a desire to understand why the church performs its elaborate rituals.

From the very first chrismation I observed, I have noted a desire to capture language that effectively explains what anointing with chrism means. There was never a question of whether or not something important happened, because the ritual and its solemn celebration spoke for itself: God was there and poured out abundant blessings on the one being initiated and all who gathered. It was during my graduate studies at The Catholic University of America that I discovered that Catholics also recognized the anointing with chrism as a sacrament in which something happened, and were also looking for appropriate language that effectively communicates this reality. This book is an attempt to explain to readers of all backgrounds the rich meaning of the anointing with chrism in the Byzantine Orthodox tradition. Readers will note that I draw upon dozens of authors and books to develop this explanation. This prefatory statement is an acknowledgment that my inquiry into the issue was equally inspired by celebrating baptisms and chrismations in real life, with real people.

---

[1] I had the privilege of participating in the reception of the renowned church historian Jaroslav Pelikan into the Orthodox Church through the anointing with Chrism.

Acknowledgments

This project began as a paper presented to the Christian Initiation Seminar of the North American Academy of Liturgy in 2011. After presenting the initial paper, I approached Hans Christoffersen of Liturgical Press, who expressed interest in the project and has supported me throughout this process. I am grateful to Hans and the editorial board of Liturgical Press for their support and patience. Special thanks to the Very Rev. Mark Morozowich, dean of the School of Theology and Religious Studies at The Catholic University of America, who shared his insights and excerpts from his seminal study on Holy Thursday in the Byzantine tradition. I extend special gratitude to the many friends and colleagues who generously donated time to read drafts: the members of the Christian Initiation Seminar of NAAL, Fr. Peter McGrail, Sr. Margaret Schreiber, OP, Adam DeVille, Donna Hawk-Reinhard, and especially Fr. Michael Plekon. I am also grateful to Tom Fisch and Fr. Dominic Serra, who offered insightful feedback during a memorable dinner conversation, and to my colleagues of the theological studies department at Loyola Marymount University, who consistently offer cheerful and enthusiastic encouragement. Last, but by no means least, I thank Tresja and Sophia, my wife and daughter, for contributing joy to this project.

Abbreviations

BAR	Stefano Parenti and Elena Velkovska, eds., *L'eucologio barberini gr. 336*, 2nd ed. (Rome: Edizioni liturgiche, 2000)
BES	*Codex Grottaferrata Gb 1*, a thirteenth-century Euchologion frequently referred to as "Bessarion"
BELS	Bibliotheca Ephemerides Liturgicae Subsidia
EOC	Evangelical Orthodox Church
GBN	*The Great Book of Needs*, expanded and supplemented, vol. 1: *The Holy Mysteries*, trans. St. Tikhon's Monastery (South Canaan, PA: St. Tikhon's Seminary Press, 1998)
NAAL	North American Academy of Liturgy
NPNF	*Nicene and Post-Nicene Fathers*
OCA	Orthodox Church in America
PG	J.-P. Migne, ed., *Patrologia Graeca*
SCOBA	Standing Conference of Orthodox Bishops in America
TGC	"Typikon of the Great Church," in *Le Typikon de la grande église: Ms. Sainte-Croix no. 40, X siécle*, vol. 1, Juan Mateos, ed., OCA 165 (Rome: Pontificium institutum orientalium studiorum, 1962)
UGCC	Ukrainian Greco-Catholic Church
UOC-KP	Ukrainian Orthodox Church-Kyivan Patriarchate

Introduction

Sometimes, the best symbols of community events can be found after they have concluded. The odors of physical exertion hang in the air of gyms and locker rooms after an athletic event, confirmed by the sight of sweaty socks and soiled jerseys. One can still smell roasted meats, gravy, and baked bread after a family holiday meal, and crumbs on the floor, spills on tablecloths, half-full glasses of water and wine, and barren bones on soiled plates hint toward a story with a longer narrative. One can experience the same phenomenon after a graduation party, or even an assembly of four-year-olds who gathered to honor one of their peers with chicken nuggets and macaroni and cheese. The effect of the experience is tangible. The hosts feel the aftereffects of the event with weary feet and legs, ringing ears, and an almost inexplicable feeling of personal fatigue. Hosts and attendees sense the energy of the event with its conversations, laughter, joy, accidents, and quiet encounters, even after it is over.

I begin this book on chrismation in the Byzantine tradition by using examples of the aftereffects of daily and domestic gatherings because they tell us something strong about the event, even though the event itself has concluded and the guests have gone home. For most of my life, I have taken for granted the way an empty Byzantine Rite church communicates its liturgy.[1] My brother and I had the privilege of spending most of our weekends with our grandparents, which entailed staying in the rectory next door to my grandfather's Ukrainian Orthodox parish. As children, we fully participated in the liturgy and replayed the entire Eucharist on the staircase connecting the first and second floors of the rectory. We sang the Trisagion, used the handle of a bag containing a loaf

---

[1] Throughout this book, I will use the titles "Byzantine Rite" and "Orthodox" interchangeably. When the liturgical practices or teachings of the Orthodox differ from the Catholic Churches using the Byzantine Rite, I will precisely state the traditions I am discussing.

of bread for the censer, and received and distributed Holy Communion from a coffee cup and dessert plate. One of our favorite activities was to accompany Grandpa to the church as he prepared a homily or cleaned the carpet in the sanctuary. We enjoyed the sacred space of the church because it always retained something from the previous liturgy, the faint smell of incense in the air, the fragrance of the sweet wine used for the *zapivka* the altar boys prepared for communicants after communion, the smell of the fresh charcoal waiting to be enflamed for the incense, the almost-melted candles of the candelabra and the smell of the wax that littered the floor.[2] No Byzantine Rite church is ever devoid of people, either, not only because Christ is present in the reserved gifts on the altar, but also on account of the many icons bearing the presence of Christ, Mary, and the saints who are always in the church, waiting for the people of God of the parish to heed God's call and assemble to worship him. Perhaps the most telling symbol is one that is not really tangible or sensible but certainly no less legitimate or true: the energy of the assembly that has temporarily departed but will return with all its joys and sorrows, sins and virtues, and petitions asking God to impart divine mercy.

As an adult who served as a full-time choir director, graduated seminary, and exercised diaconal ministry for more than ten years, I sense a similar energy in every church I visit, from the small, Missouri Synod Lutheran parish just down the street to the beautiful edifice constituting Our Lady of the Angels Cathedral in downtown Los Angeles. The visual symbols communicate meaning with great clarity: the cathedral's large baptismal font horizontally oriented toward the eucharistic table speaks of entering God's life, from font to table. Many liturgical symbols communicate meaning with similar clarity. A baptismal font is designed with cruciform or octagonal shape and a particular depth to connote metaphors of burial and birth. Some ambos are constructed so that the lector ascends to an impressive height, which facilitates both visibility

---

[2] *Zapivka* is a mixture of sweet red wine and hot water given to communicants after communion in some Byzantine Rite churches. This drink is offered as a way to consume any remaining particles of Holy Communion.

and the acoustical effect of the proclamation of the word of God in psalmody, Scripture, and homily. The relics of a saint are often preserved in an elegant case and strategically positioned for public veneration. The iconostasis of the Byzantine Rite church serves as a portal to the sanctuary beyond, inviting people, when the iconostasis is well designed, to participate in the life of the age to come. These examples depend on skilled design and arrangement of sacred space.

But not every church or chapel enjoys the benefit of professional and skilled design and arrangement. Many Byzantine Rite churches do not have vertically arranged ambos, quality chairs for their presiders, or liturgical vessels such as baptismal fonts and chalices visible to the observer. When one enters the church in a nonliturgical setting, all the doors attached to the iconostasis used by the celebrants and their assistants are closed, along with the curtain drawn so that the sanctuary and eucharistic table itself is invisible. Contemporary issues of sacred space, their design and arrangement, and how they communicate the mystery of salvation history should be taken up elsewhere.[3] However, in this space I argue that even impoverished sacred spaces still communicate the meaning of a liturgical event through liturgical movement. During the Divine Liturgy, the curtain and doors are opened, and the clergy bring the gospel into the midst of the assembly at the Little Entrance. The lector reads the epistle lection from the midst of the assembly and the deacon reads the gospel from the same place, both ministers carrying the book high for all to see and venerate as they stand in the middle of the nave. The ministers also bring the offering of bread and wine into the midst of the assembly and place them on the table, from which all who dare to approach are fed.

These liturgical movements invite and ignite participation, and they require intense energy. However one assesses the current state

---

[3] For an overview of the Orthodox concept of sacred space, see Alexander Grishin, "Eastern Orthodox Iconography and Architecture," in *The Blackwell Companion to Eastern Christianity*, ed. Ken Parry (Malden, MA / Oxford, UK: Blackwell Publishing, 2007), 371–87. For a comprehensive survey on Byzantine architecture, see the seminal work by Cyril Mango, *Byzantine Architecture* (New York: Harry N. Abrams, Inc., 1976).

of liturgical distribution of communion—I have in mind the Byzantine practice of literally spoon-feeding communion to recipients—its distribution is still accompanied by singing. One can smell the sweet wine in the cup, and even the smallest taste of communion can be memorable to both the one who imparts and the participant. The Slavic tradition encourages communicants to kiss the cup, an act of venerating the vessel containing the Lord's precious blood. This act of venerable kissing is important to the people; parents and grandparents gently encourage small children to kiss the cup, and clergy instruct baptized visitors unfamiliar with the practice to kiss, often in several languages. A sense of relief and fatigue accompanies the conclusion of communion, the taste and smell of wine and incense lingering. A similar feeling occurs at baptisms, especially when those who are not baptized are impacted by the mess that inevitably happens when an infant or adult is immersed in the water three times.

Whether it is the liturgy itself or the postliturgical environment, one's senses say that a community did something significant here. The senses unveil cloaked mysteries. Wet spots, bread crumbs, wax on the floor, the fragrance of incense and wine, and the inadvertent marks of lipstick on a glass case protecting relics or icons reveal the worship that recently concluded. The people who participated in this worship recall its meaning through vivid images and sounds, humming the tunes of the hymns they just sang while remembering the touch of cold metal on their lips when they kissed the chalice. Despite the closed curtains and huge iconostases obscuring one's vision of the sanctuary, the liturgy unveils the meaning of mystery and initiates the participant into it.

I have offered this introduction because, for some reason, the various rites of anointing with chrism, known as "chrismation" in the Eastern rites, seem to present themselves as exceptions to this rule. Like confirmation, its Western sibling, chrismation appears to be a cloaked mystery. Extracting the meaning of chrismation is no easy task because of the variety of ways it is celebrated. The most common celebration of chrismation occurs after the immersion in the baptismal font. A presbyter anoints the neophyte (usually an infant, sometimes older children or adults) on the forehead, nose, lips, ears, breast, hands, and feet, symbolizing an anointing of the entire body. This postbaptismal anointing occurs in the course of the same liturgical rite as baptism. After the neophyte exits the font and dries herself, the lector chants Psalm 31, and the neophyte puts on the white garment and a neck cross. Then, with no pause, introduction, or special demarcation in the euchologion, the celebrant recites the prayer of chrismation and anoints the neophyte, saying "the seal of the gift of the Holy Spirit" at each anointing, with the people responding, "Amen." The rite of baptism continues with a procession around the font, the assembly singing "As many as have been baptized into Christ have put on Christ. Alleluia!" (Gal 3:27), followed by the epistle (Rom 6:3-11) and gospel (Matt 28:16-19) lections. After the rites of ablution, tonsuring, and churching, the neophyte participates in the Eucharistic Liturgy, ideally on the same day, but most frequently whenever the next liturgy is celebrated.[4]

In Orthodox practice, chrismation occurs in another context, construed as equally meaningful with the postbaptismal anointing with chrism. The Orthodox Church typically receives Christians who were baptized in another church through the anointing with chrism. There are variations in the process and rituals for receiving non-Orthodox Christians employed by the different Orthodox Churches in the world. A small but vocal minority baptizes everyone who joins the Orthodox communion, even if those who are received have been baptized with water in the name of the Trinity. There were long periods in history when Orthodoxy received Catholics through confession and participation in the Eucharist. The most common method of reception, though, is through anointing with chrism, also known as chrismation among Orthodox. The variations of this rite are many. As a rule, the rite occurs in a single liturgical celebration with a litany and other prayers, renunciation of heresies and confessions of faith, absolution from sin, a prayer of chrismation which differs from the one used with baptism, and the anointing with chrism.

---

[4] In some parishes, the neophyte immediately receives communion from the reserved sacrament.

The term "chrismation," then, applies to a rite of receiving baptized Christians into the Orthodox Church who represent a wide variety of ages, religious backgrounds, and life experience. Most Orthodox Christians are infants when they receive chrismation as part of the rite of baptism and have no memory of the sacrament. Some Orthodox Christians received chrismation as the main ritual of passage into the Orthodox Church when they were adults and have strong memories of the ritual.

Faithful members of Orthodox communities have a mixture of memories when it comes to chrismation. Private baptism and chrismation remains prevalent in Orthodoxy, and even adults who become Orthodox through chrismation do so in a liturgical context outside of the Sunday Eucharistic Assembly. While some parishes make a conscious effort to integrate baptisms or chrismations into the Sunday Eucharistic Liturgy, the rites of baptism and/or reception via chrismation usually occur before the liturgy begins so that many people are absent. The Orthodox Church does not appoint a particular date of the liturgical year for baptism. The Vesperal Liturgy of Holy Saturday is the original Paschal Vigil for the Byzantine Rite, a rich baptismal liturgy consisting of fifteen Old Testament lessons, with the Epistle to the Romans and the vesting of the church paraments and the clergy in white betraying the original baptismal provenance of the Vigil.[5] When the practice of baptizing neophytes on Pascha began to fade from Byzantine liturgical practice and the monastic rites for Pascha with the canon of St. John of Damascus became the highlight of the Paschal liturgical offices, the original Paschal Vigil was repositioned to a celebration earlier in the day. The monastic hymnography developed around the core structure of the Vigil and redefined the Paschal Vigil as Holy Saturday, a mimesis of Jesus' Sabbath rest before his resurrection in the

---

[5] On this topic, see the seminal study by Gabriel Bertoniere, *The Historical Development of the Easter Vigil and Related Services in the Greek Church*, Orientalia christiana analecta 193 (Rome: Pontifical Oriental Institute, 1972). Also see Alkiviadis Calivas, *Great Week and Pascha in the Greek Orthodox Church* (Brookline, MA: Holy Cross Press, 1992), 113–14; and Nicholas Denysenko, "Psalm 81: Announcing the Resurrection on Holy Saturday," *Logos: A Journal of Eastern Christian Studies* 50, nos. 1–2 (2009): 55–88.

Byzantine version of the Paschal Triduum. In its earlier cathedral context, the church community knew that the neophytes had just been baptized and chrismated, since they entered the church to join the faithful, processing from the baptistery and singing "as many as have been baptized." When a predominantly baptismal Vigil became a mimesis of Jesus' Sabbath rest, and baptism became a private affair, the anointing with chrism largely disappeared from the consciousness of the Orthodox faithful.

In the course of the modern *ressourcement* movement, Catholic and Orthodox scholars alike began to research the historical sources to reconstruct the history of the liturgy. Pioneers of the study of liturgical history such as Juan Mateos and Miguel Arranz reconstructed the rites of baptism and their contexts in the Paschal liturgy of Constantinople.[6] Some Orthodox parish communities embraced the contributions of liturgical history and attempted to retrieve the baptismal origins of the Vesperal Liturgy of Holy Saturday. The results of such attempts to restore the Paschal baptismal Vigil vary, especially since there is no official encouragement on the part of Orthodox leaders to reconnect baptism with Pascha.[7] I have participated in a Vesperal liturgy with baptisms on Holy Saturday, with the baptisms occurring as part of the liturgy in the appropriate

---

[6] See Juan Mateos, ed., *Le Typikon de la grande église: Ms. Sainte-Croix no. 40, X siécle* vol. 2, Orientalia christiana analecta 166 (Rome: Pontificium Institutum Orientalium Studiorum, 1963), 76–77. Arranz published several articles presenting the euchology and sacramental theology of baptism in the Byzantine Rite, particularly the Constantinopolitan tradition. The most important of these are "Les sacrements de l'ancien euchologe constantinopolitain, pt 6: l'illumination' de la nuit de Pâques," *Orientalia christiana periodica* 51 (1985): 60–86; "Les sacrements de l'ancien euchologe constantinopolitain, pt 7: l'illumination' de la nuit de Pâques," *Orientalia christiana periodica* 52 (1986): 145–78; "Les Sacrements de l'ancien Euchologe constantinopolitain (9), pt 4: Ch 6, l'illumination' de la nuit de pâques," *Orientalia christiana periodica* 55 (1989): 33–62; and "Les sacrements de l'ancien Euchologe constantinopolitain (8): l'illumination' de la nuit de Pâques," *Orientalia christiana periodica* 53 (1987): 59–106.

[7] For an exception, see Peter Galadza, "Schmemann between Fagerberg and Reality: Towards an Agenda for Byzantine Christian Pastoral Liturgy," *Bolletino della Badia Greca di Grottaferrata* 4 (2007): 9–12.

place. I have also concelebrated the Holy Saturday liturgy with baptisms (of neophytes) and chrismations (of other baptized Christians becoming Orthodox) scheduled before the beginning of the liturgy, a pastoral decision to expedite the sequence of liturgical events. In the former case, the baptism and chrismation occurred in the midst of the assembly. In the latter, observing the fullness of the burdensome requirements of the Holy Saturday liturgy superseded integration of baptism into the Eucharistic Liturgy. In fact, most parishes have low attendance for the Holy Saturday liturgy and abbreviate it. Holy Saturday has become more an occasion to bless the baskets of food people traditionally enjoy on Pascha, having fasted from savory foods since the beginning of Lent, a pastoral assent to people's demands. In short, while baptism and chrismation have been partially reintegrated into the life of the parish, as a rule, most Orthodox observe or participate in the rite of chrismation rarely.

Despite the infrequent and sporadic celebration of chrismation, its celebration with baptism and as the main rite for becoming Orthodox reveals it as a mystery with profound meaning for the whole church. Chrismation is certainly important for Eastern Orthodox Christians, but it is equally important for Catholics, who view it as the Eastern equivalent of confirmation. The obvious reason for this assumption is the similarity in the position and execution of the parallel sacraments. Confirmation and chrismation are postbaptismal, and they both include a bodily anointing with chrism that was consecrated by a bishop at the Eucharistic Liturgy on Holy Thursday. Confirmation and chrismation also appear to share a common theology of the Holy Spirit. The Roman Church viewed the similarities between the two sacraments as so strong that it adopted the Byzantine formula of chrismation as the new formula for the anointing with chrism at the rite of confirmation. The Catholic Church also employs confirmation as the rite for receiving baptized Christians into the full communion of the Catholic Church, another similarity with the Orthodox version of chrismation.[8] Theologically, Catholics view confirmation as imparting the

---

[8] Paul Turner, *When Other Christians Become Catholic* (Collegeville, MN: Liturgical Press, 2007).

Christic ministries of priest, prophet, and king to neophytes, a view shared by many Orthodox theologians of the twentieth century.[9]

While they share similarities, confirmation and Byzantine chrismation also have many differences. Some differences are admittedly minor, but even the lesser differences point to diverse accents in ecclesiology, theological anthropology, and the meaning of the gift of the Holy Spirit. Let us begin with the origins of chrism. Catholics create chrism by adding balsam to olive oil, and the Catholic Church annually blesses the oils for healing and anointing the catechumens and consecrates chrism under the presidency of the diocesan bishop in his cathedral at the chrism Mass on Holy Thursday. While the Orthodox Church also consecrates chrism on Holy Thursday, the celebration is not annual—it occurs only when there is a pastoral need for more chrism—and only the first bishop of a synod has the authority to consecrate chrism, which means that it is a synodal, and not a diocesan event. The discrepancy between the two practices reveals diverse pastoral agendas and ecclesiological accents concerning authority and the nature of the local church.

The most glaring difference between the Orthodox and Catholic rites of chrismation occurs in its mode of celebration. Catholics anoint neophytes with chrism twice in the baptism for children. The first anointing occurs immediately after baptism and is performed by a presbyter, followed by a short prayer.[10] The second anointing technically belongs to the office of bishop and occurs with the laying on of hands, which was a venerable tradition connoting the imparting of the gift of the Holy Spirit in Western traditions.[11] The Catholic Church now allows some presbyters to impart

---

[9] Numerous *ressourcement* scholars advanced this notion. The most important Catholic contribution is by Yves Congar, "Sur la trilogie: prophìte-roi-prêtre," *Revues des sciences philosophiques et théologiques* 67 (1983): 97–115; Congar, *Lay People in the Church: A Study for the Theology of the Laity*, trans. Donald Attwater (Westminster, MD: Newman Press, 1957, 1963 reprint). Alexander Schmemann articulates the Orthodox view on king, priest, and prophet in *Of Water and the Spirit* (Crestwood, NY: St. Vladimir's Seminary Press, 1974), 81–103.

[10] *The Rites of the Catholic Church*, vol. 1, study ed. (Collegeville, MN: Liturgical Press, 1990), 403–4.

[11] Ibid., 489–91.

anointing with chrism, but only through the principle of subsidiarity. Furthermore, the first anointing occurs immediately after baptism but is granted only to infants. Adolescents and adults who are baptized receive only the anointing included in confirmation. Children who were baptized and anointed as infants receive confirmation at varying ages, most often between seven and eighteen, and the Catholic Church allows conferences of bishops to determine the appropriate age, beginning with seven (the age of reason).[12] Because confirmation is deferred to an older age in most cases, it is frequently preceded by a formal process of faith formation.

The Byzantine Rite celebration of chrismation differs from Roman confirmation. The normal celebrant of chrismation is a presbyter, who also presides at baptism. His celebration at both sacraments is seamless, since chrismation follows baptism with no fanfare or division in the rubrics. Byzantine chrismation does not include a handlaying gesture, which is a notable difference between the two rites, given the prominence of the handlaying gesture in the history and theology of Catholic confirmation. As mentioned above, for the vast majority of Orthodox, there is no criterion of age in celebrating chrismation; it is given to everyone who is baptized as part of one seamless ceremony. Consequently, there is one postbaptismal anointing with chrism given to everyone, with no deference to age.

The differences between confirmation and chrismation that I have briefly outlined illuminate divergent theologies. These divergent theologies can be explored through the experiential aspect of ritual. For a Christian of the Byzantine Rite who received baptism and chrismation as an infant, little can be said about the experience of either sacrament. Conversely, Byzantine Rite Christians fully participate in the Eucharistic Liturgy from infancy. For children, it is normal to approach and receive Holy Communion at every Eucharistic Liturgy. Byzantine Rite Christians can refer to the Eucharist as an event in which they have participated for their

---

[12] Ibid., 482–83. For a comprehensive historical treatment of this issue, see Paul Turner, *Ages of Initiation: The First Two Christian Millennia* (Collegeville, MN: Liturgical Press, 2000).

"whole lives," a ritual experience shared in common with family members and friends. Orthodox generally do not have a solemn occasion marking First Communion for a child; First Communion occurs immediately after baptism.[13] A typical child's first memory of sacramental participation is in eucharistic participation. The phenomenon of remembering is not limited to mere memory but of full participation in the community event, with no ecclesially sanctioned prohibitions on partaking of Holy Communion. Theologically, if we assume that baptism initiates one into the life of the Triune God, we can assert that children begin participating in the communion of the Holy Spirit (to paraphrase the liturgies of John Chrysostom and Basil the Great) as infants. There are no prohibitions concerning age for the people of the church. Consequently, each person, regardless of gender, race, or age experiences belonging at two levels: they belong to the holy people of God, and likewise belong to the Triune God.

The experience of the Catholic child differs. After baptism, Catholic children receive the first of two different anointings with chrism. Catholic children then participate in sacramental confession in preparation for First Communion, which will occur around the age of seven. The most rigorous and involved preparation happens before confirmation. Once candidates have completed the preparatory program, they receive confirmation and are now fully initiated into the body of Christ, having received the gift of the Spirit. The major difference from the Orthodox model is that Catholic children receive the gift of the Spirit through the laying on of hands and anointing with chrism at a deferred age. The different sequence of rites of initiation introduces a difficult theological question: when is one ready to receive the gift of the Spirit? Many related questions come to mind: what kind of preparation is needed for full initiation into the church? How can a community determine a threshold for determining when the gift of the Spirit should be given?

Catholic Christians who are confirmed as adolescents speak from experience in defending the necessity of deferred confirmation.

---

[13] Many Orthodox parishes in America follow the tradition of a solemn "first confession," which usually occurs at the age of reason.

Allow me a personal anecdote to elaborate the point. When I teach the sacrament of confirmation in the classroom, my students, both undergraduate and graduate, tend to vigorously defend confirmation as a sacrament of maturity and insist on the necessity of faith formation programs as a prerequisite, so Catholics will be able to recite their baptismal vows with the proper intention. Such defensive postures prevail regardless of my historico-theological presentations. Students speak from personal and pastoral experience. Having prepared for confirmation, some of them view it as a transformative event, a true rite of passage into the full communion of the Catholic Church. For them, the meaning of the sacrament is not veiled by mystery; they truly view themselves and those they prepared as having attained the necessary maturity to receive the Holy Spirit and live a Christian life of witness and service. They belong to a group of people of similar age and experience set aside for formation, and the memory of that formation and its ritual recognition—confirmation—empowers them.

This cursory comparison of Catholic confirmation and Byzantine chrismation yields both ritual and experiential differences. Byzantine Rite Christians baptized as infants have no frame of reference for remembering chrismation, but they enjoy the blessings of full participation in the body of Christ and can testify to it through lifelong participation in the Eucharist. Catholic Christians often have a powerful transformative experience in adolescent confirmation, yet their participation in the body of Christ is limited until they are confirmed. The ritual and experiential differences yield several crucial questions. These include: what blessings does chrismation confer, and how do these blessings relate to those imparted at baptism and the Eucharist? When and how is one ready to receive the gift of the Holy Spirit? What are the potential benefits one reaps by receiving chrismation with baptism at infancy? How do the sacraments of baptism, chrismation, and Eucharist initiate one into the life of the Triune God, and how can one speak of the meaning of participating in divine life? What kinds of liturgical rituals are appropriate for marking important thresholds of life such as adolescence and adulthood? The diverse ways in which the church employs anointing with chrism initially yields more confusion than clarity, and this is the chief reason I have referred to chrismation as a sacrament unlike most of the others, one that remains veiled in mystery because it is not well known in Orthodoxy, and its relationship with its sibling sacrament is confusing.

The purpose of this book is to unveil the mystery of chrismation and manifest it as a sacred mystery of initiation into the life of the Triune God that seals unity with Christ and creates a covenant of belonging with a parish community. This notion of belonging is crucial, because it is tangibly experienced within real faith communities and is also a gift from the Triune God to humanity, the privilege of being a citizen of God's kingdom. Recently, Graham Ward identified liturgy and liturgical celebration as a key source to be explored for addressing the crisis of belonging experienced across the globe, especially questions of ecclesial belonging, or finding a community where one feels at home worshipping God with others.[14] In this study, I endeavor to demonstrate how the rites of chrismation communicate a strong sense of belonging by illuminating chrismation as a rite of entering into a meaningful covenant with the church and the Triune God. God imparts numerous blessings through this twofold covenant, most notably the capacity to gradually become like God, better known as *theosis* in the Byzantine tradition.

I also believe that a robust theology of chrismation has much to offer the Roman Catholic Church in facilitating the process of identifying and developing a theology of confirmation. In the chapters that comprise the body of this book, I will clarify the relationship of chrismation to the sacraments of baptism and Eucharist, explain the trinitarian theology of chrismation with reference to the dynamic relationship of Christology and pneumatology, and discuss how chrismation communicates an identity of belonging to the participant. My discussion of identity will analyze the twentieth-century emergence of an ecumenical theology defining chrismation as imparting the Christic gifts of priest, prophet, and king to

---

[14] Graham Ward, "Belonging to the Church," in *Liturgy in Migration: From the Upper Room to Cyberspace*, ed. Teresa Berger (Collegeville, MN: Liturgical Press, 2012), 14–16.

participants. My presentation will also explore several related issues including the innate sacramentality of chrismation and its value of the materiality of the cosmos, the ecumenical lessons one can glean by comparing confirmation and chrismation in this post-ecumenical period of Christian history, and pastoral initiatives church leaders should consider to illuminate the transformative and life-giving power of chrismation.

METHOD AND TASK

My task in this work requires an interrogation of liturgical sources. I will primarily analyze the rites related to the anointing with chrism as a way of gleaning their liturgical theology. It is my conviction that the liturgical theology will provide an initially satisfying response to the questions I have raised above. Readers should note that this is primarily a work of sacramental theology, when one probes rites, structures, components, and their interpretation to parse out the theological threads, assess their relationships with one another, and establish a course for the next stage of theologizing. One of the most important parts of this work is historical research, and it is crucial to note that many excellent scholars have established a solid historical foundation of chrismation. This work is not primarily a history of chrismation in the Byzantine Rite, and I will not be devoting multiple pages to exploring how and when the prebaptismal anointings that so inspired Christians of Syria and Antioch came to be repositioned as a postbaptismal anointing in the Byzantine Rite. Scholars such as Gabriele Winkler and Maxwell Johnson have magisterially explored the dynamics of ritual development as it pertains to chrismation.[15] Others such as Hugh Riley and Donna Hawk-Reinhard have expertly addressed one of the most important instances of postbaptismal anointing with chrism, namely, the meaning of the anointing with chrism in the Mysta-

---

[15] Maxwell Johnson, *The Rites of Christian Initiation: Their Evolution and Interpretation*, rev. ed. (Collegeville, MN: Liturgical Press, 1999, 2007), 52–63; Gabriele Winkler, "The Original Meaning of the Prebaptismal Anointing and Its implications," in *Living Water, Sealing Spirit: Readings on Christian Initiation*, ed. M. Johnson (Collegeville, MN: Liturgical Press, 1995), 58–81.

gogical Catecheses by Cyril of Jerusalem in the late fourth century.[16] The reader will also recognize the foundational historical work on the rites of baptism, chrismation, and the consecration of chrism performed by the inimitable Jesuit scholar of Byzantine liturgy of blessed memory, Miguel Arranz, and the excellent analysis of the history of the consecration of chrism by Mark Morozowich.[17] Other scholars made seminal contributions on the history of the reception

---

[16] For details on the formation of the baptismal liturgy in Jerusalem and the formation of the postbaptismal anointing, see Johnson, *The Rites of Christian Initiation*, 142–44; Bernard Botte, "Postbaptismal Anointing in the Ancient Patriarchate of Antioch," in *Studies in Syrian Baptismal Rites*, ed. J. Vellian, Syrian Churches Series 6 (Kottayam: J. Vellian, 1973), 63–71; Juliette Day, *The Baptismal Liturgy in Jerusalem: Fourth and Fifth Century Evidence from Palestine, Syria and Egypt*, Liturgy, Worship and Society Series (Aldershot, Burlington: Ashgate, 2007), 105–20; Donna Hawk-Reinhard, "From Χριστιανοί to Χριστοφόροι: the Role of the Eucharist in Christian Identity Formation according to Cyril of Jerusalem" (PhD diss., St. Louis University, 2011), 80–91. For the theology of chrismation, see N. Joseph Torchia, "The Significance of Chrismation in the Mystagogical Lectures of Cyril of Jerusalem," *Diakonia* 32, no. 2 (1999): 128–44; Cyrille Argenti, "Chrismation," in *Ecumenical Perspectives on Baptism, Eucharist and Ministry* (Geneva: World Council of Churches, 1983), 46–67; and Hugh M. Riley, *Christian Initiation: A Comparative Study of the Interpretation of the Baptismal Liturgy in the Mystagogical Writings of Cyril of Jerusalem, John Chrysostom, Theodore of Mopsuestia, and Ambrose of Milan*, The Catholic University of America Studies in Christian Antiquity, no. 17, ed. Johannes Quasten (Washington, DC: The Catholic University of America Press, Consortium Press, 1974), 349–409. On Cyril's hagiopolite forerunner, see Macarius of Jerusalem, *Macarius of Jerusalem: Letter to the Armenians, AD 335*, intro., trans. Abraham Terian (Crestwood, NY: St. Vladimir's Seminary Press, St. Nersess Armenian Seminary, 2008), 62, 86–87, 126. Terian dates Macarius's letter to 335.

[17] In addition to the sources listed in note 6 above, see Miguel Arranz, "Évolution des rites d'incorporation et de réadmission dans l'Église selon l'Euchologe byzantin," in *Gestes et paroles dans les diverses families liturgiques: Conferences Saint-Serge XXIVe semaine d'etudes liturgiques, 1977*, ed. A. Postoia and A. Triacca, Bibliotheca Ephemerides Liturgicae Subsidia 14 (Rome: Centro Liturgico Vincenziano, 1978), 31–75; Arranz, "La saint consécration du saint myron: les sacrements des l'Euchologe constantinopolitain 10," *Orientalia christiana periodica* 55 (1989): 317–38; and Mark Morozowich, *Holy Thursday in Jerusalem: The Liturgical Celebrations from the Fourth to the Fourteenth Centuries*, Orientalia christiana analecta (forthcoming). I am grateful to Fr. Morozowich for sharing his manuscript-in-progress with me for this study.

of converts in the Byzantine tradition, including John Erickson, John Klentos, and Alkiviadis Calivas.[18] I use their work as a basis and offer historical insights and questions when the sources offer them. My work is then organized according to the following order.

Liturgical Sources: Consecration of Chrism and Postbaptismal Chrismation

My investigation begins with the beginning of chrismation: the consecration of chrism on Holy Thursday at the Divine Liturgy. I explore the ancient and contemporary texts and use the prayer for the consecration of chrism to commence development of the theological anthropology of chrismation. The eucharistic context of the consecration of chrism is foundational for understanding how the sacraments relate to one another. The Eucharist is the origin of the chrism itself, and the Eucharistic Assembly asks God to create chrism that will initiate new people into the eucharistic community. In other words, the Eucharist is the source, the alpha and omega of chrismation, and the consecration of chrism thus reveals the inseparability of the two sacraments.

The next section analyzes the postbaptismal anointing with chrism and establishes its context as a crucial component in a sequence of ritual actions. Chrismation is not demarcated as divided or distinct from baptism and essentially belongs to it. The ritual context of chrismation embellishes its meaning as imparting forgiveness of sins and sealing people in Christ through the Spirit. An

---

[18] John Erickson, "The Reception of Non-Orthodox into the Orthodox Church: Contemporary Practice," *St. Vladimir's Theological Quarterly* 41 (1997): 1–17; Erickson, "Divergences in Pastoral Practices in the Reception of Converts," in *Orthodox Perspectives on Pastoral Praxis: Papers of Intra-Orthodox Conference on Pastoral Praxis Celebrating 50th Anniversary of Holy Cross*, ed. Theodore Stylianopoulos (Brookline, MA: Holy Cross Orthodox Press, 1988), 149–77; Archbishop Peter L'Huillier, "The Reception of Roman Catholics into Orthodoxy: Historical Variations and Norms," *St. Vladimir's Theological Quarterly* 24 (1980): 75–82; John Klentos, "Rebaptizing Converts in the Orthodox Church: Old Perspectives on a New Problem," *Studia Liturgica* 29 (1999): 216–34; and Alkiviadis Calivas, "Receiving Converts into the Orthodox Church: Lessons from the Canonical and Liturgical Tradition," *Greek Orthodox Theological Review* 54, nos. 1–4 (2009): 1–76.

analysis of the historical development of the formula texts accompanying the bodily anointing further illustrates the development of a theology of holiness. A tabular comparison of texts from the consecration of chrism and the prayer of chrismation describing the gifts of God follows to establish a coherent theology of chrismation gleaned from the entire liturgical process: consecration of chrism, baptism, chrismation, and participation in the Eucharist.

The Reception of Converts and Anointing with Chrism

The next chapter of the book examines the particular Eastern Orthodox practice of receiving converts via the anointing with chrism. This practice is universally known throughout the Orthodox world as chrismation, so when people refer to chrismation in conversation, they mean either the postbaptismal anointing with chrism or the liturgical celebration marking their entrance into the Orthodox communion. The chapter begins with an overview of the history of the reception of converts in Orthodoxy. The most frequent practice of the Orthodox Church has been to receive converts via a confession of faith and eucharistic communion or through the anointing with chrism. On some historical occasions and occasionally today, Orthodox communities receive converts via baptism, even if the candidate has already been baptized elsewhere.

The chapter then analyzes the structure, texts, and contexts of the reception of converts, primarily by presenting and analyzing the rites as they appear in the English translation of the *Great Book of Needs*.[19] Liturgical components of special interest are the renunciations of heresies required by candidates, the confessions of faith, the revision of the prayer of chrismation to fit the context of conversion, and remarks on the other liturgical components' contribution to the liturgical theology of conversion. My examination of the rite

---

[19] *The Great Book of Needs*, expanded and supplemented, Vol. 1: *The Holy Mysteries*, trans. St. Tikhon's Monastery (South Canaan, PA: St. Tikhon's Seminary Press, 1998), hereafter cited as GBN. For the celebration of this service in the Greek Orthodox tradition, see "Service for the Reception of Converts into the Orthodox Church," Greek Orthodox Metropolis of Denver website, accessed December 17, 2012, http://www.denver.goarch.org/teleturgical_encyclicals/te-23-encl.pdf.

of reception yields an emphasis on the cognitive dimension of faith in the process of entering the communion of the Orthodox Church, as the candidates are asked to renounce tenets of faith that do not cohere with Orthodox theology, and profess tenets of faith held by the Orthodox communion. Thus, the decision to enter the Orthodox community requires the acquisition of cognitive certainty on certain aspects of faith. While the process of conversion involves the whole person, it accentuates the cerebral process of professing faith. In this model, the candidate must rehearse and essentially master the process of being of one mind with the community she seeks to enter. One might describe the process as engaging and entering more deeply into a permanent state of belonging to the Orthodox communion.

The next and final part of the chapter is an attempt to test the liturgical theology of the rite of reception through anointing with chrism by examining select narratives of conversion by men and women who have become Orthodox. This section employs Amy Slagle's important ethnographic profiles of Orthodox converts in America and also consults Oliver Herbel's study of renowned converts.[20] This portion of the chapter parses out the metaphors converts use to describe the process of becoming Orthodox. I attend to notions of belonging, entrance, and journey in this discussion, and also analyze problematic terms such as catechumenate and conversion. The chapter concludes by comparing convert narratives with the liturgical theology of the rite of reception.

Orthodox Theologians on the Meaning of Chrismation

Chapter 3 builds on the previous ones by exploring the contributions of select Orthodox theologians on the meaning of the anointing with chrism. I examine the works of Nicholas Cabasilas, Nicholas Afanasiev, Alexander Schmemann, Boris Bobrinskoy, and Paul Evdokimov. Cabasilas, Schmemann, and Bobrinskoy in particular attempt to explain the meaning of chrismation in its

---

[20] Amy Slagle, *The Eastern Church in the Spiritual Marketplace: American Conversions to Orthodox Christianity* (DeKalb, IL: Northern Illinois University Press, 2011); D. Oliver Herbel, *Turning to Tradition: Converts and the Making of an American Orthodox Church* (Oxford: Oxford University Press, 2013).

postbaptismal context, whereas Afanasiev and Evdokimov present chrismation as a sacrament initiating participants into the universal priesthood of the laity. My analysis focuses on three important and related areas: the place of the anointing with chrism in the sequence of liturgical actions occurring in baptism and the Eucharist; the dynamics of the transformative activity of the Triune God in these ritual actions; and the interpretation of chrismation as the sacrament that confers the Christic ministries of king, priest, and prophet (henceforth "trilogy") to all recipients. I compare the Orthodox view of chrismation and the trilogy of Christic gifts to contemporary Roman Catholic magisterial teaching on the trilogy of gifts, baptism and confirmation, and the lay apostolate.

This chapter concludes with an attempt to reconcile the Orthodox theology of chrismation and the liturgical theology gleaned from my analysis of the rites in the previous two chapters. The conclusion includes a proposal for new models of identity formation that represent the increasing diversity of lived Christian experience in the world and also retrieve the patristic spirit of identity formation.

Orthodox and Catholics in Dialogue: Toward a Theology of Confirmation

Chapter 4 brings an Orthodox theology of chrismation into dialogue with Western Christians, especially Roman Catholics. I attempt to employ a model of ecumenical gift exchange in this chapter by presenting aspects of an Orthodox theology of chrismation that might benefit Western Christians, and also by considering elements of Roman confirmation that might illuminate Orthodox pastoral practice. I begin the chapter by describing Catholic confirmation as "a sacrament in search of a theology," an oft-repeated moniker. A survey of confirmation's complex liturgical history and its historical development follows, largely following the historical studies of Maxwell Johnson, Aidan Kavanagh, and Gerard Austin.[21] Paul Turner's presentation of models of confirmation sets the stage to analyze the most prominent issues confronting confirmation in

---

[21] Aidan Kavanagh, *Confirmation: Origins and Reform* (New York: Pueblo Publishing Company, 1988); Gerard Austin, *Anointing with the Spirit: The Rite of Confirmation: The Use of Oil and Chrism* (New York: Pueblo Publishing Company, 1985).

the West: its position in the sequence of sacramental celebration; the theology of the Holy Spirit; and the question of the appropriate age for confirmation.[22]

An important part of my analysis is a suggested reconfiguration of confirmation, where it is construed as originating from the Eucharistic Assembly, since chrism is consecrated at the Eucharist. The principle I employ for offering an Orthodox gift to Catholics is a call for Catholics to retrieve the best of their own native liturgy and sacramental theology. My suggestions concern the rich history in the Roman liturgy of chrismating infants and of viewing the Eucharist as a repeatable sacrament that regularly imparts the gift of the Holy Spirit to participants. I also propose that one cannot earn the gift of the Holy Spirit, but that the churches should allow the gift to be given as a seed one cultivates in advancing toward God in this life, a process known as becoming like God, or *theosis*.[23] I also call upon Orthodox to consider certain strengths from the Catholic tradition as tools to strengthen Orthodox Church life. These Catholic accents include the annual practice of consecrating chrism in the diocesan cathedral, which functions as a model for anticipating the building up of the body of Christ through new baptisms. The Western interpretation of confirmation as a rite of strengthening and maturity also holds appeal for people in various stages of life, like adolescents, who seek a ritual in the churches that communicates stronger senses of belonging and service.

In conclusion, this is a book that attempts to bridge the academic and the pastoral. The book attempts to break open the meaning of the rites of chrismation as they are practiced in the Orthodox world

---

[22] Paul Turner, *Confirmation: The Baby in Solomon's Court*, rev. and updated (Chicago: Hillenbrand, 1993, 2006). Also see Thomas Marsh, *Gift of Community: Baptism and Confirmation* (Wilmington, DE: Michael Glazier, Inc., 1984); Liam Walsh, *Sacraments of Initiation: A Theology of Life, Word, and Rite*, 2nd ed. (Chicago: Liturgy Training Publications, 2011), 145–214; and Timothy Radcliffe, *Take the Plunge: Living Baptism and Confirmation* (London: Bloomsbury, 2012), 185–214.

[23] For an accessible survey of *theosis* in the Greek patristic tradition, see Norman Russell, *Fellow Workers with God: Orthodox Thinking on Theosis*, Foundations Series (Crestwood, NY: St. Vladimir's Seminary Press, 2009).

for the Catholic reader. Readers will learn how postbaptismal chrismation envisions the creation of a holy people of God who share communion with God while bearing his presence in service to this world. Readers will learn how the Byzantine tradition presents the rites of initiation as a unified and indivisible celebration beginning and ending with the Eucharist, the repeatable sacrament in which participants receive the gift of the Holy Spirit anew. Most important, I hope that by the end of the book, readers will join me in viewing anointing with chrism as a ritual moment that fills both the body of Christ and the empty sacred space of the church with a sense that an incredible event filled with divine energy has taken place, one so powerful that one can feel it with her senses.

CHAPTER 1

Chrismation in the Byzantine Rites of Initiation

INTRODUCTION

In the introduction, I stated that the most striking similarity between confirmation and chrismation is that they are both sacraments in search of a theology. In the case of chrismation, its theology is multivalent because of its frequent celebration for diverse purposes in pastoral liturgy. Chrismation's place as the sacrament bridging baptism and Eucharist in a unified liturgical process is not in question. However, chrismation has become the primary celebration for the reception of converts in many Orthodox churches. Orthodox churches use the sacrament of chrismation even for converts who are entering the Orthodox Church from other Christian churches who have been baptized and confirmed. Some Orthodox churches receive converts through full participation in the Eucharistic Liturgy, and Catholic priests are received via vesting, without chrismation. In these instances, the definition of chrismation is extended to receive some converts from other Christian churches, whereas baptism or the Eucharist is used to receive other converts in various stages of ecclesial membership. Based on practice, chrismation is used to seal the gifts of the Spirit given at baptism and to receive some Christians converting from other churches.

This chapter endeavors to explore the theology of chrismation in the Byzantine Rite by analyzing its liturgical theology and historical development within the liturgical context of the rites of initiation, specifically in relationship to baptism and Eucharist. I begin by examining the most ancient Byzantine liturgical components of chrismation in the eighth-century Euchologion *Barberini 336*, which represents Constantinopolitan liturgical practices preserved in southern Italy with some Palestinian monastic influence.[1]

This examination attends to the consecration of chrism (also called "myron") on Holy Thursday and concludes with the prayers and rubrics for postbaptismal anointing with chrism. Methodologically, the consecration of chrism and postbaptismal anointing with chrism must be interpreted together.[2] In the history of the Byzantine Rite, the process of preparing the chrism began on Holy Thursday and culminated with baptisms at the Paschal Vigil, an instance where the liturgical year fused the preparation of chrism with baptism. The liturgical act of postbaptismal anointing completes the fusion, since the anointing uses the chrism consecrated at the Eucharistic Liturgy of Holy Thursday. Thus, chrismation can be understood only through the broad contextual hermeneutic encompassing the consecration of chrism and postbaptismal anointing (chrismation).

THE CONSECRATION OF CHRISM

The sacrament of chrismation actually begins with the consecration of chrism celebrated on Holy Thursday in the Byzantine Rite. Macarius, the fourth-century archbishop of Jerusalem, wrote in his Letter to the Armenians (in 335) that the blessing of the oil of holiness is performed by the chief bishop of a synod.[3] There is also evidence of the use of chrism in the sacraments of initiation of the

---

[1] *L'Eucologio Barberini gr. 336*, 2nd ed., eds. S. Parenti, Stefano and E. Velkovska, Bibliotheca Ephemerides Liturgicae Subsidia 80, eds. A.M. Triacca and A. Pistoia (Rome: Edizioni liturgiche, 2000), hereafter BAR.

[2] See Paul Turner, *Confirmation: The Baby in Solomon's Court*, rev. and updated (Chicago: Hillenbrand, 1993, 2006), 26. The Byzantine liturgical sources in Greek and Slavonic consistently refer to the oil of chrismation as "myron." I will employ "myron" when citing the liturgical sources and will employ "chrism" in the body of the text (for simplicity).

[3] "The chief-bishop alone shall bless the oil of holiness. But by reason of distance and weighty circumstances, at the command of the archbishop, two or three bishops may meet together [to bless it]," in *Macarius of Jerusalem: Letter to the Armenians*, ed. and trans. A. Terian (Crestwood, NY: St. Vladimir's Seminary Press, St. Nersess Armenian Seminary, 2008), 88–89. It is evident that Macarius is referring to chrism since he distinguishes the "oil of holiness" from

East from the Council of Laodicea in Phrygia (360–390).[4] Thus, the consecration of chrism for the sacraments of initiation in the Byzantine Rite originated in Jerusalem and Constantinople, and the consecration occurred on Holy Thursday. In his seminal study of the liturgies of Holy Thursday in the Byzantine tradition, Mark Morozowich suggests that the consecration of chrism originated in an Antiochean milieu, and was the subject of numerous commentaries throughout the Christian East.[5] An eleventh-century liturgical book describing the services of Holy Week in Jerusalem, the Anastasis Typikon, contains a complete description of this service.[6] Morozowich provides a complete description and explanation of the splendid and ostentatious consecration of chrism in Jerusalem, and calls for further study of its relationship with other Antiochean chrism liturgies.[7] The lack of the text for the prayer of the consecration of chrism in the Jerusalem liturgy precludes a more rigorous analysis of its meaning and relationship with other rites.[8]

Liturgical evidence demonstrates the consecration of chrism on Holy Thursday in Constantinople as well. The so-called Typikon of the Great Church (TGC), a synaxarion representing ninth- to tenth-century Constantinopolitan cathedral liturgy at Hagia Sophia, makes a terse reference to the consecration of chrism during the Eucharistic Liturgy of Holy Thursday, providing no detail other

---

"the oil of anointing for the dead and the sick and for those to be baptized," which can be blessed by priests and bishops individually.

[4] Mark Morozowich, *Holy Thursday in Jerusalem: The Liturgical Celebrations from the Fourth to the Fourteenth Centuries* (Rome: Orientalia Christiana Analecta, forthcoming). I am grateful to Fr. Morozowich for sharing his manuscript with me for this paper.

[5] For a list of commentaries, see ibid.

[6] The text of the Anastasis Typikon is published in A. Papadopoulos-Kerameus, "Τυπικὸν τῆς ἐν Ἱεροσολίμοις ἐκκλεσίας" in Ἀνάλεκτα Ἱεροσολύκῆς Σταχυολογίας II (St. Petersburg, n.p., 1894), 1–254. For a description of this liturgical source, see Gabriele Bertonière, *The Historical Development of the Easter Vigil and Related Services in the Greek Church*, Orientalia christiana analecta 193 (Rome: Pontifical Oriental Institute, 1972), 12–18.

[7] Morozowich, *Holy Thursday*.

[8] Ibid. Morozowich bemoans the absence of a hagiopolite Euchologion accompanying the *Anastasis Typikon*.

than the recitation of the prayer of the chrism at the liturgy.[9] In 1989, Miguel Arranz provided a study of the consecration of chrism on Holy Thursday in the ancient Constantinopolitan euchologion tradition.[10] Arranz's study was intended to complement a doctoral thesis by Pavlos Menevisoglou in 1972 at the University of Thessalonica on the contemporary practices for the consecration of chrism in the Ecumenical Patriarchate.[11] Arranz reviews several Euchologia representing the Constantinopolitan liturgical tradition dating generally from the end of iconoclasm (843) to the Fourth Crusade (1204). Morozowich completes his study of the consecration of chrism on Holy Thursday by presenting the structure of the celebration according to the Constantinopolitan tradition.[12]

In contemporary practice, the consecration of chrism is rarely celebrated.[13] The Patriarch of Constantinople celebrates the conse-

---

[9] Juan Mateos, ed., *Le Typikon de la grande église: Ms. Sainte-Croix no. 40, X siécle* Vol. 2. Orientalia christiana analecta 166 (Rome: Pontifical Oriental Institute, 1963), 76–77.

[10] Miguel Arranz, "La saint consécration du saint myron: les sacrements des l'Euchologe constantinopolitain 10," *Orientalia christiana periodica* 55 (1989): 317–38.

[11] Pavlos Menevigoslou, Τὸ ἅγιον μύρον ἐν τῇ Ὀρθοδόξῳ Ἀνατολικῇ Ἐκκλησίᾳ ἰδίᾳ κατὰ τὰς πηγὰς καὶ τὴν πρᾶξιν τῶν νεωτέρων χρονῶν τοῦ Οἰκουμενικοῦ Πατριαρχείου, Analecta Vlatadon 14 (Thessalonica, 1972).

[12] Morozowich, *Holy Thursday*, 222–32.

[13] Arranz, "La saint consécration du saint myron," 335. Several Internet resources offer brief explanations and interpretations of the consecration of chrism, including: "The Sanctification of Holy Chrism," Greek Orthodox Archdiocese of America website, accessed October 17, 2011, http://www.goarch.org/ourfaith/ourfaith8420; and "The Holy Myron," The Ecumenical Patriarchate of Constantinople website, accessed June 21, 2013, http://www.patriarchate.org/patriarchate/holymyron. S.A. Vaniukov produced a Russian-language essay surveying the historical formation of the consecration of chrism in "Освящение мира" (The Consecration of Myron), *Московские Епархиальные Ведомости* nos. 7–8 (2007), accessed June 21, 2013, http://www.mepar.ru/library/vedomosti/2/420/. Also see George Wagner, "La consécration du myron," in *Les bénédictions et les sacramentaux dans la liturgie : conf Saint-Serge, XXXIVe semaine d'études liturgiques, Paris, juin 1987*, ed. A. Postoia and A. Triacca, Bibliotheca Ephemerides Liturgicae Subsidia 14 (Rome: Centro Liturgico Vincenziano, 1988), 285–94.

cration of chrism with the first bishops of other ancient Orthodox churches as a sign of unity, while other Orthodox patriarchates consecrate their own chrism in fidelity to their autonomy.[14] Arranz notes that the ritual for the consecration of chrism presented by Menevisiglou relies on the rituals prepared in 1890, 1912, 1951, and 1960. The gaps of time in between these publications of the rites of consecration of chrism do not necessarily represent the time that elapsed between the actual celebrations of rituals, but the infrequent celebration of the consecration of chrism in Orthodox churches is notable.[15] One can only speculate on the reasons, which would include the longevity of the chrism, and the lack of need for chrism with baptism and chrismation celebrated infrequently by churches under persecution.[16] That these churches infrequently consecrated chrism reveals the state of Orthodox Church life and the need (or lack thereof) for chrism for the sacraments of initiation.

In BAR, the consecration of chrism occurs during the Eucharistic Liturgy of Holy Thursday. Not surprisingly, the euchology identifies the bishop as the liturgical presider at this event. The title for the consecration of chrism in BAR number 141 is "The prayer or making of chrism celebrated on Holy Thursday of Great Week by one bishop."[17] The liturgy of the consecration of chrism begins as

---

[14] Arranz, "La saint consécration du saint myron," 335. The hagiopolite practice could be an antecedent to the Orthodox tradition of the chief bishop of a synod consecrating chrism, as evidenced by the testimony of Macarius of Jerusalem, *Letter to the Armenians*, ed. and trans. Terian, 88–89.

[15] Arranz, "La saint consécration du saint myron," 335. Arranz also states that in 1912, the Patriarchate of Constantinople reformed the rite of consecration of myron by replacing the Constantinopolitan prayer of BAR with the second prayer from the Cypriot euchologion known as "Allatanium," which dates to the late sixteenth century (330).

[16] Arranz wrote in 1989, when the Ecumenical Patriarchate was under Turkish duress (and remains so today) and the churches of Russia, Serbia, Romania, and Bulgaria were under communist rule.

[17] BAR no. 141, 2nd ed., eds. Parenti and Velkovska, 143. Also see Arranz, "La saint consécration du saint myron," 324–25. The title and description for the consecration of chrism is a bit different in three other euchologia Arranz examined. *Codex Grottaferrata Gb 1*, a thirteenth-century Euchologion frequently referred to as "Bessarion" (BES) as it has been widely interpreted

the anaphora concludes. One of the presbyters brings a container of oil and places it on the altar table near the diskos holding the consecrated bread for the Eucharist.[18] After the intonation of "Let us attend," the presider bows forward and recites the prayer for the consecration of chrism. The text of BAR's prayer is as follows:

> Lord of mercies and Father of lights, by whom this good gift and this perfect grace is given, grant to us who are unworthy grace for the service of this great and life-giving mystery, as you gave it to Moses your faithful servant, and to your servant Samuel, and to the holy apostles, and send your all-holy Spirit upon this myron and make it a royal chrism, a spiritual chrism, a protector of life, sanctification of souls and bodies, oil of great joy, both binding to law and the light of the New Testament: with it you anointed priests and high priests, prophets and kings, and through it anointed your holy apostles, and all of those who through the bath of regeneration are born again by them, and continued by the bishops and presbyters up until today. Yes, Master, God Almighty, show it, by the descent of your adorable and Holy Spirit, to be a vesture of incorruption and a seal of perfection, imprinting upon those who have received divine baptism your holy name and of your only-begotten son and of your Holy Spirit, that they would become knowledgeable in your view as your citizens, your children and servants, sanctified in soul and in body, free from every evil and

---

as a gift from Cardinal Bessarion to the monastery of Grottaferrata during the fifteenth-century milieu of the Council of Florence, is regarded as a copy of a Constantinopolitan patriarchal euchologion. *Athens gr. 662* is an important twelfth–fourteenth century monastic euchologion renowned for its comprehensive coverage of Byzantine liturgical celebration. *Sinai Gr. 959* is a Constantinopolitan patriarchal euchology, though it may also contain Palestinian influences. While their descriptions differ, *Bessarion* and *Athens 662* likewise identify the archbishop as the celebrant. Clearly the consecration of chrism is an episcopal liturgical ministry. For more background on these core Constantinopolitan liturgical sources, see M. Arranz, "Les Sacrements de l'ancien Euchologe constantinopolitain," *Orientalia christiana periodica* 48 (1982): 284–335.

[18] BAR and *Sinai Gr. 959* state that the oil is placed to the left of the diskos, while Bessarion and *Athens 662* simply say "near" the diskos (Arranz, "La saint consécration du saint myron," 324–25). Also see Morozowich, *Holy Thursday*.

redeemed from sin, by the vesture of your incorruptible glory, and that they would be known by this holy sign by the holy angels and archangels and by all the heavenly powers, and that they would be strong against evil and impure spirits, so that they would become for you a chosen people, a royal priesthood, a holy people, sealed through this your pure myron, and having your Christ in their hearts for your dwelling, God and Father in the Holy Spirit: For You are holy, our God, and unto You we send up glory.[19]

After the "Amen," the presider offers the Peace, and the deacon commands the assembly to bow their heads. The presider then recites the following prayer:

> To You God and king of all, offering you thanksgiving, we bend the neck of our heart, that being unworthy, you have made us worthy to minister these divine mysteries; proclaiming the abundant mercy which you have poured out on us, we beseech that you would grant your sanctification as myron upon the head, so that myron would be emptied out in the name of your only-begotten Son Christ our God, in whom the whole visible and invisible world is made fragrant. And to you are due all worship and thanksgiving, to the Father.[20]

Morozowich's comprehensive examination of Constantinopolitan manuscripts reveals a liturgy defined by "pageantry," especially since compatible Constantinopolitan sources depict the entrance of the chrism into the church as the equal to the preparation of the eucharistic gifts, since the chrism was accompanied by ripidia (fans), and deacons, with the liturgical officials exhibiting a disposition of solemn veneration toward the element of chrism.[21] The following analysis retains the imagery of this pageantry as shaping the liturgical environment while engaging a rigorous interpretation of the euchology.

---

[19] My translation of BAR's Greek text into English.
[20] My translation of BAR's Greek text into English.
[21] Morozowich, *Holy Thursday*.

The contemporary rite for the consecration of chrism is quite similar to its Constantinopolitan ancestor.[22] The rite begins on Monday of Holy Week, when the first hierarch of the synod blesses the ingredients for the chrism.[23] The main component of the initial rite is the blessing of water, which is used to sanctify the ingredients of the chrism. The ingredients include oil, wine, resins, and other fragrances. A cooking pot is prepared, the chief bishop pours blessed water into the pot, and the clergy add oil and a little wine. Priests read the gospel during the cooking process that continues until 4:00 p.m. on Wednesday of Holy Week. A priest adds wine to the mixture on Tuesday and Wednesday mornings, and the aromatic essences are added when the chrism has cooled on Wednesday. The chrism is poured into the containers used for storage and placed on a table near the table of oblation in the sanctuary. At the liturgy for the consecration of chrism, the chrism is placed on the altar table and the consecration occurs after the anaphora.[24] The metropolitan

---

[22] For the contemporary version, I am employing the English Language Rite titled "The Order of the Consecration of Holy Chrism for the Orthodox Church in America" ("OCA Chrism Rite" hereafter). I am grateful to Alexis Liberovsky, archivist of the Orthodox Church in America, for providing me with the text used for consecrating chrism in 2004. Mr. Liberovsky sent me this text via e-mail on January 31, 2012.

[23] "OCA Chrism Rite" states that this is the metropolitan, who is the first hierarch of the Orthodox Church in America.

[24] The contemporary rite has retained the pageantry of the ancient Constantinopolitan Rite, as described by "OCA Chrism Rite": "Before the Divine liturgy on Great and Holy Thursday, the Metropolitan, fully vested, takes the holy chrism from its place of safekeeping. He gives it to the senior priest and the procession is made to the church in which the consecration is to take place. The procession is led by the cross and candles. Fans are held over the holy chrism. The holy chrism is placed on the table of oblation . . . The Vesperal Divine liturgy begins as usual. At the Great Entrance, the senior priest carries the vessel of holy chrism, flanked by the fan-bearers. He is followed by the holy gifts and then by the clergy carrying the chrism that is to be consecrated. The Metropolitan first receives the vessel of holy chrism at the royal doors and places it upon the holy altar, to the right and slightly behind the holy Gospel. He then receives the holy gifts as usual. The clergy then enter with the chrism to be consecrated and place it on the holy altar, near the edges. After the consecration of the holy gifts . . . the containers of new chrism are opened. The

recites the prayer for the consecration of chrism followed by the prayer for the bowing of the heads.[25] The metropolitan blesses and closes each container and the Divine Liturgy continues. A unique ritual concludes the rite of consecration, accompanied by the chanting of Psalm 45:

> After the Divine Liturgy, a few drops of the old holy chrism are poured into the containers of the new holy chrism and then the old container of holy chrism is filled with the new holy chrism.[26]

ANALYSIS

The liturgies of the consecration of chrism in the ancient Constantinopolitan Rite and in "OCA Chrism Rite" offer several insights into the purpose of the chrism. The consecration is celebrated in the context of the Eucharistic Liturgy, after the gifts have been consecrated and before Holy Communion. The placement of the vessel containing the chrism on the altar table near the diskos accords the oil honor. One can view this placement functionally, since the oil needs to be placed somewhere, but the meticulous description of placing the oil near the diskos with the bread conveys the image of the connection between the chrism and the Eucharist. The contemporary rite evidences an intriguing development with the inclusion of the existing chrism that was consecrated on a Holy Thursday at an earlier date. Besides the inclusion of this chrism and its placement on the altar, the adding of old chrism to the new bottles and new to the old is a topic worthy of exploration. One possible explanation comes to mind: the mixture of the two chrisms establishes the sacramental viability of the old chrism. The new chrism is not replacing something that is no longer valuable, but is a significant addition to the church's supply of chrism. The new chrism continues the function of the old.

Metropolitan blesses each container three times saying, 'in the name of the Father, and of the Son, and of the Holy Spirit. Amen.'" The prayer for the consecration of the holy chrism follows.

[25] The English texts for this prayer and the prayer at the bowing of the heads in "OCA Chrism Rite" are essentially identical to those of BAR.

[26] "OCA Chrism Rite."

The beginning of the prayer for the consecration of chrism refers to God as the Lord of mercies and father of lights. The context is clearly established: God is the father of lights because of the anticipated celebration of baptism, a title drawn from James 1:17. While the phrase obviously draws from James's letter, there is also a secondary reference to baptism by introducing the notion of God as the source of light that illuminates darkness. The sequence of sacramental celebration is almost literally portrayed on the altar table. The church asks God to bless the chrism in anticipation of the Eucharist itself. Arranz argues that the euchology's use of "mystery" (μυστήριον) makes the chrism the equal of the Eucharist itself.[27] The placement of the chrism on the altar table and the recitation of the prayer affirm this hypothesis, but the broader context of the euchology illustrates a more sophisticated sacramental theology. The references to the Eucharist and baptism in the euchology anticipate the building up of God's holy people in the church, sealed in Christ, and go beyond the sacramentality of the elements of oil, bread, and wine themselves. The consecrated eucharistic gifts are received at the final stage of the baptismal process, so the oils are placed near them as an image of the church's journey.[28]

The prayer for the consecration of chrism presents a dilemma, as it appears to have two unique epicleses. The epicleses certainly differ in the language and verbs they employ, but they could also be interpreted as complementary.

Table 1.1 compares the two anamnesis-epiclesis sets:

---

[27] Arranz, "La saint consécration du saint myron," 337.
[28] Ibid.

Table 1.1 Epicleses in BAR: Consecration of Chrism

Anamnesis-Epiclesis 1:	**Anamnesis-Epiclesis 2:**
Lord of mercies and Father of lights, by whom this good gift and this perfect grace is given, grant to us who are unworthy grace for the service of this great and life-giving mystery, as you gave it to Moses your faithful servant, and to your servant Samuel, and to the holy apostles. Send (Κατάπεμψον) your all-holy Spirit upon this myron and make it (ποίσον αὐτὸ) a royal chrism, a spiritual chrism, a protector of life, sanctification of souls and bodies, oil of great joy, both binding to law and the light of the New Testament: with it you anointed priests and high priests, prophets and kings, and through it anointed your holy apostles, and all of those who through the bath of regeneration are born again by them, and continued by the bishops and presbyters up until today.	Yes, Master, God Almighty, manifest (ἀνάδειξον) it, by the descent of your adorable and holy Spirit, to be a vesture of incorruption and a seal of perfection, imprinting upon those who have received divine baptism your holy name and of your only-begotten son and of your Holy Spirit, that they would become knowledgeable in your view as your citizens, your children and servants, sanctified in soul and in body, free from every evil and redeemed from sin, by the vesture of your incorruptible glory, and that they would be known by this holy sign by the holy angels and archangels and by all the heavenly powers, and that they would be strong against evil and impure spirits, so that they would become for you a chosen people, a royal priesthood, a holy people, sealed through this your pure myron, and having your Christ in their hearts for your dwelling, God and Father in the Holy Spirit.

The anamnesis leading into the first epiclesis is remarkably terse, briefly mentioning the granting of grace to Moses, Samuel (God's servant), and the holy apostles. This brief anamnesis concerns the liturgical ministry of the presider and his concelebrants, who are the servants of this particular mystery. The first epiclesis actually lacks a preceding anamnesis, as the prayer immediately asks God to send his Holy Spirit upon the myron to become chrism, with a description of the blessings the chrism confers upon those who will be anointed: royalty and spiritual gifts, punctuated by the sanctification of souls and bodies. The epiclesis reverts to an anamnesis of past anointing, specifically of priests and high priests, prophets and kings, and everyone who has been baptized. The absence of particular references to events in salvation history in the language of the prayer is the most noteworthy characteristic. The prayer provides a general description of God's grace given in sanctification and protection to those who have been anointed in the past and have been baptized.

A second epiclesis follows the conjunction "Yes" (Ναί), asking God to show (ἀνάδειξον) the oil to be the vesture of incorruption and seal of perfection for those who have received baptism in the name of the Trinity. The second epiclesis appears to elaborate the bullet-like list of blessings described by the first epiclesis. Neophytes are the recipients of these gifts, and the chrism serves as their courier into the life of the Trinity, described as the imprinting of the name of the Holy Trinity.[29] The chrism also seals them into a group of people who are identified by citizenship in God's kingdom. The priority of the second epiclesis appears to be the continuing transformation of the neophytes into people who live as citizens of God's kingdom, confirmed by angelic recognition of their worthiness. The act of sealing with the holy chrism provides vesture of incorruption, a motif which receives extra emphasis since the second epiclesis mentions vesture and incorruption twice. The chrism seals incorruption because it helps protect the neophytes from sin, which the second epiclesis covers twice, particu-

---

[29] "Neophytes" is my abbreviation of the prayer's elongated description of the recently baptized: "ἐντυποῦσαν τοῖς τὸ θεῖόν σου λουτρὸν δεχομένοις."

larly in its reference to strength against impure spirits. Incorruption is evidenced by a community of holy people, an ecclesiological motif rooted in 1 Peter 2:9. The angels, archangels, and heavenly powers recognize the transformation of these people, which completes the ecclesiological motif. Thus, the anointing with chrism makes the neophytes incorrupt, and escorts them into the life of the Trinity, a holy people whom the angels recognize.

The second epiclesis functions to elaborate the brief description of blessings introduced by the initial epiclesis, illustrated by table 1.2:

Table 1.2: Epicletic Blessings in the Consecration of Chrism

Epiclesis 1	Epiclesis 2
royal chrism (χρῖσμα βασιλικόν)	Royal priesthood (βασίλειοω ἱεράτευμα)
sanctification of souls and bodies (ἁιαστικὸν ψυχῶν καὶ σωμάτων)	sanctified in soul and in body (ἡγιασμένους ψυχῇ καὶ σωμάτι)
protector of life (ζωῆς φυλακτήριον)	free from every evil and redeemed from sin; (ἀπηλλαγμένους πάσης κακίας καὶ πάσης ἁμαρτίας λελυτρωμένους) strong against evil and impure spirits (φοβεροὺς πᾶσιν ὑπάρχειν τοῖς πονηροῖς καὶ ἀκαθάρτοις πνεύμασιν)
those who were born again through baptism (πάντας τοὺς διὰ λουτροῦ παλιγγενεσίας)	those who have received divine baptism (ἐντυποῦσαν τοῖς τὸ θεῖόν σου λουτρὸν δεχομένοις)

Table 1.2 proves informative in analyzing the structure of the prayer and in hypothesizing the intent of its composition. Epiclesis 1 asks God to send the Holy Spirit and make (ποίησον) the myron in such a fashion that the myron is now chrism and has the capacity

to grant spiritual gifts such as sanctification and fidelity to God's law. Epiclesis 2 expands the vision of the first epiclesis by explicating how those who are anointed with the chrism benefit from the gifts infused into it. The theological themes of the two epicleses are consistent and the essential idea is this: God transforms the oil into chrism containing the divine powers of protection and sanctification. Those who are anointed with this chrism receive the gifts of protection from evil and the capacity to become holy.

In conclusion, the two epicleses of the prayer for the consecration of chrism in BAR are complementary, as they ask God to infuse the chrism with his power to bless newly baptized Christians with spiritual blessings that reveal them as God's holy people, whose life in the Triune God has already commenced. The anticipatory style of the prayer's language is particularly noteworthy, as the chrism is consecrated on Holy Thursday, with baptisms presumably occurring three days later at the Paschal Vigil. The consecration of chrism identifies several blessings that can be categorically summarized in terms of theological anthropology, ecclesiology, and eschatology. The theological anthropology of the prayer anticipates the emergence of a person who is vested in incorruption, protected from sin, and faithful to both the scriptures and the New Testament. The ecclesiology of the prayer draws from the language of St. Peter's first epistle by envisioning the new community as a royal and chosen people. The eschatology of the prayer anticipates the people's participation in the life of God and their recognition by the heavenly hosts as God's people.

Two other qualities are consistent throughout the prayer: the chrism introduces participants to intimate communion with the Holy Trinity, a variant of sacramental *theosis*, affirmed by the concluding phrase envisioning them as "having your Christ in their hearts for your dwelling, God and Father in the Holy Spirit."
The consecration of chrism also identifies a clear purpose for the chrism: it is to seal the Christian life in the royal priesthood shared by all the neophytes. The absence of references to other uses for the oil in the euchology is notable, even if officials employed the oil for noninitiatory purposes. The euchology identifies the neophytes as the ones who should receive chrismation. The multiple references

to baptism in the prayers suggest that the postbaptismal anointing with chrism continues what was begun at baptism, and that its liturgical and spiritual contexts are postbaptismal.

AN ANALYSIS OF CHRISMATION IN THE CONSTANTINOPOLITAN EUCHOLOGION

This section follows the method employed above, and closely examines the euchology for the prayer and postbaptismal anointing with chrism in the ancient Constantinopolitan euchologion.[30] My principal text of study is from BAR, and I will refer to the liturgical context of this postbaptismal anointing, and also alternate texts from the Byzantine euchologion tradition. As he did with the consecration of chrism, Miguel Arranz published and translated (into French) the texts of the rites of initiation from the Constantinopolitan euchologion tradition, and also provided a brief but substantial analysis of the postbaptismal anointing. This analysis will draw from BAR, and also from Arranz's comprehensive textual presentation and analysis.[31] First, I will begin by examining the positions of the prayer and ritual of chrismation in the context of baptism in BAR. BAR provides the euchology of the rites of initiation, which generally represents eighth-century Byzantine liturgical practice. Liturgical evidence absent from BAR but representing the Constantinopolitan liturgical tradition will be included as needed. Then, I will analyze the prayer and gestures themselves. Table 1.3 below provides the liturgical structure for baptism and chrismation in BAR:

---

[30] This section does not discuss the contemporary celebration of baptism in the Byzantine Rite because the order of the current rite is quite similar to its eighth-century predecessor.

[31] See Miguel Arranz, "Les sacrements de l'ancien Euchologe constantinopolitain (8): l'"illumination' de la nuit de Pâques," *Orientalia christiana periodica* 53 (1987): 59–106.

Table 1.3: The Order of Baptism in BAR nos. 113–26

Prayer for the entrance of a child into the church on the fortieth day of his birth (Churching)

Prayer for the making of a catechumen

Three Exorcisms (BAR nos. 115–17)

Prayer after the making of a catechumen at the hour of baptism (BAR no. 118)

Renunciation of Satan/Confession of Christ/Creed (BAR no. 119)

Diakonika of Holy Saturday for baptism (litanic biddings for the blessing of baptismal water) (BAR no. 120, includes presider's prayer of apology for himself)

Prayer for the blessing of baptismal waters ("Great are You") (BAR no. 122)

Peace/Bowing of Heads

Prebaptismal Prayer for Anointing with Oil (BAR no. 123)

Blessing of waters with Oil/Alleluia/baptism/Singing of Psalm 31.1a (BAR no. 124)

[Litany (synapte)][32]

Prayer of chrismation: "Blessed are you, Lord God almighty"

[patriarch removes baptismal vestments and puts on vestments for the Eucharistic Liturgy][33]

---

[32] Arranz presents a critical edition of texts in the form of a litany preceding the prayer of chrismation, which appears in *Sinai 959*, a ninth-century Constantinopolitan euchologion; *Grottaferrata Gb 7*, a tenth-century Italian euchologion representing Constantinopolitan liturgy; and *Sinai 973*, a twelfth-century euchologion, probably of hybrid provenance (Arranz, "Les sacrements de l'ancien Euchologe constantinopolitain (8): l'illumination' de la nuit de Pâques," 79–81.

[33] Before he anoints the neophytes with chrism, the patriarch removes his baptismal vestments and adorns those for the liturgy, according to two euchologia consulted by Arranz (*Athens 662* and the Taktikon of John Cantacuzenos); see Arranz, "Les sacrements de l'ancien Euchologe constantinopolitain (8): l'illumination' de la nuit de Pâques," 80–81.

> Singing of "As many as have been baptized into Christ have put on Christ" (Gal. 3:27, BAR 125)
>
> Anointing of neophytes with chrism: at each anointing, "[The] seal of the gift of the Holy Spirit"[34]
>
> Singing of Psalm 31.1a; the priest celebrates the holy liturgy (Eucharist) with the neophytes.
>
> [The prayer of washing] (BAR no. 126)[35]

THE CONTEXT OF CHRISMATION IN BAR

BAR presents the euchology of the baptismal rites without significant fanfare. Baptism does not have its own entry with an elaborate title. The reader identifies baptism by the title of the prayers in the order BAR provides.[36] Chrismation's appearance in the euchology follows this pattern of an orderly presentation of euchology. The reader identifies chrismation based on the order and flow of the ritual, as the euchology does not assign a title to chrismation. The lack of a title for chrismation in BAR is not unusual for the euchological style, but notable for liturgical history. Also notable is that chrismation occurs in the ritual without particular demarcation. The prayer and ritual occur as an integral part of the process of baptism, suggesting an organic connection with the preceding and successive portions of the entire ritual.

Arranz notes the interpolation of a brief synapte (series of litanic biddings) prior to the prayer of chrismation in some manuscripts.

---

[34] According to the Praxapostolos *Dresden 104*, representing Constantinopolitan cathedral liturgy, the patriarch anoints the neophytes with the chrism with the assistance of a second celebrant in the Church of St. Peter, while the people sing Gal 3:27 ("As many as have been baptized") throughout (Arranz, "Les sacrements de l'ancien Euchologe constantinopolitain (8): l'"illumination' de la nuit de Pâques," 78).

[35] The Constantinopolitan tradition completed initiation on the eighth day with the rites of ablution and tonsuring. In contemporary practice, these rites are usually celebrated on the same day as baptism.

[36] Parenti and Velkovska, the editors of the critical edition, guide the reader with the heading "Iniziazione Cristiana," but this is not a translation of the euchology.

In addition to customary litanic petitions praying for peace and for the world, this synapte contains two petitions pertaining to chrismation: "For our brothers who have been made worthy of new birth through holy baptism and will receive the grace of the Holy Spirit, let us pray to the Lord," and "That the Lord our God would maintain them spotless and blameless up to the end of their life."[37] Despite its limited appearance in the Byzantine Euchologia, the synapte's two special petitions can be consulted in analyzing the theology of chrismation.

The singing of Psalm 31.1a is noteworthy. Psalm 31 follows baptism, and BAR number 124.7 tersely indicates the following: "and after this one has been baptized, the chanter says, 'blessed are those whose faults are removed,' the incipit of the psalm.[38] The psalm appears again following the anointing of those who have received baptism and anointing with chrism, in BAR number 125.5: "and he begins, saying: blessed are those whose faults are removed, and whose sins have been covered." Arranz comprehensively examined the chanting of Psalm 31 in the Constantinopolitan Euchologion tradition.[39] The church chants select verses of Psalm 31 in the following instances: after baptismal immersion, during the procession of the patriarch and assisting bishops and presbyters from the baptistery into the church (vested in white), during the entrance into the church, and up until the patriarch and concelebrating bishops enter into the sanctuary. The singing of Psalm 31 marks the next station in the journey of the rites of initiation, as the rites culminate with the neophytes joining the rest of the people to offer and celebrate the Eucharistic Liturgy. Then, they sing Galatians 3:27 instead of the Trisagion. The chanting of the psalm essentially brackets chrismation, the source of processional psalmody after baptism, through chrismation, and going into the Eucharistic Liturgy. The replacement of the Trisagion with Galatians 3:27 symbolizes the blending of the three sacraments: the baptized are now in

---

[37] Arranz, "Les sacrements de l'ancien Euchologe constantinopolitain (8): l''illumination' de la nuit de Pâques," 80.

[38] BAR no. 124.7, in eds. Parenti and Velkovska.

[39] Arranz, "Les sacrements de l'ancien Euchologe constantinopolitain (8): l''illumination' de la nuit de Pâques," 102–3.

Christ and join his body in offering and celebrating the sacrament of the kingdom. The singing of Galatians 3:27 is a reminder that baptism and the anointing with chrism initiates neophytes into the eucharistic community over which Christ presides.

Arranz asserts that Psalm 31 is the prokeimenon of illumination, though the liturgical sources do not appoint a particular prokeimenon.[40] The evidence suggests that Psalm 31 has two functions: first, it is the selected psalm of the Byzantine rites of initiation, occasionally functioning as a prokeimenon.[41] Second, Psalm 31 significantly shapes a theology of chrismation because it accompanies the neophyte-assembly's ritual movement from the font to the anointing of chrism, and from the baptistery to the church. Thus, Psalm 31 is the church's song of chrismation, which the people sing as the mobile church proceeds from baptism, through the anointing with chrism, and to the Eucharist.

The prayer preceding the anointing with chrism in BAR is as follows:

> Blessed are you, Lord God Almighty, the spring of blessings, the Sun of righteousness, who have made the light of salvation shine for those in darkness through the appearing of your Only-Begotten Son and our God, and have granted us, unworthy though we are, the grace of blessed cleansing by this holy water, and divine sanctification by life-giving Anointing. And you have now been well-pleased to make your newly-enlightened servants to be born again through water and Spirit, and have granted him/her forgiveness of sins both voluntary and involuntary. Do you then, Master, compassionate,

---

[40] A "prokeimenon" is the responsorial psalm that begins the proclamation of the Word in Byzantine liturgical offices. Most prokeimena are composed of two selected verses from a psalm, with the first verse, chanted by the lector, functioning as the common refrain. Some prokeimena assigned to solemn festal offices have additional verses. At the Divine Liturgy, the prokeimenon introduces the epistle reading. In the daily offices, the prokeimenon is chanted without the proclamation of the Word.

[41] Arranz states that the absence of an appointed prokeimenon preceding the epistle lection of the eucharistic liturgy at the Paschal Vigil makes Psalm 31 the prokeimenon by default, in "Les sacrements de l'ancien Euchologe constantinopolitain (8): l'"illumination' de la nuit de Pâques," 103.

universal King, grant him/her also the Seal of the gift of your holy, all-powerful and adorable Spirit and the Communion of the holy Body and honourable Blood of your Christ. Keep them in your sanctification; confirm him/her in the Orthodox Faith; deliver them from the evil one and all his devices, and by your saving fear guard their souls in purity and righteousness; so that being in every deed and word well-pleasing to you, they may become sons and heirs of your heavenly Kingdom. For you are our God, a merciful God who saves, and to you we send up glory, to the Father and to the Son and to the Holy Spirit, now and forever, and to the ages of ages.[42]

The prayer introduces several themes.[43] First, it assumes that multiple people have participated in the sacrament of baptism, since the prayer consistently refers to participants in the plural. References to plural participants represent the age of BAR as an eighth-century euchologion. The Constantinopolitan Typikon of the Great Church (TGC), representing the liturgy of the imperial capital's Hagia Sophia in the ninth and tenth centuries, refers to the celebration of baptisms on Holy Saturday.[44] BAR's euchology is at least partially compatible with TGC as the diakonika, the litanic biddings (demand petitions) chanted by the deacon to introduce the blessing of the baptismal waters, are assigned to Holy Saturday (Διακονικὰ τοῦ ἁγίου σαββάτου εἰς τὸ βαπτίσαι).[45] BAR thus assumes that baptisms are celebrated at the Paschal Vigil.

The second prominent theme of BAR is that God's presence is identified with light and water. The opening doxological phrase calls God almighty and the sun of righteousness who illumines all darkness. God's light illumines those who have been in dark-

---

[42] English translation adapted from Archimandrite Ephrem Lash, Anastasis, "Service of Holy Baptism," accessed September 30, 2011, http://www.anastasis.org.uk/baptism.htm. Note the longevity of the prayer: the contemporary version of this prayer retains the text dating to the eighth century.

[43] See Arranz's brief theological analysis of the prayer in "Les sacrements de l'ancien Euchologe constantinopolitain (8): l''illumination' de la nuit de Pâques," 93.

[44] J. Mateos, Le Typikon de la grande église: Ms. Sainte-Croix no. 40, X siécle Vol. 2, 82–91.

[45] BAR no. 120.1, in eds. Parenti and Velkovska, 125.

ness. The light theme of this prayer connects it with the prayer for the consecration of chrism, which refers to God as the "Father of lights" (Πάτερ τῶν φώτων). In the prayer before chrismation, God is also the "spring" (πηγή) of blessings. "πηγή" usually refers to water, though it can also mean "source" or "origin," and Ephrem Lash translated this term as "source" in the translation grounding the English text above.[46] Translating this term as "spring" here is sensible, given the first use of "sun" (ἥλιος). "Spring" continues the pattern of thought grounded by creation, and coheres with the gift of "holy water" (literally through ἁγίῳ ὕδατι). The prayer of BAR clearly establishes God's identification with creation in enlightening the neophytes through light, and cleansing them through sanctified water. The prayer reflects on the progress of the baptismal liturgy, as the neophytes are now enlightened and have received the forgiveness of sins. The chanting of Psalm 31.1a (immediately following baptism) confirms their cleansing, and they have already received the gifts of the water and the Spirit.

Having established the neophytes as baptized through holy water and the Spirit, the prayer asks God to bestow the seal of the gift of the Spirit and the privilege of participating in eucharistic communion. Several gifts of the Spirit are delineated afterward, though the prayer does not specifically assign them to the anointing or the Eucharist. Neophytes receive the following gifts: preservation of the gift of holiness, surety in purity and righteousness, protection from evil spirits, and membership in God's family of the kingdom.

The lack of clarity in whether chrismation or Eucharist bestows these gifts is not alarming. The prayer's ambiguity on this front suggests that participation in both sacraments leads to the imparting and reception of these gifts. An implication of the frequent imparting of these spiritual gifts is that the sacraments of baptism, chrismation, and Eucharist are not necessarily sequential in the Byzantine Rite. When one partakes of the Eucharist, he or she receives the gifts bestowed at baptism and chrismation anew, at each eschatological encounter in the heavenly kingdom. Since the prayer

[46] Ibid.

explicates participation in the Eucharist, and the rubrics likewise indicate that the assembly proceeds from chrismation into the Eucharistic Liturgy, one can conceive of chrismation as a part of baptism that naturally leads into the Eucharist.

The structure of the sequence of the initiatory rites and the prayer of chrismation points to the Eucharist as the destiny of the journey of initiation. It is important to note that the neophyte is initiated into a community of people who offer and celebrate the Eucharist. This eucharistic celebration is both frequent and regular, and each member of the eucharistic community partakes of holy communion, a communion described by the Eucharistic Liturgy itself as "communion of the Holy Spirit," a phrase taken from 2 Cor. 13:14 and embedded throughout the Eucharistic Liturgy.[47] The Eucharist is the repeated sacrament in which each person of the community participates and receives the blessings originally imparted at baptism and chrismation anew. The prayer of chrismation does not explicate this theology, but it is not necessary for the prayer to do so because the structure of the rites of initiation illuminates a journey of initiation into a eucharistic community.[48] "Communion of the Holy Spirit" connotes a communion with God. The implications of this assertion are bold: essentially, the rites of initiation begin a process of restoring each neophyte, regardless of age or social status, to communion with the Triune God, a gradual process of spiritual perfection better known as *theosis*, or deification.[49]

---

[47] The Byzantine eucharistic liturgy contains references to the Communion of the Holy Spirit in the anaphoras attributed to Basil the Great and John Chrysostom which is taken from Paul's second letter to the Corinthians (2 Cor. 13:14). "Communion of the Holy Spirit" also appears and the litany of supplication preceding the Lord's Prayer, and again in the collect prayer of the Lord's Prayer. For the contemporary texts, see "The Divine Liturgy of St. Basil the Great" and "The Divine Liturgy of St. John Chrysostomos" at the Greek Orthodox Archdiocese of America website, accessed June 26, 2013, http://www.goarch.org/chapel/liturgical_texts.

[48] A thorough examination of the blessings imparted by participation in the eucharistic liturgy is outside the scope of this study.

[49] For a magisterial explanation of the meaning of the Communion of the Holy Spirit in the Byzantine Eucharistic *lex orandi*, see Alexander Schmemann,

The prayer of chrismation is followed by the chanting of "As many as have been baptized in Christ have put on Christ," from Galatians 3:27.[50] BAR's text then indicates the ritual action of anointing with the chrism: "and the priest anoints those who have been baptized with the holy myrrh making the sign of the cross on the eyes, the nose, the mouth, and on two ears saying, 'seal of the gift of the Holy Spirit.'"[51] Arranz mentioned that anointing the eyes, nose, mouth and ears with the chrism dates to the late fourth century, as the seventh canon of the Council of Constantinople of 381 stipulates that heretics desiring restoration to the church are to be received through anointing with chrism on the forehead, mouth, nostrils and eyes with the same formula, "seal of the gift of the Holy Spirit."[52] It is likely that this canon was retroactively attributed to the Council of Constantinople, and actually represents a later, fifth-century practice of receiving converts.[53] The text appears in several canonical and liturgical texts dating from the fourth century and later, including canon 95 of the Council in Trullo (692).[54] I will

---

The Eucharist: Sacrament of the Kingdom, trans. Paul Kachur (Crestwood, NY: St. Vladimir's Seminary Press, 1987), 222–27.

[50] Note that the rubrics only mention the chanting of this text; there is no indication of an accompanying action.

[51] "Σφραγὶς δωρεᾶς πνεύματος ἁγίου ," in BAR no. 125.4, in eds. Parenti and Velkovska, 131.

[52] Arranz, "Les sacrements de l'ancien Euchologe constantinopolitain (8): l'"illumination' de la nuit de Pâques," 83, 89.

[53] G. W. H. Lampe, *The Seal of the Spirit: A Study in the Doctrine of Baptism and Confirmation in the New Testament and the Fathers,* 2nd ed. (London: SPCK, 1967), 283.

[54] For a brief synopsis of the text's history, see John Erickson, "Divergences in Pastoral Practices in the Reception of Converts," in *Orthodox Perspectives on Pastoral Praxis: Papers of Intra-Orthodox Conference on Pastoral Praxis Celebrating 50th Anniversary of Holy Cross,* ed. Theodore Stylianopoulos (Brookline, MA: Holy Cross Orthodox Press, 1988), 162–66. Arranz appears to accept the text as belonging to the Council of Constantinople in 381 in Arranz, "Évolution des rites d'incorporation et de réadmission dans l'Église selon l'Euchologe byzantine," in *Gestes et paroles dans les diverses families liturgiques,* eds. A. Postoia and A. Triacca, Bibliotheca Ephemerides Liturgicae Subsidia 14 (Rome: Centro Liturgico Vincenziano, 1978), 70–71. See the Greek, Latin, and English translations

address the Byzantine practice of receiving converts through the ritual anointing with chrism elsewhere; in this section of the study, I analyze the formula within the context of the rites of initiation.

The use of the word "seal" (Σφραγὶς) in the Byzantine euchology is provocative. Throughout its history, both within and outside of Christianity, "seal" connotes multivalent meaning, including the identification of authority, ownership, and particularly in the Christian context, the notion of Christians belonging to God. G. Lampe performed a contextual study of the lexical use and interpretation of "seal" in the rites of baptism and confirmation in a dated work (1967), and warned of the danger in attempting to directly connect "seal" with a sacrament, since the term has a "bewildering variety of meaning."[55] Eldon Woodcock surveyed the manifold meanings of "seal," and in particular, he attended to the connection between anointing and chrism in the Scriptures and the New Testament.[56] He asserts that in the New Testament, the anointing "equips Christians to serve," assures sufficient knowledge of spiritual truth, and naturally advances toward God's sealing them with the Holy Spirit, affirming their belonging to God.[57] None of the euchological texts contain an explanation of seal, but as a repeated acclamation at chrismation, accompanying the ritual act of anointing, the acclamation clearly helps to interpret the ritual action. Thus, the actual liturgical context can help define how the Byzantines understood "seal," since it can only be interpreted in particular contexts, given its plurality of meaning.

The ritual postbaptismal anointing with chrism echoes the phrase "seal of the gift of the Holy Spirit," which was mentioned with greater elaboration in the prayer recited before chrismation in

---

of Trullo's 94th canon in G. Nedungatt and M. Fatherstone, eds., *The Council in Trullo Revisited*, Kanonika 6 (Rome: Pontifical Oriental Institute, 1995), 174–77.

[55] Lampe, *The Seal of the Spirit*, 7.

[56] Eldon Woodcock, "The Seal of the Holy Spirit," *Bibliotheca Sacra* 155 (1998), 154–55.

[57] Ibid.

BAR.[58] While the formula of anointing in BAR is simple, the Constantinopolitan Euchologion contains numerous variants of the formula, evidencing significant historical development. Arranz identified nine variants of the formula diffused throughout the Euchologia.[59] Table 1.4 lists the first six variants presented by Arranz:

Table 1.4: Variant Formulas of Anointing with Chrism

"Seal of the gift of the Holy Spirit" (without Amen, recited once only)

"Seal of the gift of the Holy Spirit, Amen" (recited once only)

"Seal of the gift of the Holy Spirit, Amen" (recited after each anointing)

"Seal of the gift of the Holy Spirit, in the name of the Father, and of the Son, and of the Holy Spirit, now and ever . . ." (recited once only)

"Seal of the gift of the Holy Spirit, for the fullness of wisdom for the obedience of faith, now and ever" (recited once only)

"Seal of the gift of the Holy Spirit, Amen. For the obedience of faith, Amen" (recited once only)

In addition to these six formulas, Arranz presents three additional formulas for the anointing with chrism that are followed by other formulas for each bodily anointing. As an illustration of the textualization of this ritual anointing, I present Arranz's seventh example of the formula taken from *Sinai 981*, a fourteenth-century Byzantine

---

[58] "χάρισαι αὐτοῖς καὶ τὴν σφραγῖδα τῆς δωρεᾶς τοῦ ἁγίου καὶ παντοδυνάμου καὶ προσκυνατοῦ σου πνεύματος," BAR no. 125.2, in eds. Parenti and Velkovska, 131.

[59] Arranz, "Les sacrements de l'ancien Euchologe constantinopolitain (8): l'"illumination' de la nuit de Pâques," 84–88.

Euchologion, with variant formulas accompanying each bodily anointing in table 1.5:[60]

Table 1.5: Postbaptismal Chrism Anointing Formulas

"Seal of the gift of the Holy Spirit" (forehead)
"Holy chrism of indissoluble life" (eyes)
"chrism (a) pledge of the heavenly kingdom" (ears)
"chrism unto preservation of souls and bodies" (throat)
"Vestment of royal dignity" (breast)
"Fullness of the gift of the Holy Spirit" (back)
"Armor of faith and of truth" (exterior of hands)
"Path of divine way" (feet)
"Seal of the gift of the Holy Spirit"

Arranz's remaining examples draw from Euchologia dated as late as the seventeenth century. He concludes that the proliferation of formulas accompanying the ritual anointing is not a particularly late development, since a renowned ninth-century Euchologion representing Constantinopolitan cathedral worship, *Sinai 957*, contains variant formulas particular to the part of the body being anointed.[61] Such elaborate formulas contrast with the simple one of BAR.[62] Arranz found an explanation he attributes to Metropolitan Cyril II, who justified the practice of using the simple formula

---

[60] Arranz takes this example from the fourteenth-century Euchologion *Sinai 981* in "Les sacrements de l'ancien Euchologe constantinopolitain (8): l'"illumination' de la nuit de Pâques," 86 and n. 46.

[61] Arranz, "Les sacrements de l'ancien Euchologe constantinopolitain (8): l'"illumination' de la nuit de Pâques," 86, 90. *Sinai 957* begins with "Seal of the gift of the Holy Spirit." The formula for eyes: "Charism of the gift of the Holy Spirit"; back: "fullness of the gift of the Holy Spirit and of the armor of faith and of truth."

[62] Arranz notes that the simple formula of BAR occurs in at least thirteen other manuscripts, many of them early, ibid., 84.

with anointing on the forehead, eyes, nose, and breast to Cyril, the fourth-century bishop of Jerusalem.[63] Arranz discovered that Cyril's mystagogical catecheses do not refer to the main formula, "seal of the gift," and thus concluded that this chief formula is particular to Constantinople (and not Jerusalem), which simply expanded the number of anointings to include the breast, hands, and feet.

Arranz's seminal research on the question of the formula of postbaptismal anointing with chrism illuminates the Constantinopolitan liturgical development of the seal of the gift of the Spirit without resolving how this core ritual anointing coheres with the prayer's theology.[64] Allowing for the possibility that BAR does not include each acclamation accompanying bodily anointing, its ritual formula is simple. Thus, the tendency for later liturgical sources to include verbose formulas accompanying each bodily anointing is an instance of the textualization of ritual. The liturgical celebrants who edited their books increasingly imposed their theological interpretations of chrismation on the actual formulas. Such ritual textualization contributes to the liturgical theology of chrismation, as the elongated formulas presumably represent the editors' interpretation of the ritual action.[65] It is also possible that the textual development of the simple formula "seal of the gift of the holy Spirit" demonstrates an attempt to capture a more precise theological interpretation of the simple formula containing the keyword "seal." In examining samples of anointing formulae from the eleventh through the seventeenth centuries, Peter Galadza suggests that the Byzantine euchology enumerates multiple gifts granted to the participant who

---

[63] Ibid., 91–92.

[64] Arranz attempts to connect the two, but claims that the prayer's themes are not clearly related to the anointing, ibid., 93.

[65] It is possible that the textualizing of the postbaptismal anointing formulas is an instance of Anton Baumstark's law no. 6, that "the later it is, the more liturgical prose becomes charged with doctrinal elements," in *Comparative Liturgy*, 3rd ed., ed. Bernard Botte, trans. F. L. Cross (Westminster, MD: Newman Press, 1958), 60–61; and also the discussion by Robert F. Taft in "Anton Baumstark's Comparative Liturgy Revisited," in *Acts of the International Congress Comparative Liturgy Fifty Years after Anton Baumstark (1872–1948), Rome, 25–29 September 1998*, ed. R. F. Taft and G. Winkler, Orientalia christiana analecta 265 (Rome: Pontifical Oriental Institute, 2001): 199, 204–5.

is anointed with chrism.[66] One can reasonably suggest that the solemnity of the ritual moment functioned as a catalyst in shaping an emerging theology of the gift of the Holy Spirit, an instance of the textualizing of ritual. Because the prayer preceding chrismation and ritual anointing constitute the chief components of this liturgical unit, the theological relationship between the prayer and the anointing deserves further examination and can contribute to the theological interpretation of chrismation as a process.

ANALYSIS OF PRAYER AND RITUAL ANOINTING WITH CHRISM IN BAR

Assuming that anointing the neophytes on their senses ritualizes the delineated blessings of the prayer of chrismation, one can conclude that the anointing grants the following blessings to participants: sanctification, surety in faith, deliverance from evil spirits, and growth toward the kingdom of God.[67] In the ritual, the anointing of the senses represents the Christian life of the person receiving the anointing, as the mind will direct personal activities through sensual perception and operation in seeing, hearing, and smelling.[68] The examples of formulas for the postbaptismal ritual anointing summarized in table 1.5 above shows that the blessings iterated by the prayer are verbally repeated in the formulas accompanying the ritual anointings. Table 1.6 illustrates examples of reiterations of the prayer's blessings in the formulas of postbaptismal ritual anointing:

---

[66] Peter Galadza, "The Holy Spirit in Eastern Orthodox Worship: Historical Enfleshments and Contemporary Queries," in *The Spirit in Worship—Worship in the Spirit*, ed. Teresa Berger and Bryan Spinks (Collegeville, MN: Liturgical Press, 2009), 125–27.

[67] A simple summary from the prayer's iteration of blessings: "Keep them in your sanctification; confirm him/her in the Orthodox Faith; deliver them from the evil one and all his devices, and by your saving fear guard their souls in purity and righteousness; so that being in every deed and word well-pleasing to you, they may become sons and heirs of your heavenly Kingdom."

[68] In the contemporary postbaptismal anointing, the neophytes are also anointed on the breast, hands, and feet. See Archimandrite Ephrem Lash, "Baptism," accessed October 17, 2011, http://www.anastasis.org.uk/baptism.htm.

Table 1.6: Comparison of Chrismation Blessings between Prayer and Anointing Formulas

Prayer of chrismation	Formulas of postbaptismal anointing
Sanctification	"Chrism of participation in immortal life," (*Sinai 981*, 14th c.)[69]
surety in faith	"Armor of faith and of truth"
deliverance from evil spirits	"To tread on serpents and scorpions and on all the power of the enemy," (*Pantokrator 149*, 15th c.)[70]
growth toward the kingdom of God	"Chrism of the guarantee of the kingdom of God" (*Sinai 958, Sinai 981, Sinai 982*)[71]

The select examples in table 1.6 illustrate the inscribing of the blessings iterated by the prayer onto the formulas of postbaptismal anointing. Arranz's critical edition of the text of the prayer demonstrates that the text does not considerably develop throughout history, so BAR's variant is fairly stable up until the *textus receptus*. While the themes of the formulas cohere with the prayer, one cannot conclude that the prayer alone inspired the inscribing of new texts for the formulas, due to a lack of clear connecting evidence.

However, the liturgical environment of postbaptismal anointing with chrism provides a space where the blessings iterated by the prayer echo and are creatively reiterated in the formula texts for the anointing. Every blessing iterated by the prayer finds a common theme in the anointing formulas. Although "sanctification" has no direct equivalent in the formulas, it has many formulaic synonyms. Formulas such as "fullness of the gift of the Holy Spirit" (*Sinai*

---

[69] Arranz, "Les sacrements de l'ancien Euchologe constantinopolitain (8): l'"illumination' de la nuit de Pâques," 86.
[70] Ibid., 88.
[71] Ibid., 87.

981, 957, 958) and "holy chrism of Christ God and unassailable seal, Amen" (*Sinai 958*) represent attempts to articulate the idea of sanctification.[72] Arranz made two noteworthy observations about the textualization of the ritual formulas: seven manuscripts reserve the original, simple formula for the anointing of the forehead, and develop more elaborate texts for the anointing of other body parts.[73] He also asserted that the appearance of more developed formulas is not a late occurrence, because it is evident in Euchologia as old as *Sinai 957* and *Sinai 958*, which date to the ninth and tenth centuries, respectively.[74] However, the cluster of thirteen Euchologia preserving the simple anointing formula, including classical Constantinopolitan cathedral sources such as BAR, *Bessarion*, *Athens 662*, and *Porfyry-Leningrad 226* simply shows that the process of textualization began early, but the core formula remained predominant in the Constantinopolitan Euchologion tradition. Theologically, the addition of texts to the postbaptismal anointing coherent with the prayer of chrismation shows that throughout Byzantine liturgical history, practitioners of the Byzantine Rite recognized an organic coherence of euchology and ritual action in chrismation.

The organic coherence between euchology and ritual action elucidated in the above section on chrismation began with the consecration of chrism on Holy Thursday. The process of chrismation begins with the preparation and sanctification of the gifts for the people receiving them. The pageantry of the consecration of chrism, its context within the Eucharistic Liturgy and proximity to the consecrated bread and wine, and its position anticipating the celebration of baptism on Pascha constitute the beginning of the process of chrismation. Table 1.7 illuminates the continuity of themes inaugurated by the consecration of chrism and punctuated by chrismation, in euchology and ritual action:

---

[72] Ibid., 87.
[73] Ibid., 90.
[74] Ibid.

Table 1.7: Comparison of Blessings: Consecration of Chrism and Anointing with Chrism

sanctified in soul and in body	divine sanctification by life-giving Anointing; Keep them in your sanctification
[no equivalent]	confirm him/her in the Orthodox Faith
and that they would be strong against evil and impure spirits	deliver them from the evil one and all his devices
free from every evil and redeemed from sin, by the vesture of your incorruptible glory	and by your saving fear guard their souls in purity and righteousness
that they would become knowledgeable in your view as your citizens, your children and servants, a chosen people, a royal priesthood, a holy people	so that being in every deed and word well-pleasing to you, they may become sons and heirs of your heavenly Kingdom

The phrases in the left column are taken from the second epiclesis of the prayer for the consecration of chrism, which expresses the blessings to be given to the neophytes at their postbaptismal anointing. The right column contains the iteration of blessings from the prayer of chrismation. Clearly, the prayer for the consecration of chrism is more elaborately developed, and the blessings of the chrismation prayer are not lexically equivalent. References to confirmation in the Orthodox faith are absent in the prayer of consecration of chrism, and the language expressing citizenry in God's kingdom differs. While the allusion to the anointing of Moses and Samuel in the consecration of chrism is not echoed in the prayer of chrismation, Arranz emphasizes that this biblical anamnesis recalls the significance of chrism in the Old Testament as grace given from God to the people.[75] Interpreting the postbaptismal anointing with chrism from this perspective demands an emphasis on the gift of prophecy. Thus, the continuity between the prayers of consecration of chrism and the rite of anointing with chrism in initiation in the Constantinopolitan euchological tradition is thematic, and the evidence strongly suggests that the prayers received mutually independent processes of redaction throughout their history.

CONCLUSION

The analysis above presents the historical structures of the rites of consecrating chrism and anointing neophytes with chrism after baptism. In the preceding presentation, I established an initial sacramental theology of chrismation. Now, I shall conclude this chapter by elaborating the most salient theological points from this examination of the rite involving the consecration of and anointing with chrism. These points are, in order, the seamless and blended structure of the rites of initiation, the solemnity of the consecration of chrism and its resemblance to the Eucharistic Liturgy, and how the rites of chrismation communicate an image of a Christian as a holy person belonging to a holy community.

Chrismation in the Context of the Rites of Initiation

The history of the rite of chrismation reveals it to be one of multiple liturgical components constituting initiation. Essentially, chrismation is a component of baptism and not a separate sacrament. The treatment of postbaptismal chrismation as a separate sacrament is influenced by Western scholarly study on confirmation and the attempt to ascertain the proper position and definition of confirmation today. This chapter's analysis of chrismation illumi-

---

[75] Miguel Arranz, "Évolution des rites d'incorporation et de réadmission dans l'Église selon l'Euchologe byzantine," in *Gestes et paroles dans les diverses families liturgiques: Conferences Saint-Serge XXIVe semaine d'etudes liturgiques, 1977*, ed. A. Postoia and A. Triacca, Bibliotheca Ephemerides Liturgicae Subsidia 14 (Rome: Centro Liturgico Vincenziano, 1978), 61–62.

nates it as a crucial component in a large and complex series of rites contained under the umbrella of initiation. The rites clearly demonstrate that chrismation is truly inseparable from the whole, a necessary part of the journey that begins with baptism and culminates with entrance into the eucharistic community and the fellowship of the Holy Spirit.

The consequence of separating chrismation from baptism and Eucharist is an isolated theology, exiled from its native home, and thus sentenced to impoverishment. This consequence also applies to the consecration of chrism and the reception of converts into the communion of the church. The liturgical evidence suggests that initiation begins with the consecration of chrism, which is then used for diverse purposes: initiating neophytes and receiving converts.

Thus, chrismation belongs to the whole complex of initiating people into the church. Its prayers and liturgical context are theologically potent, but they can be interpreted only through the contextual lenses of baptism and Eucharist. The implications of identifying chrismation as part of a larger program that includes baptism and Eucharist are manifold. For example, in contemplating the meaning of consecrating chrism, we must remember that this process begins with the assembly of a eucharistic community that petitions God to change the oil into chrism. In other words, the process of chrismation actually begins in the Eucharist—the eucharistic community asks God to sanctify oil for the purpose of building up the body of Christ, and introducing new people to the eucharistic community. Another example of articulating the theology of chrismation through a contextual lens of baptism and Eucharist occurs when we attempt to glean pneumatology from the prayer of chrismation. It is not sufficient to view the prayer as a petition of the descent of the Spirit upon the neophytes to seal them into the Triune God and the community. The prayer refers back to baptism and forward to the Eucharist. The reference backward refers to the activity of the Spirit throughout the baptismal portion of the journey.

For example, the Spirit descended upon the baptismal waters and made Christ present in them, allowing the catechumens to die and rise with Christ and thus become one with him. The Spirit continues to act in chrismation by sealing the neophytes into the eucharistic community. It is in this eucharistic community where the Spirit acts continuously and repeatedly, providing an entrance into the presence of the Triune God for the holy community where it receives the blessings of the Spirit anew. Chrismation, then, is crucial and exudes a powerful sacramental theology, but it does not stand alone; it is intimately linked to both baptism and Eucharist, and it is thoroughly ecclesiological because it literally ritualizes initiation into a particular community as a rite of passage.

The Solemnity of the Consecration of Chrism

The consecration of chrism is essential to the celebration of chrismation, and it is intimately linked with and representative of the Eucharist. The survey above demonstrates how the process of preparing for the postbaptismal anointing with chrism closely parallels the Eucharistic Liturgy in structure, pageantry, and lexicon. The eucharistic consecration of gifts follows a pattern of prayer over the gifts with an iteration of blessings for participants imparted through the parallel ritual actions of preparing/consecrating gifts and distributing them for ritual use (consumption). In chrismation, the church follows the same pattern of preparing/consecrating, and imparting for ritual use (anointing). Like the eucharistic anaphora, the consecration of chrism asks God to consecrate the chrism so that the participants would receive the iterated spiritual blessings upon receiving the anointing.

The context of consecrating chrism during the Eucharistic Liturgy and in close proximity to the eucharistic gifts, punctuated by the chrismation prayer's reference to partaking of the Eucharist, definitively demonstrates the organic inseparability of chrismation and Eucharist in the Byzantine liturgical tradition. The history of the consecration of chrism reminds us of the solemnity of this event in the arrangement of the altar, since the chrism was placed on the altar table itself adjacent to the holy gifts of the Lord's body and blood. It is as if the altar was an image of the initiation journey, since the anointing with chrism would initiate new people into the community that celebrates and offers this very Eucharist in thanksgiving to God.

The Eucharist shapes the theology of chrismation and contributes to its ecclesiological tenets. Figure 1.1 depicts how the Eucharistic

Assembly inaugurates the process of initiation by anticipating baptism and invoking God to sanctify the chrism required to anoint holy ones who will join the priestly assembly that thanks God and receives the communion of the Holy Spirit at each Divine Liturgy:

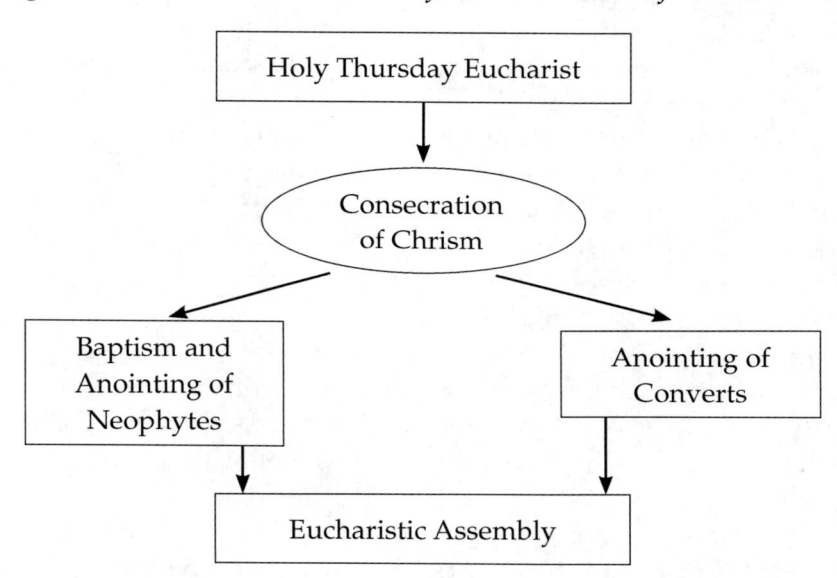

Figure 1.1: The Eucharist as Source of the Consecration of Chrism

```
        ┌─────────────────────────────┐
        │   Holy Thursday Eucharist   │
        └─────────────┬───────────────┘
                      ▼
              ╱───────────────╲
             │  Consecration   │
             │   of Chrism     │
              ╲───────────────╱
              ↙               ↘
┌──────────────────┐      ┌──────────────────┐
│  Baptism and     │      │   Anointing of   │
│  Anointing of    │      │    Converts      │
│   Neophytes      │      │                  │
└────────┬─────────┘      └─────────┬────────┘
         ▼                          ▼
        ┌──────────────────────────────┐
        │   Eucharistic Assembly       │
        └──────────────────────────────┘
```

A Byzantine peculiarity of the consecration of chrism is the rarity of its celebration on Holy Thursday. The Byzantines assign liturgical presidency to the chief bishop of a synod, as opposed to a diocesan bishop, exposing a noteworthy ecclesiological motif. The context of the consecration of chrism with all or most of the bishops of a local church concelebrating highlights the Orthodox emphasis of synodality. The difference between the Orthodox and Catholic variants of consecrating chrism is important. While the occasion is Paschal for both, the reservation of this celebration for all the hierarchs of a synod in Orthodoxy has the capacity to emphasize the vertical gaps between the orders of the church since the audience of the ritual is largely hierarchical. The rarity of its celebration is purely pastoral: chrism is consecrated only when a need for it is ascertained by the Synod.

Chrismation Imparts Holiness: Theosis

The ritual context of chrismation clearly identifies the neophytes, the newly baptized, as the liturgical audience, which raises questions about using chrism for other canonical purposes.[76] The prayers and formulas also iterate what liturgical participation in chrismation does: it seals the participants in the divine life of the Triune God, marked by their citizenship in God's kingdom, envisioning angelic recognition of their becoming God's chosen, holy, and chosen people. The Byzantine tendency to search for words and phrases that capture the theology during the ritual anointing reveals a desire to demonstrate the solemnity of the liturgical celebration, where the postbaptismal anointing completes their entrance into the eschatological stage of life with God, sustained by regular participation in the Eucharist. The prayers emphasize that the chrism is the vesture of incorruption, sealing in these gifts and defining the content of life for the neophytes.

Two potentially overlooked liturgical components provide insight into the way chrismation communicates *theosis* in Byzantine theology. First, postbaptismal anointing with chrism refers to the covenant forged with Christ at baptism by defining the people to be anointed as keeping Christ in their hearts. The fourteenth-century Byzantine mystagogue of Thessalonika Nicholas Cabasilas interpreted chrismation as the mystery firmly uniting the participant with the person of Christ himself.[77] Cabasilas's description of chrismation as completing the union between Christ and the neophyte accentuates the covenantal quality of chrismation.[78] Cabasilas also

---

[76] The chief question is using chrism as the main rite for receiving converts into the church. I survey this aspect of chrismation in chapter 2 of this study.

[77] Nicholas Cabasilas, *The Life in Christ*, trans. Carmino J. deCatanzaro, intro. Boris Bobrinskoy (Crestwood, NY: St. Vladimir's Seminary Press, 1974). The critical edition of the text: *La vie en Christ, Livres I–IV*, ed. Marie-Hélène Congourdeau, Sources Chrétiennes 355 (Paris: Cerf, 1989). Congourdeau has also provided the introduction with critical text, translation, annotation, and index in *La vie en Christ, Livres V–VII*, Sources Chrétiennes 361 (Paris: Cerf, 1990).

[78] "So the effect of this sacred rite is the imparting of the energies of the Holy Spirit. The chrism brings in the Lord Jesus Himself, in whom is man's whole salvation and all hope of benefits. From Him we receive the participation in the Holy Spirit and through Him we have access to the Father. . . . the gifts

points to participation in the Eucharist as the perfection of baptism and chrismation, because in receiving communion, the participant experiences a union with Christ so intimate that Christ's body and blood are described as flowing through the communicant.[79] Receiving the Spirit to forge union with Christ, a union sustained by frequent participation in the Eucharist, is a priority of chrismation evidenced by its euchology, and also the ritual singing of Galatians 3:27 ("As many as have been baptized into Christ have put on Christ: Alleluia!") at the first Eucharistic Liturgy neophytes partake of.[80] This reference to the prayer for consecrating the chrism reminds us that the Triune God is the active agent of *theosis*. It is not sufficient to say that chrismation is pneumatological because it requests the imparting of the gift of the Spirit. The prayer asks that those who are anointed with chrism will become one with Christ, and through and in him, enjoy fellowship with God the Father. The trinitarian dimension of initiation was already manifested by the descent of the Spirit upon the baptismal waters, making Christ present in them so that those who entered would die and rise with

---

which the chrism always procures for Christians and which are always timely are . . . godliness, prayer, love, and sobriety," in Cabasilas, *The Life in Christ*, 106–7.

[79] "O how great are the mysteries! What a thing it is for Christ's mind to be mingled with ours, our will to be blended with His, our body with His body and our blood with His blood! What is our mind when the divine mind obtains control? What is our will when that blessed will has overcome it?" in Cabasilas, *The Life in Christ*, 116. Cabasilas could be drawing from and elaborating the fourth-century teaching of Cyril of Jerusalem here, who makes a similar statement in Mystagogical Catechesis no. 4.3: "For thus we come to bear Christ in us, because his body and blood are diffused through our members; thus it is that, according to the Blessed Peter, we become partakers of divine nature," in Cyril of Jerusalem, *Catéchèses mystagogiques*, ed. and trans. A. Piédagnel, Sources Chrétiennes 126 (Paris: Cerf, 1966), 136–37. Translation from Piédagnel, *Lectures on the Christian Sacraments*, ed. F. L. Cross (Crestwood, NY: St. Vladimir's, 1995), 68.

[80] Arranz attempts to address the question of when the seal occurs in "Évolution des rites d'incorporation et de réadmission dans l'Église selon l'Euchologe byzantine," in *Gestes et paroles dans les diverses families liturgiques*, eds. A. Postoia and A. Triacca, Bibliotheca Ephemerides Liturgicae Subsidia 14 (Rome: Centro Liturgico Vincenziano, 1978), 60.

Christ. The double epiclesis of the prayer of consecration demonstrates another instance of this pattern of the Triune God acting in initiation: God sends the Spirit on the chrism to grant it the properties of adhesion to Christ. When receiving the anointing, the Spirit blesses the neophytes with Christ's communion, which grants them access to fellowship with God the Father. In other words, those who have been bathed with water and anointed with chrism have been granted the privileges of sharing life with God and having the capacity to become worthy citizens of his kingdom. This is how chrismation contributes to the process of *theosis*, which occurs progressively in Christian life.

Chrismation's context in the rites of initiation also illuminates an image of the kind of Christian foreseen by initiation. The use of Psalm 31 as the church's song (responsorial psalmody) contributes another noteworthy dimension, namely, the expectation that the neophytes, clothed in Christ, would adopt and perfect the practice of living without sin. The psalm is an integral component of the entire liturgical context of chrismation, bracketing it and accompanying the neophytes' ritual movement. The psalm punctuates the recalling of forgiveness of sin, and expectation that neophytes would not abandon these gifts and return to a life in sin. The euchological association of chrism with vesture is quite telling. The prayer for the consecration of chrism refers to the chrism as a vesture of incorruption. Given the popular emphasis on the white robe put on by neophytes at baptism, the notion of chrism as vesture seems surprising. It is helpful to recall how the ritual of anointing occurs in several places on the body. The multiple anointings with chrism symbolize the idea that a neophyte is completely covered with the chrism. The ritual experience is quite sensory, given the fragrance emitted by the chrism and the sensation experienced by being touched with oil on several parts of the body. The euchology effectively theologizes the sacramentality of chrism by defining it as the new vesture of the Christian.

It is not surprising that the notion of chrism as the Christian's vesture has an important antecedent in Christian history. The association of holy chrism with incorruption helps explain why the fourth-century bishop Cyril of Jerusalem, in Mystagogical

Catechesis number 3.7, twice urges the neophytes baptized in Jerusalem to "keep this unspotted [. . .] Having been anointed, therefore, with this holy ointment, keep it unspotted and unblemished in you, pressing forward by good works."[81] Cyril's instruction confirms that the notion of postbaptismal anointing with chrism capacitating neophytes to live without sin existed as early as the fourth century. His instruction, together with the Byzantine prayer for consecrating chrism, reminds the community of how the bodily anointing with chrism communicated a new and holy way of living worthy of the twofold covenant with the Triune God and local Christian community. The sensible experience and memory of anointing reminds Christians of their obligation to the covenant, symbolized by their invisible vesture.

The image of chosen and holy people expressed by the prayer of the consecration of chrism can find its fulfillment only in people whose faithfulness to Christ is manifested by their daily lives. Liturgical theology often expresses bold visions for its participants, and in chrismation, this bold theology is summarized in the chosen and holy people who participate in the life of God through their entrance into the eschaton in Christ.

---

[81] Cyril of Jerusalem, *Catéchèses mystagogiques*, ed. Auguste Piédagnel, trans. Pierre Paris, Sources chrétiennes 126 (Paris: Cerf, 1966), 130–33. Translation from Cyril, *Lectures on the Christian Sacraments*, ed. F. L. Cross (Crestwood, NY: St. Vladimir's, 1995), 66–67.

CHAPTER 2

Chrismation and the Reception of Converts

The previous chapter presented a theology of chrismation by interpreting the liturgical theology of the texts and rituals of chrismation in the Byzantine Rite, with some reference to historical models. Now we turn to the ritual of anointing with chrism as the preferred way of receiving converts into the church.[1] My examination of these rituals contributes to my thesis for several reasons. First, the inner relationship between chrismation as an integral part of the rite of initiation and anointing with chrism as a way of receiving converts into the church needs to be fleshed out. The previous chapter illuminated chrismation as an almost invisible ritual within initiation, which makes it difficult to speak of it as a separate mystery. When the anointing with chrism is used as the rite for receiving converts into the church, it is detached from baptism and becomes independent in both ritual and meaning. Second, history demonstrates that anointing with chrism was not the only ritual used for receiving converts into the church. The eventual coronation of anointing with chrism as the preferred mystery for receiving converts suggests that the ritual confers something new that was absent from the previous rites. I will seek to identify and articulate such new ideas. Third, the nature and process of conversion has evolved throughout Christian history, and conversion today has serious pastoral implications. Many converts to Eastern Christianity were baptized and formed in another Christian community. The process of conversion they experienced cannot be equated simply with that of their historical antecedents, who came into the church

---

[1] "Converts" refers to baptized Christians joining the communion of the Orthodox Church. I realize that some readers will view this term as problematic. I have decided to retain the term "converts" in this study because it is deeply embedded in the nomenclature of Orthodox vocabulary in English.

from marginalized "heretical" groups, or had no particular religious affiliation, because today's converts to Eastern Christianity retain their past religious associations through family and community connections, as well as through their own memories. A presentation of their experiences as narrated in memoirs and sociological studies is a suitable partner to presenting the liturgical theology of chrismation as a way to construct a comprehensive theology of chrismation in all its complexity. This chapter will begin by briefly presenting the history of the reception of converts in the Byzantine Rite, to be followed by an analysis of the current rituals for receiving converts. I will then present and analyze select narratives on the process of converting through the rite of anointing with chrism in completing the construction of a theology of chrismation.

HISTORY OF THE RECEPTION OF CONVERTS

The history of the reception of converts in the Byzantine Rite reveals diverse practices in the processes and rituals used for receiving converts that never achieved uniformity. In fact, in the contemporary Orthodox world, plurality continues to reign, and there is no single rite used for receiving converts. The seminal work produced on the reception of converts in the Byzantine Rite is largely attributable to John Erickson, Miguel Arranz, John Klentos, and most recently, Alkiviadis Calivas. Arranz surveys the Constantinopolitan euchological tradition to establish the practice of receiving converts, while Erickson plunges deep into the Byzantine patristic and canonical tradition for complementary evidence.[2] Erickson,

---

[2] For an overview, see Miguel Arranz, "Évolution des rites d'incorporation et de *réadmission* dans l'Église selon l'Euchologe byzantine," in *Gestes et paroles dans les diverses familles liturgiques : Conferences Saint-Serge XXIVe semaine d'etudes liturgiques, 1977*, ed. A. Postoia and A. Triacca, Bibliotheca Ephemerides Liturgicae Subsidia 14 (Rome: Centro Liturgico Vincenziano, 1978), 31–75; John Erickson, "The Reception of Non-Orthodox into the Orthodox Church: Contemporary Practice," *St. Vladimir's Theological Quarterly* 41 (1997): 1–17; Erickson, "Divergences in Pastoral Practices in the Reception of Converts," in *Orthodox Perspectives on Pastoral Praxis: Papers of the Intra-Orthodox Conference on Pastoral Praxis Celebrating the 50th Anniversary of Holy Cross*, ed. Theodore Stylianopoulos (Brookline, MA: Holy Cross Orthodox Press, 1988), 149–77; Archbishop Peter L'Huillier, "The Reception of Roman Catholics into Orthodoxy:

Klentos, and Calivas discuss the current practices of receiving converts and their implications in the contemporary milieu. Their discussions are, in fact, somewhat dated. This section will briefly survey the historical development of the reception of converts to establish the foundations for the current diverse practices in the Eastern Orthodox Church.

The history of receiving converts draws upon conciliar, patristic, and liturgical sources. The patristic sources date to the third century and the controversies on readmitting apostates to the church. These controversies pertain to Cyprian's insistence on rebaptizing heretics who had received baptism outside of the church.[3] The practice of rebaptism emerged in the Orthodox world in the eighteenth century, under the influence of Constantinopolitan Patriarch Cyril V and St. Nikodemus the Hagiorite.[4] The Greek rigorists were responding to the proselytizing activities of Catholic missionaries and injected polemic into the process of receiving converts from Roman Catholicism by associating them with heretics such as Arians or Sabellians.[5] Klentos notes that the trend of rebaptism among the Greek Orthodox eventually faded and the Greeks reverted to accepting converts by anointing with chrism at the turn of the twentieth century, but we should note the politico-religious context that ignited the possibility of rebaptizing people who were born Roman Catholic: interfaith conflict in a context and period of

---

Historical Variations and Norms," *St. Vladimir's Theological Quarterly* 24 (1980): 75–82; John Klentos, "Rebaptizing Converts in the Orthodox Church: Old Perspectives on a New Problem," *Studia Liturgica* 29 (1999): 216–34; and Alkiviadis Calivas, "Receiving Converts into the Orthodox Church: Lessons from the Canonical and Liturgical Tradition," *Greek Orthodox Theological Review* 54, nos. 1–4 (2009): 1–76.

[3] See Erickson, "Divergences in Pastoral Practice in the Reception of Converts," 149–55; and Klentos, "Rebaptizing Converts," 217–19. Also see Maxwell Johnson, *The Rites of Christian Initiation: Their Evolution and Interpretation*, rev. ed (Collegeville, MN: Liturgical Press, 1999, 2007), 69–71.

[4] Calivas comprehensively treats this topic in "Receiving Converts," 16–26; also see Klentos, "Rebaptizing Converts," 221–22.

[5] Calivas, "Receiving Converts," 16–26; and Klentos, "Rebaptizing Converts" 221–22.

duress that restored painful memories of the Byzantine Empire's legacy, namely, the Latin sacking of Constantinople in 1204. The restoration of rebaptism as an option for receiving converts is relevant to the contemporary Orthodox world because some churches have retained rebaptism as their preferred method for receiving converts. We will turn to the implications of these practices in our analysis of receiving converts later in this chapter.

Besides rebaptism, the Byzantine Church had two distinct ways of receiving converts into the church.[6] The first process entailed the convert presenting a libellus renouncing his or her heresies, receiving the anointing with chrism with a special prayer, and concluded with a rite of ablution on the eighth day after the anointing. The second process required a libellus renouncing heresies and the reception of Holy Communion at the Eucharistic Liturgy. These processes generally accord with the most authoritative canonical evidence from Byzantium's antiquity, namely, the 95th canon from the Council in Trullo, which requires baptism via immersion in the name of the Trinity, anointing with chrism, and a profession of faith.[7] The convert's background dictated the process of reception engaged. For example, Arians and Macedonians were required to receive anointing with chrism, whereas Nestorians and Monophysites were readmitted by issuing the libellus and receiving Communion.[8] Arranz hypothesizes that the distinction in ritual practice relates to the degree of deficient faith of the groups of converts. In other words, Nestorians and Monophysites had a much lower degree of deficiency in their Christology and thus required only readmittance to communion, whereas Arians and Macedonians required anointing with the Spirit, which would capacitate the

---

[6] See Erickson, "The Reception of non-Orthodox," 2; Klentos, "Rebaptizing Converts," 224–25; Arranz, "Évolution des rites d'incorporation," 70–73; and Calivas, "Receiving Converts," 6–16.

[7] Erickson, "The Reception of non-Orthodox," 2. Arranz seems to believe that this practice is older, dating it to the seventh canon of the Council of Constantinople in 381, Erickson, 70. See the Greek, Latin, and English translations of this canon in *The Council in Trullo Revisited*, ed. G. Nedungatt and M. Fatherstone, Kanonika 6 (Rome: Pontifical Oriental Institute, 1995), 174–77.

[8] Arranz, "Évolution des rites d'incorporation," 75.

development of faith in the divine Son of God.[9] The history suggests that a more rigorous liturgical practice of receiving converts parallels an intense period of catechesis, an implication to which we will turn when discussing the contemporary situation below. Arranz also comments on the surprising tolerance of the Byzantine Church before iconoclasm, since the church did not require notorious heretical groups such as Arians and Macedonians to return to the church via rebaptism, and even anointing with chrism was not required of all groups.[10] He also notes a shift in the policy of receiving converts after 1204 (the sacking of Constantinople), when reception via anointing with chrism became the norm.

It is frequently and falsely assumed that the reception of converts via anointing with chrism is equivalent to chrismation, and Klentos aptly clarifies that the ritual used for receiving converts with a chrism anointing was not identical to the chrismation liturgical structure within baptism. Table 2.1 furnishes Klentos's presentation of the Constantinopolitan Rite for the reception of converts:[11]

Table 2.1: Ancient Constantinopolitan Rite for Receiving Converts (Eighth Century)

---

1) Public renunciation of heresy and adherence to Orthodox articulation of trinitarian faith;

2) Triple affirmation of Orthodox trinitarian faith;

---

[9] Ibid. Klentos provides a helpful distinction in his overview of the history: "Heretics who had a divergent Christological confession were received by means of a libellus and Eucharist; . . . those who differed in their theology of the Trinity were required to submit a libellus, fast, pray, learn the Creed (which implies a more serious dogmatic deviation), publicly renounce their heresy, and be anointed with myron before receiving communion," in Klentos, 224–25.

[10] Arranz, "Évolution des rites d'incorporation," 74.

[11] Klentos, "Rebaptizing Converts," 226. Klentos draws upon BAR no. 146, in eds. Parenti and Velkovska, 151–52. For commentary on the Constantinopolitan rite, see Calivas, "Receiving Converts," 40–43.

> 3) Prayer of anointing;
>   anointing with Myron (chrism), accompanied by the standard anointing formula "seal of the gift of the Holy Spirit";
> 4) Prayer for the anointed;
> 5) Reception of Holy Communion.

The prayer recited for anointing converts with chrism differs from the postbaptismal chrismation prayer:[12]

> O God our Savior, you desire that all people be saved and arrive at the knowledge of truth; receive your servant (N.) who comes to repudiate his error, and who truly desires to arrive at knowledge of the truth. You have said: I have other sheep who are not of this flock. I must bring them also and they will listen to my voice; and there will be one flock and one shepherd. Therefore, guide him/her in your glory toward knowledge of the truth according to the statement of your saints and glorious apostles; make him/her worthy of the seal of the holy anointing and participation in your precious Body and Blood; make him/her a perfect servant, so that you may count him/her among the flock for the glory and praise of your glory.

The key distinction between this prayer and the one recited at chrismation in the context of initiation is the journey to the "knowledge of the truth," a phrase repeated three times in a relatively short prayer. Consequently, the prayer conveys a message of restoration, placing more emphasis on setting the right path on the journey to knowledge of God as opposed to the shaping of the whole person communicated by the postbaptismal prayer of chrismation.[13]

An important historical shift occurred in the seventeenth century that has shaped the ritual practice of the reception of converts in

---

[12] Klentos, "Rebaptizing Converts," 227. For the earliest Greek recension of this prayer, see BAR no. 146.10, in eds. Parenti and Velkovska, 152.

[13] For Klentos's comparative analysis of the two prayers, see Klentos, "Rebaptizing Converts," 228–29.

the Orthodox Church. Peter Mohyla, the embattled metropolitan of Kyiv, used the rite for anointing with chrism taken from the rites of initiation as the method for receiving mainline Protestants and unconfirmed Roman Catholics.[14] Confirmed Latin and Eastern Catholics were to be received by confession of the Orthodox faith and reception of Holy Communion, since they had already received the sacrament of confirmation.

Two developments are particularly notable here. First, we see a transition from the Greek rite of anointing with chrism to simply using the chrismation liturgical structures from the rites of initiation. Erickson and Klentos discuss these issues by referring to Mohyla's complex environment of scholastic theology, where Mohyla attempted to demonstrate the legitimacy of Orthodox sacraments by showing that Orthodoxy had seven (including chrismation), and validity could be verified through the presence of matter and form.[15] Erickson positively appraises Mohyla's reform of the reception of converts, rendering it a "clear and coherent modern application of Trullo canon 95."[16] Erickson does not assess the problem of applying the theology of chrismation as it is celebrated in initiation to converts who have already been baptized in another tradition.

The second development illustrates the evolution of context, as the rite is concerned with converts from Latin and Eastern Christianity and mainline Protestantism, an environment quite remote from the Constantinopolitan milieu of Arians, Nestorians, and Monophysites, among others. If the rite itself and the categorizations of converts demonstrate change, one important item remained the same in this process: the church's ecclesiological definition of converts was the main factor shaping the rite of the reception of converts. Erickson categorizes this rite as a "Russian" approach for convenience, which represents its popularity among the churches that generally follow the liturgical practices of the Moscow Patriarchate. This version of the rite is widely (but not univer-

---

[14] This section follows Erickson, "The Reception of non-Orthodox," 4–6. Also see Klentos, "Rebaptizing Converts," 220–21, 226.

[15] See Erickson, "The Reception of non-Orthodox," 6; and Klentos, "Rebaptizing Converts," 226.

[16] Erickson, "The Reception of non-Orthodox," 6.

sally) used in the Orthodox world today, and is the most authentic representation of chrismation as a rite of receiving converts.

A notable instance of diversity in the rites for receiving converts appears in the history of receiving Latin converts into the Orthodox Church. Peter L'Huillier attends to the history of the reception of Latin Catholics in the medieval period, and mentions a complaint issued at the Fourth Lateran Council in 1215 that some Greeks were rebaptizing Roman Catholics.[17] Calivas treats the decision of the Constantinopolitan Synod of 1484, an event in Greek ecclesial history marking a new development in the reception of Catholics.[18] This office of reception differs from the eighth-century one in BAR, as the convert is to repudiate Latin erros in dogma, including the *filioque* clause, the use of *azymes* in the bread for the Eucharist, and the decree of the defunct Council of Florence.[19] Earlier, we noted the eighteenth-century Constantinopolitan requirement of rebaptism for Catholics, which cleverly viewed Roman Catholic baptism as invalid since Catholics customarily baptized via affusion instead of immersion, a practice that did not fulfill the requirements of the Council in Trullo. These models of receiving Roman Catholics are exceptionally rigorous and diverge from the fairly tolerant perspective of Mohyla, who accepted Roman Catholic confirmation. We should also note the method used for receiving Roman Catholic priests in the Orthodox Church. Priests are received via vesting. Like the laity, they offer a profession of Orthodox faith, but then they simply put on traditional Byzantine vestments and take their place within the ordered Eucharistic Assembly. The divergences of methods for receiving Catholics into the Orthodox Church are instructive and informative, as they clearly illuminate the enormous influence ecclesiological perspectives have had on the liturgy of conversion in Orthodoxy.

---

[17] L'Huillier, "The Reception of Roman Catholics into Orthodoxy," 77.

[18] Calivas, "Receiving Converts," 11, 43–45. Also see Erickson, "The Reception of non-Orthodox," 7–8.

[19] Calivas, "Receiving Converts," 43. Calivas notes that this rite of receiving converts is one of reconciliation and not an adaptation of postbaptismal chrismation (44).

History, then, proves informative in helping us understand the development of the rite for receiving converts, especially when it includes anointing with chrism. First, history demonstrates that the rituals used for receiving converts have always been shaped by particular ecclesiological perspectives, especially concerning the deficiencies converts might have to overcome to enter Orthodoxy. There is some unity within the diversity, in the form of constant liturgical elements. These elements include the renunciation of heresy, profession of faith, and restoration to the Eucharistic Assembly. Surprisingly, while the anointing with chrism is canonically required and easily the most prominent ritual gesture in history, it is not always present; the Eucharist, however, is, though it is implicit, since the rituals simply assume that the convert enters the Orthodox Eucharistic Assembly. When chrism is used, its liturgical context has not always been constant, as evidenced by the variant prayers accompanying it. History's greatest contribution is its identification of diverse liturgical rites used to receive converts and the contribution of ecclesiological perspectives to the shaping of rite. History is silent on a most important factor, however, that we must explore in this ecumenical endeavor: the real life implications of conversion, including renunciation, for the actual convert. We simply do not know how converts interiorized the process of conversion with its polemic language so colored by politico-religious contexts, and we will consider this reality as part of our assessment of the contemporary rites.

CONTEMPORARY BYZANTINE RITES OF CONVERSION

If the history of the reception of converts in the Byzantine Rite illustrates diversity in the rituals for conversion, contemporary practices exhibit consistency with this pattern. Erickson and Klentos offer a dated but reasonably accurate and comprehensive overview of the reception of converts. Both Erickson and Calivas begin their assessments of receiving converts with an overview of the SCOBA guidelines of 1966 that result in diverse rites of reception.[20] Before

---

[20] Erickson, "The reception of non-Orthodox," 1–3; and Calivas, "Receiving Converts," 4–6. SCOBA was the Standing Conference of Canonical Orthodox

turning to their essentially uniform presentation, however, we must mention that rebaptism remains one of the options for receiving converts occasionally employed by Orthodox churches of the world. The Orthodox who practice rebaptism tend to justify it in ecclesiological terms, by stating that the communities from which converts hail had some kind of deficiency that kept them from being an authentic church.[21] Currently, rebaptism is employed as a way of delegitimizing schismatic bodies within Orthodoxy, and the best-known instance is the practice of the Moscow Patriarchate of rebaptizing and reordaining people who were initiated or ordained in the Ukrainian Orthodox Church of the Kyivan Patriarchate (UOC-KP).[22] The logic underpinning this practice is the perceived illegitimacy of the Kyivan Patriarchate's hierarchy, especially since the Moscow Patriarchate deposed Patriarch Filaret (the primate of the UOC-KP) and anathematized him from the church for disobedience in 1992.[23] The UOC-KP insists on the legitimacy of its

---

Bishops in America. The Orthodox Churches realigned SCOBA in 2009 and renamed it the Assembly of Canonical Orthodox Bishops in North and Central America.

[21] Clearly, the Orthodox who practice rebaptism do so in defiance of the World Council of Churches' strong discouragement of rebaptism: "Baptism is an unrepeatable act. Any practice which might be interpreted as 'rebaptism' must be avoided," in No. 13, *Baptism, Eucharist, and Ministry*, Faith and Order Paper no. 111 (Geneva: World Council of Churches, 1982).

[22] See Serhiy Luchnanin, "Про повторні звершення таїнств в Московському патріархаті" (On the Repetition of the Celebration of Sacraments in the Moscow Patriarchate), Ukrainian Orthodox Church Kyivan-Patriarchate website, accessed October 15, 2012, http://www.cerkva.info/en/publications/articles/2256-tainstva.html. A noteworthy development is the Ukrainian Greco-Catholic Church's (UGCC) official recognition of the validity of the sacraments celebrated in the Kyivan Patriarchate as evidenced by a recent letter from Archbishop Sviatoslav Shevchuk (leader of the UGCC) to Patriarch Filaret, "Викладено позицію УГКЦ щодо дійсності Таїнства Хрещення в УПЦ КП" (Announcement on the Position of the UGCC on the Validity of the Sacrament of Baptism in the UOC-KP), Ukrainian Orthodox Church-Kyivan Patriarchate website, accessed November 5, 2012, http://www.cerkva.info/uk/publications/articles/2824-bapt-ugcc.html.

[23] For an official account of the Russian Orthodox Church's deposition of Filaret, see "акт об отлучении от Церкви монаха Филарета (Денисенка)" (The

sacraments since all of its bishops have received apostolic succession via a line of successive ordinations from Orthodox bishops.

The contemporary rite for receiving converts by anointing with chrism illustrates the Orthodox Church's retention of its heritage without any adjustment to its ecclesiological perspective. The so-called "Russian" rite of receiving converts using the postbaptismal rite of chrismation and the "Greek" practice of anointing with chrism prevail, but new, conflated practices have also emerged.[24] One example is the confusing rite developed within the Orthodox Church in America (OCA) in 1989, which attempts to resolve deficiencies among converts coming from churches that do not have the same ecclesiological system of sacramental orders as Orthodoxy. The main development in this rite from its parent "Russian" rite is the anointing of Catholic converts with chrism on the forehead, a curious development that seems self-contradictory since Catholics would already have received the anointing with chrism at baptism and confirmation. Erickson assesses this development as "lacking in historical resonance," and calls on the OCA to amend it at its first opportunity.[25] The emergence of such new conflations alongside the divergent practices of rebaptism, chrismation, and anointing with chrism with alternate prayers only adds to the confusion, and suggests that the rite of receiving converts is indeed in search of a theology.

Within the group of Orthodox churches that employ the "Russian" tradition of receiving converts, one will find diversity and variety when closely examining the actual liturgical content. For example, Orthodox parishes in North America using the translation

---

act of deposing the monk Filaret (Denysenko) from the Church), Moscow Patriarchate website, accessed October 26, 2012, http://www.patriarchia.ru/db/text/417804.html.

[24] Erickson, "The Reception of non-Orthodox," 10–13; and Calivas, "Receiving Converts," 14–16.

[25] Erickson, "The Reception of non-Orthodox," 13. Erickson includes a similar conflation in the 1987 Greek Orthodox "Priest's Handbook," which universally requires chrismation for all converts, even though the history of the reception of converts clearly shows that chrismation was required only for Protestant converts (see Erickson, 10–11).

of the Russian Orthodox Church's *Great Book of Needs* will find three distinct liturgical offices for conversion.[26] The following section will present and analyze selections from the three preparatory rites with particular emphasis on the offices of conversion for Christians who have already been baptized, to illuminate the dynamics of conversion before receiving anointing with chrism. Then, the rite of anointing with chrism will be presented and analyzed.

CONVERSION: PREPARATORY RITES BEFORE CHRISMATION

The rite for receiving converts with a valid Christian baptism begins with an initial renunciation of heresy in an interrogation exercised by the celebrant.[27] After an initial prayer requesting the removal of the candidate's former errors, the candidate faces West and renounces all heresies in an expanded interrogation. The heresies are not explicated in this section, but generalized, exemplified by the following excerpt: "Do you renounce all ancient and modern apostasies, heresies, and founders of heresies, and cast them off because they are contrary to God?" "I cast off all ancient and modern apostasies, heresies, and founders of heresies because they are contrary to God." The parallel section in the office for receiving converts from the Roman Catholic and Reformed traditions is much more explicit. After beginning with a question asking the candidate to renounce "transgressions and errors," a prayer follows, titled "In Thy Name, O Lord God of truth." It is notable that this prayer is absent from the contemporary Greek rite for the reception of converts. This prayer occurs in the offices of the reception of converts for non-Orthodox Christians and for Armenians, though the versions of the prayer differ, as the text is longer and contains trinitarian

---

[26] *The Great Book of Needs*, expanded and supplemented, vol. 1: *The Holy Mysteries*, trans. St. Tikhon's Monastery (South Canaan, PA: St. Tikhon's Seminary Press, 1998). Hereafter cited as GBN. For the celebration of this service in the Greek Orthodox tradition, see "Service for the Reception of Converts into the Orthodox Church," Greek Orthodox Metropolis of Denver website, accessed December 17, 2012, http://www.denver.goarch.org/teleturgical_encyclicals/te-23-encl.pdf. For an excellent assessment of the Greek Rite of receiving converts, see Calivas, "Receiving Converts," 46–57.

[27] GBN, 62–64.

extensions in the office for the reception of those with valid baptism but raised in heresy, as illustrated by the text in table 2.2:

Table 2.2: *Text of Prayer at the Laying-on-of-Hands*

Prayer at the Laying-on-of-Hands for the Reception of Converts Who Were Baptized in a Christian Community	Prayer at the Laying-on-of-Hands for Receiving Armenians into the Orthodox Church[28]
In Thy Name, O Lord God of Truth, and of Thine Only-begotten Son, and of Thy Holy Spirit, look down upon Thy servant, N., whom Thou hast found worthy to have recourse unto Thy Holy Orthodox Church, and to be kept under the shelter of her wings. Remove from him (her) his (her) former errors, and fill him (her) with the True Faith, and hope, and love which are in Thee. Grant him (her) to walk in all Thy commandments, and to fulfill all things that are pleasing unto Thee; for if a man shall do these things, there shall be life in them. Write him (her) in Thy book of Life. Join him (her) to the flock of Thine inheritance, that Thy holy Name may be glorified in him (her), together with that	O Lord God of Truth, look down upon Thy servant, N., who seeks to make haste unto Thy Holy Orthodox Church, and to take refuge under her shelter. Turn him (her) from his (her) former error to the path of the true faith in Thee, and grant him (her) peace to walk in Thy commandments. Let Thine eyes ever look upon him (her) with mercy, and Thine ears hearken unto the voice of his (her) supplication, and that he (she) may be numbered with Thine elect flock. [Exclamation]

---

[28] Ibid., 73. GBN notes that this office can be used for converts coming from any "non-Chalcedonian" community.

> of Thy beloved Son, even our Lord Jesus Christ, and of Thy life-giving Spirit. Let Thine eyes ever look upon him (her) with mercy, and Thine ears hearken unto the voice of his (her) supplication. Make him (her) to rejoice in the works of his (her) hands, that he (she) may confess Thee, worshipping and glorifying Thy great and exalted Name, and ever praise Thee all the days of his (her) life. [Exclamation]

The prayer asks God to continue the process of conversion inaugurated by the candidate, who has performed her initial renunciation. The prayer asks God to "remove from him his former errors and fill him with the True faith, and hope, and love which are in Thee."[29] One of the two versions of the prayer was edited either by addition or abbreviation, but the core theology underpinning the two prayers is the same: God is to remove all remaining error in matters of faith and join the candidate to the Orthodox Church. The prayer is crucially positioned to show that God is an active participant in the process of conversion from the very beginning of the ritual, with the candidate, the assembly, and God acting together in completing the journey of conversion.

The celebrant then asks the candidate to renounce specific teachings belonging to his or her original faith tradition. For example, the question posed to "non-Chalcedonians" asks "do you renounce the false opinion that in our Lord Jesus Christ there are not two

---

[29] Ibid., 62. The shorter version of the prayer in the office for receiving non-Byzantine Orthodox Christians asks God to "turn him from his former error to the path of true faith in Thee, and grant him the grace to walk in Thy commandments," ibid., 73.

natures, Divine and human, but one only, the human nature being swallowed up by the divine?"[30] The second question for converts of "Roman-Latin" origin reads, "Do you renounce the erroneous supposition that the holy Apostles did not receive from our Lord Jesus Christ equal spiritual power, but that the holy Apostle Peter was their prince; and that the Bishop of Rome alone is his successor and that the Bishops of Jerusalem, Antioch, Alexandria and the others are not, equally with the Bishop of Rome, successors of the Apostles?"[31] The second question posed to candidates who were Lutheran is also illustrative: "Do you renounce the erroneous opinion that in the eucharistic mystery the bread is not transformed into the Body of Christ, yet does not become the Body of Christ, and that the wine is not transformed into the Blood of Christ, yet does not become the Blood of Christ?"[32] The response to each question is "I renounce it/them," or "I forsake it/them." Again, it is notable that these particular renunciations are absent from the Greek rite, which contains a general renunciation of heresy.[33] The distinction between general and particular renunciations is relevant to the experience of the candidate and illustrates the magnitude of the change the church expects her to embrace. The language of the renunciation texts is ecumenically problematic and poses a formidable challenge to the candidate, who will have to navigate potentially painful personal contexts and relationships, assuming the candidate truly interiorizes the renunciations.

As in baptism, a series of confessions of faith follow the renunciations. The first confession of faith is the Nicene-Constantinopolitan Creed, with a second interrogation concerning the particulars of

---

[30] Ibid., 73.
[31] Ibid., 75.
[32] Ibid., 76.
[33] The candidate says, "I renounce all false doctrines and erroneous teachings," in "Service for the Reception of Converts into the Orthodox Church," Greek Orthodox Metropolis of Denver website, accessed December 17, 2012, http://www.denver.goarch.org/teleturgical_encyclicals/te-23-encl.pdf. Calivas likewise notes the absence of dogmatic recantations in the contemporary Greek rite in "Receiving Converts," 50.

the newly adopted faith held by the candidates.[34] Each confession of faith begins with "I believe." This section is organized by the Byzantine ecclesiological interpretation of the hierarchy of articles of faith. The candidate professes faith in the following: the canons of the ecumenical councils; seven mysteries of the church; the true presence of the Body and Blood of Christ; the communion of saints and the legitimacy of venerating relics; the veneration of icons; the efficacy of ecclesial prayers offered for the dead; the church's authority to bind and loose sins; Jesus Christ as the only head of the church; the church as the bride of Christ; and obedience to the bishop. As with the renunciations, particular confessions of faith are to be made in accordance with one's faith of origin. For example, Roman Catholics are to reject purgatory in favor of the efficacy of the eucharistic prayers offered for the dead, whereas Lutherans and Reformed Christians must accept the Eastern method for interpreting Scripture.[35] This section exhibits a pattern of ritual consistency, generality, or particularity in renunciation models along with generality and particularity in confession. Practically speaking, the confessions of faith have the capacity to significantly impact the candidate, as they define the parameters of faith to which the candidate is to adhere. Candidates who retain strong familial or community relationships with the faith community they just renounced have the challenge of integrating these new tenets of faith they have just voluntarily adopted into their personal orbits. The celebrant then leads the candidate into the church, processing toward a table with the gospel book and a cross while a reader chants Psalm 66.[36] The candidate then kneels down (before the gospel and cross) while the celebrant chants the final verses

---

[34] See GBN, 66–67.

[35] "Do you believe that, what heals departed souls is not a purifying fire which does not exist, but that alms and prayers, and most of all, the Bloodless Sacrifice, carries to them great liberation and consolation? . . . Do you promise to examine and understand Sacred Scripture according to the interpretation given us by the fathers and Church teachers, and which are held by the Eastern Church?" Ibid., 82.

[36] The celebrant's command to the candidate: "Enter into the Orthodox Church, and utterly rejecting the errors wherein you have dwelt, honor the

of Psalm 66. The usage of Psalm 66 in the office of reception is an important point of distinction from the celebration of chrismation as a rite of initiation together with baptism, because Psalm 66 essentially replaces Psalm 31. The previous chapter presented the importance of Psalm 31, which immediately follows immersion in the baptismal water, as a demonstration of baptism's power to cleanse all sin and transgression. Psalm 66 explicates the covenant between God and humanity, including repetitive petitions to God to bless the people with gifts, with the people's response to the gift offered in thanksgiving. The final part of the psalm, chanted by the celebrant, is epicletic, asking God to "send forth Thy Spirit," and "return." Psalm 66 envisions the covenant into which the convert enters and provides a subtle hint at the content of the life expected of the convert: to continually offer thanksgiving to God for God's gifts. Psalm 66 is a thematic preview of the eucharistic life the convert will, presumably, regularly engage upon completing the process of conversion.

After the psalm, the celebrant then offers a prayer thanking God for making the candidate worthy of irrevocable reception into the church, and to be made a "pure vessel and the abode of Thy Holy Spirit."[37] The celebrant then commands the candidate to "stand aright. Stand with fear" and make a final confession of faith before the gospel and cross.[38] The candidate offers the following vow:[39]

> The Orthodox-Catholic Faith, which I now voluntarily confess, I will firmly maintain whole and inviolate even until my last breath, God helping me, and I shall strive to fulfill its precepts zealously and joyfully, preserving my heart in purity, as far as possible. In confirmation of this, my vow, I kiss the words and cross of my Savior. Amen.

The candidate then ritualizes the vow by kissing the cross and gospel book, and kneels again; the celebrant absolves the candidate

---

Father almighty, His Son, Jesus Christ, and the Holy Spirit who proceeds from the Father, the Trinity one in essence and undivided," ibid., 84.

[37] Ibid., 85.
[38] Ibid., 86.
[39] Ibid.

of her sins and restores her to the church's communion. The actual anointing with chrism occurs at this point. Table 2.3 outlines the structure of the preliminary rites of the reception of converts by the anointing with chrism:

Table 2.3: Preliminary Rites of Chrismation

First interrogation and renunciation of heresies

Prayer: "In Thy Name, O Lord God of Truth" or "O Lord God of Truth" (absent from Greek variant)

Second Interrogation and renunciation of heresies (general or particular)

Bow and Confession of Faith

Confession of Nicene-Constantinopolitan Creed

Confession of articles of Faith in the Eastern Church (Particular articles by original faith tradition)

Entrance into Church, procession to table with gospel and cross; kneeling

Psalm 66

Prayer of Reception: "O Lord God Almighty"

Rising

Vow of obedience; kissing of gospel and cross

Prayer of Absolution

In conclusion, the preliminary rites of receiving converts by chrismation incorporate many of the rituals and themes of baptism. In baptism, the convert's renunciation and confession are tightly centered on community covenants. The covenant with Satan is rejected, as repetitively demonstrated by the exorcisms and the casting out of demons from the baptismal water, and life in the Trinity begins when the candidate confesses God. The conversion that occurs in these preliminary rites is different in the references to particular teachings in GBN. The rites of receiving converts acknowledge, though not always eloquently, that the candidate may already be adhered to the covenant with God. In the rite of receiving converts, a new covenant is forged with the Orthodox Church. Candidates reject particular teachings and articles of faith, a significant step in conversion connoting a change of mind and raising questions about the convert's new relationship with her previous faith tradition. Candidates coming from Reformed communities must reject the notion of *sola scriptura*; candidates coming from the Roman tradition must reject Papal infallibility. For some, this process might not pose any challenges, but in an increasingly pluralistic religious milieu, agreeing to such sharp and even polemical ecclesial verbiage must be difficult for others, especially people whose spouses or families are Christians in non-Byzantine or Orthodox churches.

Some pastors have modified the language of these texts, or even eliminated whole sections and structures, in an attempt to show that the candidate's journey took a new direction, and that changing course does not necessarily entail rejection. Candidates who enter the Orthodox Church through the Greek tradition offer only a general renunciation.[40] Thus, there is no universal pastoral practice on the content in the renunciations that can be edited or retained in such instances. The liturgical theology of the ritual and its structure clearly suggest something sharply distinct about the process of conversion in chrismation: the conversion is a matter of the whole person, and the preliminary rites inaugurate a new covenant emphasizing the cognitive dimension since the content largely centers on articles of faith. The conversion of mind is not isolated from a conversion of heart; this is just a point of emphasis, designed to show that the content of one's belief really does matter, and synergy between mind and heart is necessary for the person to profess true faith.

CHRISMATION IN THE RECEPTION OF CONVERTS

Having established and initially analyzed the preliminary rites of the reception of converts with the anointing with chrism, we now turn to the main ritual gestures and its prayers.[41] The anoint-

---

[40] See Calivas, "Receiving Converts," 50–51.
[41] GBN, 88–95.

ing with chrism begins with the bringing forth of the chrism and placing it on the table in the middle of the church. The first distinct aspect of this liturgical office is the Litany of Holy Chrismation. This litany stands out because in the context of baptism, there are no special litanic petitions established for the chrism, so these petitions refer to the anointing with chrism for the reception of converts, and in instances when a person has been baptized in the church without chrismation (which very rarely occurs). After the opening doxology ("Blessed is the Kingdom"), the church sings the hymn of Pentecost, "Heavenly King," and then proceeds to the litany. The eight petitions pertaining to anointing with chrism begin with petition number 6. Petition number 6 asks that divine power be granted to the convert for protection from evil spirits.[42] Petition number 7 requests that the convert become a "valiant and victorious soldier of Christ our God" by the descent of the Holy Spirit, establishing a link between the descent of the Spirit at Pentecost and the anointing with chrism. Petition number 8 asks that the convert remain strong in the faith, and petition number 9 requests that converts would have the courage to confess the "Name of Christ our God," even if it requires one to die for his sake. Petition number 10 requests increase in virtue and prosperity in commandments, and number 11 asks for "holy fear" for the preservation of the convert's soul. Petition number 12 asks "that he may ripen unto a perfect man (woman), unto the measure of the stature of the fullness of Christ."[43] Petition number 13 transitions to general concluding petitions by asking God to deliver the converts from afflictions, and then the litany concludes. Each special petition refers to the ritual act of anointing with chrism by interpolating the following phrase: "by the anointing of the all-holy chrism."[44] Petitions 7 and 12 specifically mention the "power, operation, grace, and descent

---

[42] "That he (she) may remain steadfast, and strong, and unshakeable in the Orthodox Faith, and in love and hope, by the anointing of the all-holy Chrism, all the days of his (her) life, let us pray to the Lord," ibid., 90.

[43] Ibid.

[44] Petition no. 6, first of the special petitions, has an elongated phrase, "that through the anointing with the all-holy, beneficial and all-perfect Chrism," ibid., 89.

of the most Holy Spirit," clear references to epicleses. These invocations ask God to send the Spirit upon the actual convert, and not the chrism, since the chrism has already been consecrated, so the petitions refer to the present activity of the Spirit as another layer of grace. The petitions iterate the desired blessings given by God to the converts during the ritual action of anointing with chrism. We can summarize these blessings as follows: protection from evil, advocate of God, steadfastness in the faith and willingness to confess it under duress, growth in virtue, preservation of the soul, and progress in perfection.

The office immediately proceeds to the prayer of chrismation, in the case of the Russian Rite, the one also used in the context of baptism and established in the seventeenth century by Mohyla. The version of this prayer for the reception of converts contains an important modification that distinguishes the prayer as suitable for receiving converts. It is notable that the Greek Rite does not include this modification, so converts entering the church through the Greek tradition hear a slightly different translation of the original prayer of chrismation in the left column of table 2.4.[45] Table 2.4 illustrates the modification in the context of the two parallel prayers, with the modified portion in the second column:

Table 2.4: Comparison of Prayers of Chrismation

Prayer of Chrismation in Rites of Initiation	Prayer of Chrismation Reception of Converts
Blessed art Thou, O Lord God Almighty, fountain of good things, Sun of righteousness, who shinest unto them that are	Blessed art Thou, O Lord God Almighty, fountain of good things, Sun of righteousness, who shinest unto them that are

---

[45] For the Greek version of this prayer, see "Service for the Reception of Converts into the Orthodox Church," Greek Orthodox Metropolis of Denver website, accessed December 17, 2012, http://www.denver.goarch.org/teleturgical_encyclicals/te-23-encl.pdf.

in darkness the light of salvation, through the manifestation of Thine only-begotten Son, and our God, and Who grantest unto us who are unworthy blessed cleaning in holy water, and divine sanctification in life-giving anointing	in darkness the light of salvation, through the manifestation of Thine only-begotten Son, and our God, and Who grantest unto us who are unworthy blessed cleaning in holy water, and divine sanctification in life-giving anointing
And Who art now well-pleased for Thy newly-illumined servant to be born again through water and the Spirit, and Who grantest unto him (her) remission of sins, both voluntary and involuntary	And Who art now well-pleased for this, Thy servant, N., to come unto the knowledge of Thy truth and make haste unto deep compassion, to be joined to Thine elect flock, and Who grantest unto Him (her) remission of sins through me, Thine unworthy servant.
Do Thou Thyself alone, O Compassionate King of All, grant him (her) also the seal of Thy Holy, All-powerful, and Worshipped Spirit	Do Thou Thyself alone, O Compassionate King of All, grant him (her) also the seal of Thy Holy, All-powerful, and Worshipped Spirit

The modification of the prayer of chrismation for the reception of converts is informative and establishes the chief priority of the anointing with chrism in the reception of converts. The convert has come to the knowledge of God's truth and is admitted to the church (God's flock) in an act of compassion. This readmission to the church includes the forgiveness of sins, which the chrismation prayer of initiation also references. The key in the reception of converts is that sins are forgiven through the mediation of the celebrant. Two theological points are crucial to the reception of converts, and only implied in the revised prayer of chrismation for receiving converts. First, the reference to compassion suggests the mercy of God and the church in readmitting the convert to the true flock. Second, the mediation of the celebrant in forgiving sins illustrates the ecclesiological mechanism used to establish order in the church, since a bishop or priest must first verify the candidate's readiness for readmission before the anointing can occur.[46] This reading of the prayer of chrismation also shows that the theological blessings envisioned by the initial litany are not particular to the reception of converts. Each blessing finds a parallel in the prayer for chrismation in the rites of initiation, with the exception of the reference to soldiers.

The convert is then anointed with the chrism on the forehead, eyes, nostrils, lips, both ears, the breast, hands, and feet, each anointing accompanied by the formula, "The seal of the gift of the Holy Spirit. Amen." A brief prayer follows the anointing:[47]

> O Lord our God, who hast vouchsafed to show this, Thy servant, N., perfect, through the True faith which is in Thee, and through the seal of the gift of the Holy Spirit, in Thy holy and most-heavenly anointing: Do thou, Master of all, preserve in him (her) the true faith, bring him up in righteousness and truth, and adorn him with all Thy gifts. For Thou art our God.

This prayer simply repeats the iterated blessings requested earlier, namely, preservation in the faith and growth in righteousness and truth. The celebrant then offers the Peace, and the following prayer at the bowing of the heads:[48]

> He who has put on thee, Christ and our God, now bows his head unto Thee, together with us. Keep him always a warrior invincible in every attack of those who struggle against him (her) and us. And show all of us victors even unto the end, through Thine incorruptible crown.

---

[46] This reference to the mediation of the celebrant in forgiving sins also reveals the provenance of the modification, since explicating the mediation of a priest in absolving sins is a Western theological idea permeating Byzantine theology in the liturgical reforms of Peter Mohyla. See Paul Meyendorff, "The Liturgical Reforms of Peter Moghila: A New Look," *St. Vladimir's Theological Quarterly* 29 (1985): 110–13.

[47] GBN, 92.

[48] Ibid., 93.

This prayer at the bowing of heads (a clue that dismissal is near) seems to be the euchological source of military language. But the prayer actually originates from the rites of initiation, and is the second prayer recited after the ablution and before the ritual tonsure, an offering of the neophyte to God in the vein of a sacrificial motif. The prayer appears in the Byzantine rite of baptism in *Bessarion*, a thirteenth-century Constantinopolitan Euchologion, and *Athens Greek 662*, a twelfth- to fourteenth-century Euchologion.[49] The prayer occurs in the contemporary rite of the reception of converts to fortify the military theme of chrismation in the reception of converts, so that the convert would be protected from attacks by the devil. On one hand, the content of the prayer itself is not unusual, as it appears to add merely another thematic layer of protection from evil to the rite. However, the grafting of this prayer on to the rite of receiving converts removes it from its original liturgical context. In initiation, the prayer shapes the thematic context for one of its final ritual gestures, the tonsuring of the new Christian. In the rite of receiving converts, the prayer does not shape any ritual context, because the rite contains only one main gesture, the anointing with the chrism. The bowing of the heads occurs here, and typically occurs as a transition to another significant ritual action or the dismissal of the assembly, so the prayer does not shape the bowing of the heads. One could assert that the prayer fits the context of dismissal, since the new convert will depart the sacred space of the church and enter the world. In such an instance, the prayer reinforces another layer of protection for the convert to remain steadfast to the covenant with Christ forged anew by the anointing with chrism. Without additional evidence, further reflection on the motivation of the editors to graft this prayer from the rite of initiation onto the reception of converts without the ritual tonsuring is conjecture.

A brief *ektene* concludes the rite, consisting mostly of the usual petitions praying for the bishop and civil authorities, with the petition praying for the people of the church modified for the convert

---

[49] Arranz, *L'eucologio costantinopolitano agli inizi del secolo XI. Hagiasmatarion and archieratikon* (Rome: editrice pontificia università, 1996), 195–96.

and sponsors.[50] The final petition reiterates the content of life expected of the new convert: "Again we pray for the newly-illumined servant of God, N., that he (she) may be kept in the faith of a pure confession, in all piety, and in the fulfilling of the commands of Christ all the days of his (her) life."[51] The celebrant then intones the dismissal, and the rite concludes with the following rubric: "And he (she) that has received chrismation is blessed to partake of the Most-precious mystery of the Body and Blood of the Lord at the Divine Liturgy. For these things are fulfilled before the Divine Liturgy."[52] This rubric is noteworthy as a reminder that the liturgical process of receiving converts consists of more than the anointing with chrism by granting the convert entrance to the Eucharistic Assembly. The Eucharistic Assembly, then, is the sacramental goal of the process of liturgical conversion, which is consistent with the liturgical theology of chrismation in the context of the rites of initiation. In other words, the liturgy manifests multiple entrances into the Orthodox Church. Infants and some adults experience all the rites of initiation, beginning with baptism and concluding with the Eucharist. Adults who seek entrance into the church and are baptized usually receive the anointing with chrism, concluded by the Eucharist. The one common sacramental event concluding entrance into the church that everyone experiences is participation in the Eucharistic Assembly and partaking of its holy food and drink. The primary and secondary liturgical sources generally emphasize the anointing with chrism as the defining ritual gesture of conversion, but a close reading of the contexts reveals that participation in the Eucharist is always implied, though rarely explicated, and it is the theological engine powering the ecclesiological process of conversion. Table 2.5 summarizes the rite of anointing with chrism in the reception of converts:

---

[50] GBN, 94.
[51] Ibid.
[52] Ibid., 95.

Table 2.5: Rite of Anointing with Chrism in the Reception of Converts

---

Opening Doxology "Blessed is the kingdom"

Hymn: "Heavenly King"

Litany (Fifteen total petitions; Eight particular to anointing with chrism)

Prayer of chrismation: "Blessed art Thou, Lord God Almighty"

Peace

Bowing of Heads

Prayer of Inclination: "He who has put on Thee, Christ"

Ektene (Five total petitions; one particular to newly illumined servants)

Dismissal

THEOLOGICAL REFLECTIONS ON THE LITURGICAL PROCESS OF CONVERSION

The history of receiving converts in the Orthodox Church establishes the contemporary practice, and one thing has remained constant: there are multiple processes for receiving converts in the Byzantine Rite. Unity exists within the diversity in the form of recurring liturgical components, prayers, and gestures. The recurring liturgical components include renunciations of erroneous theological tenets, professions of faith, and a generally recurring prayer that the convert would come to the knowledge of the truth confessed by Christ's flock, presumably the Orthodox Church. The willingness and ability to profess the faith correctly, especially its Christological and trinitarian dimensions, emerges as the dominant motif underpinning the entire ritual process. The history of anointing with chrism to receive converts is particularly informative here, as groups that Orthodoxy has traditionally defined as outside of the church endured the process of renouncing heresies and professing true faith. A wide variety of people representing Christian communities and hailing from particular historical periods and contexts, including Arians, Macedonians, Nestorians,

Monophysites, Roman and Eastern Catholics, Lutherans, Methodists, and others have renounced various tenets of faith from their past that are defined as incoherent with Orthodoxy and professed faith in the Orthodox Church. Each person who has experienced this process has renounced some aspect of their ecclesial past and professed faith in Christ as defined and worshipped by the Orthodox Church. Clearly, most of these people have also experienced the anointing with chrism as the ritual imprinting of their entrance into the church, followed by participation in the Eucharistic Assembly and partaking of Holy Communion. Anointing with chrism as the main ritual gesture (despite divergences in the prayer texts accompanying the anointing) is inexorably connected to the ecclesiological process of renouncing one's community and joining another on the basis of its articulations of faith. Full participation in the convert's new community is defined by *regular* participation in the new community's Eucharistic Assembly. That eucharistic participation is denied until the process of conversion concludes with the anointing with chrism suggests that the Eucharist is a privilege imparted exclusively to those who profess correct faith, as defined by the Orthodox Church.

A close examination of the liturgy of receiving converts in light of history illuminates the crucial role of the sacrament in supporting Orthodoxy's ecclesiological structure. First, the exclusive privilege of celebrating and partaking of the Eucharist is reserved for those who are willing to reject the errors of other Christian groups in favor of the particular Christology and trinitarian theology of Orthodoxy. The Eucharistic Assembly is itself a sacred space containing a communitarian profession of faith engineered by the knowledge of truth, which, in short, means that the Eucharist and correct faith have a reciprocal relationship. The macro-level tenets of faith have branches that abide within the boundaries of this sacred space. A good example of this is the requirement of having a correct understanding of ecclesiology or sacramental theology. For example, according to the liturgical rite, converts from Roman Catholicism must "renounce the erroneous doctrine . . . concerning the procession of the Holy Spirit" and "the erroneous supposition that it does not suffice to confess our Lord Jesus Christ as the head of the universal Church, but that the Bishop of Rome is the head of the Church?"[53] The same converts must recite the Nicene-Constantinopolitan Creed without the *filioque* clause and also confess that "the head of the Orthodox-Catholic Church is our Lord Jesus Christ."[54] Renouncing the "error" of the *filioque* clause and then confessing the creed without the *filioque* removes the Christological, pneumatological, and trinitarian deficiencies Orthodox believe were caused by the addition of *filioque*.[55]

A similar principle applies to the renunciation of the universal jurisdiction of the Bishop of Rome over the church. Orthodoxy has defined this in Christological terms, since the pope erroneously replaces the rightful headship reserved for Jesus Christ himself. The consequences of this error are largely implied, but consistent, as an improper ecclesiological confession can presumably cause deficiencies in Christology. The same principle of large-scale ecclesial implications caused by erroneous belief is expressed in the renunciation-confession rite assigned to Lutheran or Reformed Christians. These converts are required to renounce the "erroneous opinion that in the eucharistic mystery the bread is not transformed into the Body and Blood of Christ" and subsequently to confess belief that "the faithful partake of the body and blood of . . . Christ" in the Eucharist.[56] In this case, erroneous sacramental theology represents Christological error that requires remedy. These examples illustrate the prominence of the rituals of renunciation and profession of

---

[53] GBN, 74–75.

[54] Ibid., 82.

[55] For a comprehensive treatment, see Yves Congar, *I Believe in the Holy Spirit*, vol. 3: *The River of the Water of Life (Rev. 22:1) Flows in the East and in the West*, trans. David Smith (New York: Crossroads, 2004), 73–76 and elsewhere. For an Orthodox perspective on the deficiencies caused by the *filioque* clause, see Boris Bobrinskoy, *The Mystery of the Trinity: Trinitarian Experience and Vision in the Biblical and Patristic Tradition*, trans. Anthony Gythiel (Crestwood, NY: St. Vladimir's Seminary Press, 1999), 292–303. Vladimir Lossky presented the sharpest critique of the *filioque* in *In the Image and Likeness of God*, ed. John Erickson and Thomas Bird, intro. John Meyendorff (Crestwood, NY: St. Vladimir's Seminary Press, 2001), 71–98.

[56] GBN, 78, 83.

faith consistently employed in the rite of receiving converts. Correct faith as defined and practiced by the Orthodox Church is necessary for participation in the Orthodox Eucharistic Assembly, and the anointing with chrism is the chief ritual gesture adhering one to this new expression of faith. Anointing with chrism is distinct from rebaptism because it recognizes qualities of church present in the convert's community of origin, but falls short of professing full communion with these communities.[57]

The power of the anointed chrism to equip the convert with consistently correct faith might not be initially obvious, especially since there are historical models for reception into the church by professing faith that do not include the anointing with chrism. The anointing with chrism expresses a strong theology of covenant, as revealed by the archetypal postbaptismal anointing with chrism and other liturgical rites employing oil. Chrism's covenantal quality can be found in the rite of the consecration of chrism, keeping in mind that chrism is not exclusive to postbaptismal anointing, but has also been used for the reception of converts since at least the Council of Trullo in the seventh century. The prayer for the consecration of chrism asks God to enable the converts to "bear Thy Christ in their hearts as dwelling places for Thee, the God and Father in the Holy Spirit," a phrase asserting that the anointing with chrism forges a new covenant with Christ and God in Trinity.[58] The prayer of chrismation asks God to grant the candidate the "seal of the gift of the Holy Spirit," a multivalent gift imparting many

---

[57] Paul Meyendorff aptly represents the Orthodox ecclesiological position: "The mutual recognition of Baptism is therefore a positive step towards the greater unity that we seek. Short of full communion, it nevertheless marks a degree of recognition of one another as churches. But it does not simply 'paper over' the significant issues that continue to divide Christians from one another, and which we must continue seeking to resolve in mutual love. I see this as more honest than entering into full communion while remaining fundamentally divided." In "Toward Mutual Recognition of Baptism," in *Baptism Today: Understanding, Practice, Ecumenical Implications*, ed. Thomas F. Best, Faith and Order Paper No. 207 (Collegeville, MN: Liturgical Press, 2008), 204.

[58] "OCA Chrism Rite," via e-mail with OCA Archivist Alexis Liberovsky, January 31, 2012. Also see the historical antecedent of this prayer in BAR no. 141, eds. Parenti and Velkovska, 143.

blessings, including sanctification. If the sacred space of this sanctification is community with God in the Trinity through the covenant forged with Christ, then Christ himself is the source of the sanctification. Since anointing with chrism seals the covenant of divine community, it is also used for the reception of converts.

The liturgical evidence for the reception of converts strongly suggests that a parallel covenant is forged between the convert and Christ's community through the liturgical components of renunciation/confession, and the anointing with chrism. As in baptism, the Holy Spirit works through the chrism to forge covenantal community with Christ in the reception of converts. The natural healing properties of oil are not limited to physical ailments, but also have the properties to cure the deficiencies of faith located in minds and hearts. I suggest that the multiple gifts granted by the Holy Spirit through the anointing with chrism communicate the notion of covenantal restoration of those separated from Orthodoxy.[59] The liturgical celebration of the reception of converts clearly shows that the covenant forged in conversion is twofold: to God and the Orthodox community, by the power of the Holy Spirit, and through Christ. The foundational covenant occurs during baptism, in the rites of initiation, the authentic and original context of postbaptismal anointing. The anointing with chrism capacitates the return to the original covenant, with an emphasis on its terms defined by the community: correct faith. By definition, if the convert returns to the original covenant of baptism, the covenant is also newly created with the body of Christ, the community of the church which defines, articulates, and witnesses to these articles of faith. The rite's accentuation of renouncing and professing the true faith preserved and confessed by the Orthodox Church punctuates the convert's entrance into a covenant shared by an entire living community.

---

[59] Anointing with Chrism in the reception of converts has an interesting parallel in the reconciliation of penitents to the Church practiced among some Orthodox through the celebration of the Sacrament of Holy Unction on Holy Wednesday. For more on the Byzantine tradition of healing through the Sacrament of Holy Unction, see Paul Meyendorff, *The Anointing of the Sick* (Crestwood, NY: St. Vladimir's Seminary Press, 2009), 31–61.

CHRISM AS AN AGENT OF COVENANT

Ancient and contemporary theologians offer interpretations of the covenantal quality of chrism that imparts the spiritual blessings of correct faith, protection, and belonging. Cyril, fourth-century bishop of Jerusalem, discusses the power of chrism in his third mystagogical catechesis. Cyril's context is postbaptismal anointing with chrism, imparted to the neophytes at the fourth-century hagiopolite Paschal Vigil. Cyril teaches the neophytes that their baptism in the likeness (ἐν ὁμοιώματι) of Christ makes them worthy (καταξιοῦσθε) of being crucified, buried, and raised together with him.[60] Cyril then asserts that the anointing with chrism furthers and deepens the covenant with Christ: "As he was anointed with the spiritual oil of gladness, the Holy Spirit, who is so called because he is the author of spiritual gladness, so you were anointed with Myron, having been communicants and partakers of Christ."[61] Cyril emphasizes the intimacy the neophytes share with Christ in this passage by referring to them as partakers and communicants of Christ. This intimacy grounds Cyril's calling the neophytes "Christs" and "Christians" in the context of the same lecture, a staple of his program of identity formation.[62] Cyril continues the construction of his teaching by illuminating the holy properties of the consecrated chrism:[63]

> But beware of supposing this to be plain myron. For as the bread of the Eucharist, after the epiclesis of the Holy Spirit is no longer mere bread but the Body of Christ, so also this holy Myron is no more simple Myron after the epiclesis, but the gift of Christ; and by the presence of his divinity, it causes in us the Holy Spirit.

---

[60] For critical text and French translation see Cyril of Jerusalem, *Catéchèses mystagogiques*, ed. A. Piedagnel, 124–27. I am adapting F. L. Cross's English edition, *Lectures on the Christian Sacraments*, 64–65.

[61] Piedagnel, ed., *Catéchèses mystagogiques*, 124; Cross, ed., *Lectures on the Christian Sacraments*, 64–65.

[62] For a magisterial overview of Cyril's program of identity formation, see Hawk-Reinhard, "From Χριστιανοί to Χριστοφόροι," 1–6, 287–379.

[63] Piedagnel, ed., *Catéchèses mystagogiques*, 124; Cross, ed., *Lectures on the Christian Sacraments*, 64–65.

After explaining the ritual process of anointing, Cyril then offers this provocative explanation of the significance of the anointing with chrism:[64]

> Keep this unspotted: for it shall teach you all things if it abides in you, as you have just heard declared by the blessed John, who discourses much concerning this chrism. For this holy thing is a spiritual preservative of the body and safeguard of the soul. . . . Having been anointed, therefore, with this holy myron, keep it unspotted and unblemished in you, pressing forward by good works, and becoming well-pleasing to the captain of your salvation, Christ Jesus.

Cyril's source for this passage appears to be 1 John 2, where the author laments those who have been led astray and reassures the audience that their anointing preserves the teaching about Christ they have received.

Martin Connell has recently hypothesized that the author of 1 John refers to a liturgical practice of anointing with chrism that was an alternative and perhaps controversial rite of initiation known by the Johannine community.[65] Connell's hypothesis is plausible given the plurality and diversity of liturgical rites in the apostolic era.[66] Cyril was likely unaware of the diversity of liturgical practices for the initiation of neophytes in the apostolic era, so he views this Johannine passage as a *lectio selecta* that connects the anointing with chrism and teaching about Christ. Cyril appears to integrate the connection between the anointing with chrism and the preservation of correct teaching in his own teaching to the neophytes. This section begins and concludes with an exhortation to preserve the chrism without blemish, a unique statement which would seem to pertain to the white garment traditionally given to the neophytes, but Cyril instead emphasizes the preservation of the chrism.

---

[64] Piedagnel, ed., *Catéchèses mystagogiques*, 130–31; Cross, ed., *Lectures on the Christian Sacraments*, 66–67.

[65] Martin Connell, "On 'Chrism' and 'Anti-Christs' in 1 John 2:18–27: A Hypothesis," *Worship* 83 (2009): 212–34.

[66] Connell's admonition of those who attempt to construct liturgical history through the lens of contemporary sacramental practices is apt in ibid., 231–33.

While Cyril was instructing neophytes during the week following their Paschal baptism, his instruction about the chrism itself and the gifts it imparts to participants pertains to the rite of the reception of converts. The connection between chrism and its power to sustain and preserve true teaching appears to be one of the keys to its emergence as a multivalent symbol used for the ritual of receiving converts. Much of Cyril's fourth-century description of chrism permeates later Eastern sacramental theology, since Cyril equates the anointing with chrism as imparting the ability to withstand the temptations of the devil and "stand against the power of the enemy."[67] Chrism's protective properties constitute a repetitive refrain in this study. Clearly, however, Cyril understands the ritual participation as impacting the whole person, body and soul, and consequently also connoting true teaching about Christ. Cyril's teaching recalls the ancient idea of the Spirit capacitating true belief in Christ, an idea apparently originating in the New Testament.[68]

Nicholas Cabasilas, the renowned fourteenth-century Byzantine theologian, shares views similar to Cyril on the properties of the chrism. Cabasilas's discussion of chrism, which also refers to the context of anointing with chrism as a part of initiation, refers to the anointing of kings and priests in the Old Covenant, and then refers to Jesus' own anointing, "not by receiving chrism poured on the head, but by receiving the Holy Spirit."[69] In the same vein as Cyril, Cabasilas sees the chrism as having properties that create a strong and intimate covenant with Christ:[70]

> When . . . flesh was deified and human nature gained possession of God himself by hypostatic union, the former barrier opposed to

---

[67] Piedagnel, ed., *Catéchèses mystagogiques*, 126–27; Cross, ed., *Lectures on the Christian Sacraments*, 65–66.

[68] See Connell, "On 'Chrism' and 'Anti-Christs,'" 218–20, for New Testament texts referencing anointing.

[69] Nicholas Cabasilas, *The Life of Christ*, trans. Carmino J. deCatanzaro, intro. Boris Bobrinskoy (Crestwood, NY: St. Vladimir's Seminary Press, 1974), 104. Also see Cabasilas, no. 3.2, *La vie en Christ, livres I–IV*, ed. Congourdeau, Sources Chretiennes 355 (Paris: Cerf, 1989), 238–39.

[70] Cabasilas, no. 3.5, *La vie en Christ, livres I–IV*, ed. Congourdeau, 240–41. Cabasilas, *The Life in Christ*, trans. deCantanzaro, 105.

God became joined to the chrism. The difference gave way when God became man, thus removing the separation between Godhead and manhood. So chrism represents Christ as the point of contact between both natures: there could be no point of contact were they still separate.

Cabasilas goes on to say that the gifts of the Spirit are imparted through this ritual, and that the "chrism brings in the Lord Jesus, on whom is man's whole salvation and all hope of benefits."[71] Unlike Cyril, Cabasilas does not define the chrism as connoting correct faith. This omission is outstanding since Cabasilas illustrates the chrism as enabling participants to prophesy future events, cast out demons, and heal diseases.[72] Cabasilas, then, remains faithful to the liturgical theology of the rite by interpreting the chrism's main function as ushering the participants into an intimate covenant with God in Trinity, through Christ, which one might describe as *theosis*.

Alexander Schmemann reads the liturgical sources under the assumption (like Cyril and Cabasilas) that baptism precedes chrismation in a complete rite of initiation; there is no special treatment of the anointing of chrism for the reception of converts. However, as with Cyril and Cabasilas, Schmemann's analysis of the chrism can also be applied to those who receive the anointing with chrism during the rite of the reception of converts. Schmemann emphasizes Christ as the one who imparts the gift of the Spirit in continuity with the participants' having "put on Christ" in baptism: "Christ is the Anointed and we receive his anointment; Christ is the Son and we are adopted as sons; Christ has the Spirit as his life and we are granted participation in his life."[73] Schmemann closely follows Cabasilas and the euchology of chrismation in defining the chrism as inaugurating life in the communion of the Spirit, which is another way of referring to a covenant creating life with God.

---

[71] Cabasilas, no. 3.8, *La vie en Christ, livres I–IV*, ed. Congourdeau, 244–45. deCantanzaro, trans., 106.

[72] Cabasilas, no. 3.9, *La vie en Christ, livres I–IV*, ed. Congourdeau, 244–45. deCantanzaro, trans., 107.

[73] Schmemann, *Of Water and Spirit* (Crestwood, NY: St. Vladimir's Seminary Press, 1974), 79.

Schmemann, however, further advances his thesis by claiming that chrismation is actually distinct from baptism because through it, a participant received a new gift, that of the Spirit.[74] Schmemann's explication of the novelty of chrismation is quite suggestive:[75]

> Prepared for and made possible by baptism, which thus is fulfilled in it, it takes man beyond baptism, beyond "salvation": by making him "Christ" in Christ, by anointing him with the anointment of the anointed one, it opens to him the door of theosis, of deification. Such is the meaning of this ineffable mystery, of the seal . . . its essential significance, as revealed in the anointment of the Holy chrism, is clear: it is the imprint on us of the one who owns us; it is the seal that preserves and defends in us the precious and its fragrance; it is the sign of our high and unique calling.

Schmemann emphasizes the imprint marked on participants that connotes ownership by Christ. His covenantal language is consistent with Cabasilas in emphasizing the intimacy participants share with Christ, and by stating that the mystery of chrismation results in *theosis*, union with God.

Unlike Cyril, Cabasilas, and Schmemann, Meletios Webber, a contemporary Orthodox theologian, discusses the meaning of the mystery of conversion in the context of the reception of converts by referring to his own conversion from the Church of England to Orthodoxy.[76] Webber translates chrismation as a ritual of marking that connotes belonging, and explicates the twofold covenant chrismation imparts in all of its contexts:[77]

> Belonging is described in the Orthodox Church in terms of "being in communion." This means far more than two particular people can receive Holy Communion together. It is, rather, a declaration of being "in Christ," that fundamental awareness of identity, of participating in the life of the church and the life of God. To be "in

---

[74] Ibid., 80.
[75] Ibid. Schmemann concludes this section by asserting that the entire process capacitates the participant to become temples of the Holy Spirit.
[76] Meletios Webber, *Bread and Water, Wine and Oil: An Orthodox Christian Experience of God* (Ben Lomond, CA: Conciliar Press, 2007), 131–36.
[77] Ibid., 132.

communion" is the primary sense of being within the church. It is far more significant than one's specific role or position within the church. Everyone, from the patriarch to the youngest baptized person, is 'in communion" and thus "in Christ"—a status which is both egalitarian and remarkable.

Webber effectively synthesizes the liturgical theology of chrismation articulated by the liturgical texts of chrismation, Cyril of Jerusalem, Cabasilas, and Schmemann by casting the process of conversion in terms of identity and belonging. The chrism imparts two covenants linked by Christ in one process to converts: first, a covenant in Christ and God, and second, a covenant to the community of the church. The ecclesial covenant is by definition both hierarchical and egalitarian since everyone who is in the church receives the same sacrament. Webber's analysis helps us complete this examination of chrismation because belonging to a particular communion entails sharing its values, including its articles of faith. The anointing with chrism does not necessarily examine precision in one's articulation of the Orthodox faith, but the gift of the Spirit imparted through the anointing capacitates one to grow in the faith held by the community to which he or she now belongs.

The Orthodox interpretation of anointing with chrism as forging a twofold covenant with God and the church coheres with the liturgical and theological sources, but is ecumenically problematic. Since the vast majority of Orthodox in the world receive baptized Christians into the church's communion through the rite of anointing with chrism, the question of creating a new covenant with God needs to be addressed. The Orthodox recognition of baptism in other Christian communities is an acknowledgment that those entering the Orthodox communion are already in the baptismal covenant with God. Clearly, God is not abrogating a covenant he created with Christians only to recreate it again through chrismation. It is much more preferable to view the rite of reception by anointing with chrism as a renewal of the baptismal covenant through the particular confession of faith of the Orthodox Church. Here is one possible description of how chrismation honors the twofold covenant with God and the church: when the church gathers to celebrate the reception of Christians into the communion of the Orthodox

Church, the prayers of chrismation, the confessions of faith, and the bodily anointing ritualize a deeply human experience of belonging. Christians already belong to God: when they are anointed, the covenant with God is renewed and sealed through the anointing, the confession of faith, and the church's prayer. The renewal of the baptismal covenant with God occurs simultaneously with the creation of a new covenant with the Orthodox Church. After the anointing with chrism, the newly received Orthodox Christian remains with God, for God was always with her; now, the Orthodox communicant belongs to the ecumenical Orthodox communion and promises to responsibly uphold, love, protect, and confess her faith.

BEFORE AND AFTER THE RITUAL: EXPERIENCING THE PROCESS OF CONVERSION

The *lex orandi* of the rite of the reception of converts expresses a process largely consisting of renouncing aspects of one's previous ecclesial community, particularly its tenets of faith, and joining a new community by publicly confessing its faith. The liturgical theology of the rite envisions the emergence of a new person who shares the values of the community he or she is joining and whose life will represent virtue, to the point of defending the Orthodox faith unto death. A fair and necessary question is posed here: can Orthodox conversion narratives confirm the liturgical theology of conversion presented here? If not, in what areas do converts actually differ, and how might one explain divergences? Numerous questions emerge from the initial consideration of this question and from an honest assessment of the liturgy of conversion. One might begin with the social implications of renouncing tenets of faith belonging to a particular community. When converts change communities, in many cases, their own social network of family and friends can change, or the dynamics of relationships can be altered. A good example of the implications of conversion is the well-known contemporary memoir of Sara Miles, the journalist and social activist who converted to Christianity and became active in St. Gregory of Nyssa Episcopalian Church in San Francisco.[78]

---

[78] Sara Miles, *Take This Bread* (New York: Ballantine, 2007), 66–70 and passim.

Miles's relationships were tested, stretched, and challenged during the process of her conversion. The relational challenge does not necessarily mean that everyone from her previous life abandoned her and ended the friendship, but the process of her own transformation simultaneously impacted her relationships, with some of them strained, even though she created many new friendships. Miles's narration of the elements her conversion introduced to the relationship she shared with her partner poignantly illuminates conversion as a lonely and vulnerable journey, since converts have to negotiate serious new terms with loved ones in their social networks. In Miles's case, her partner did not share her enthusiasm for her faith journey, and her daughter did not express the same interest in church involvement. This required an adjustment on everyone's part, since Fridays (the weekday Miles ran her groundbreaking food pantry through St. Gregory of Nyssa Church) and Sundays would be permanently different.

For many converts to Orthodoxy, analogous practical realignments occur, even for single people. For example, a convert who spent her lifetime celebrating Easter with her family would commemorate Easter according to the Orthodox calendar, which usually falls on a different date. Converts who observe Easter with their family might have to negotiate the Orthodox rule of fasting during Lent. Such negotiations are not only possible but pastorally encouraged, yet they still require an adjustment on the part of everyone in the social network. Furthermore, converts might find it challenging to explain why they no longer hold certain tenets of faith belonging to their original faith community. Practically speaking, for converts coming from Reformed traditions, the Orthodox veneration of saints and Mary is particularly challenging and difficult to explain.[79] I am not suggesting that all converts become lonely

---

[79] A common Orthodox liturgical refrain sung at liturgical assemblies is "Most-holy Theotokos, save us!" See Peter Gillquist, *Becoming Orthodox: A Journey to the Ancient Christian Faith*, revised and updated (Ben Lomond, CA: Conciliar Press, 1989, 1992). Also see a companion piece profiling Protestant pastors who converted to Orthodoxy: Peter Gillquist, ed., *Coming Home: Why Protestant Clergy are Becoming Orthodox* (Ben Lomond, CA: Conciliar Press, 1992).

pilgrims abandoned by family and friends, but an examination of the actual convert experience from the "other side of the coin" can be useful in helping us test and complete our thesis on the liturgical theology of conversion in the Orthodox Rite. Several contemporary sources communicate narratives of converts' experiences, and this section will illustrate the salient points of such narratives and compare them to the liturgical theology of conversion.

A handful of famous people have converted to Orthodoxy in the late twentieth and twenty-first centuries, including actor Tom Hanks, composer John Tavener, evangelist Frankie Schaeffer, church historian Jaroslav Pelikan, and NFL star Troy Polamalu. Perhaps the most renowned case of conversion occurred when a large group of evangelical Christians formerly involved in the Campus Crusade for Christ were received in the Orthodox Church in the 1980s. This group was known as the Evangelical Orthodox Church and entered the Orthodox Church in large groups via chrismation and ordination through the Antiochian Archdiocese. The group's spokesperson, Peter Gillquist, narrated the group's story in an informative and gripping memoir titled *Becoming Orthodox*, which has seen numerous revisions and updates.[80] Gillquist's account of the group's conversion to Orthodoxy contains many important points pertinent to this study. First, we should note that Gillquist does not linger on the issue of chrismation and the ritual of entrance into the church. But his description of the actual journey of conversion establishes a perspective on the various facets of the journey to Orthodoxy one experiences, and how the ritual of anointing with chrism informs the journey.

The clergy and parishes of the EOC inaugurated the search for the authentic community representing the New Testament church they loved when they sensed their ministry was not working.[81] A concerted effort to discover and reconstruct the New Testament

---

[80] Gillquist, *Becoming Orthodox*, and Gillquist, ed., *Coming Home*. For a theological assessment of this conversion and other prominent American conversion narratives, see D. Oliver Herbel's groundbreaking study, *Turning to Tradition: Converts and the Making of an American Orthodox Church* (Oxford: Oxford University Press, 2013).

[81] Gillquist, *Becoming Orthodox*, 7.

church followed, and was grounded by serious study and experience.[82] Much of the study was devoted to answering questions and filling in blanks, such as a response to the question on how communities of the apostolic era actually worshipped. The group was quite surprised by the yield of their research, which evidenced a liturgical church centered on baptism and the regular celebration of the Sunday Eucharist.[83] In their pursuit of joining the authentic New Testament church, they founded the New Covenant Apostolic Order in 1974, and began a series of encounters with the Orthodox Church in 1977.[84] The next phase of study concerned encounter with actual Orthodox communities, and their experience was both prolonged and mixed. While many Orthodox in America welcomed and encouraged them in their journey, their pilgrimage to Constantinople was a major disappointment, as the Ecumenical Patriarchate was suspicious of their motives.[85] This part of the story is crucial since the group essentially experienced rejection from the most visible authority of the Orthodox Church, a reminder that disappointment and rejection accompanies conversion journeys.

After ten years of learning about the various Orthodox groups in America, they were received into the Antiochian Archdiocese through a special arrangement following a series of negotiations with Metropolitan Phillip. Whole EOC communities were received into the Orthodox Church via mass chrismation, while the clergy of the EOC (including Gillquist) were received via chrismation with the laying on of hands and ordination immediately following.[86] This mode of reception is largely coherent with the principles established by this chapter, since the EOC communities and their

---

[82] Ibid., 3–58. Also see Herbel, *Turning to Tradition*, 106–10.

[83] Gillquist, *Becoming Orthodox*, 29–34. This section describes the EOC's program of study in detail, containing references to the group's reactions to the order of liturgy according to Justin Martyr and the Apostolic Tradition. Later sections detail their attempt to address other issues such as Tradition, the Papacy, Church orders, and Mary.

[84] Gillquist, *Becoming Orthodox*, 127–32.

[85] See ibid., 138–43 for an account of the Ecumenical Patriarch's refusal to grant them an audience.

[86] Ibid., 165–74.

clergy were already baptized, and the clergy also had to receive chrismation. The fact that the Antiochian Archdiocese was willing to expedite their sacramental process of ordination is somewhat remarkable, given their journey to Orthodoxy from the evangelical church. In other words, men who were bishops in the EOC were ordained as deacons first (to fulfill the Orthodox Church pattern of ordination to major orders), and were then immediately ordained to the priesthood.[87] The particular vocation of the EOC is notable, one proclaimed by the Antiochian Archdiocese's leader, Metropolitan Phillip, in his remarks responding to the chrismation services in which the EOC was received into Orthodoxy: "What America needs today, especially after the collapse of the electronic pulpit, is an Orthodox evangelism based on the true interpretation of the Scripture, the apostolic and patristic teachings, and the liturgical and sacramental life of the Church."[88]

The reception of the EOC into the Orthodox Church via chrismation is notable for the impact the former evangelicals had in reshaping American Orthodox identity and missiological orientation. For our purposes, the details of their journey are precious and coherent with the ritual process of chrismation as the rite of reception. First, in the preparatory process, the EOC studied in a twofold manner: through immersion in theological literature, and by encountering real Orthodox communities. This process included shock, doubt, disappointment, and courage. For the EOC, the study of church history was crucial in taking the initial step to confessing faith according to the Orthodox Church. Second, the journey included the group's addressing questions of doctrine that were formerly incontrovertible in their communities of origin, including the veneration of Mary. The group members had to honestly assess whether or not

---

[87] The men who were bishops in the EOC were not able to receive episcopal consecration in the Orthodox Church, which requires clerical celibacy. The Antiochian Archdiocese had mentioned the married episcopate as a problem requiring resolution in their original agreement with the EOC. See ibid., 151–52, for the details on the agreement.

[88] Ibid., 171. At the end of the original edition, Gillquist echoes this sentiment, stating that "it's our turn to bring America—and the West—to Orthodox Christianity," ibid., 174.

they could join a community that regularly and vibrantly praised Mary as the mother of God. Most of Gillquist's account conveys a process of encounter involving the whole person. While the cognitive consideration of tenets of faith is certainly prominent, matters of body and heart are equally integrated into the process. Finally, in considering their conversion, Gillquist uses the metaphors of entrance and journey to describe the experience: he describes conversion as a great entrance, and quotes Metropolitan Phillip who plainly told the EOC, "welcome home." In terms of Gillquist's assessment of his Christian background, one senses that Gillquist detected errors of judgment and interpretation, but not a condemnation of the Protestant heritage of the EOC.[89] The metaphor of conversion as a journey that brings one home echoes loudest, and this metaphor appears, in the absence of contradictory evidence, to be charitable to the pre-Orthodox period of the EOC's history. While the story of the EOC is of particular historical significance, one cannot describe it as modular for the convert experience because of the special circumstances surrounding their conversion, and the terms of their entrance into the church, which included the expectation that they would reshape Orthodox mission in America. For a more typical convert experience, we turn to the recent study of Amy Slagle and her presentation of convert narratives.[90]

Slagle presents a concise study of contemporary conversion dynamics as narrated by select converts to Eastern Christianity in an ethnographic study. Slagle closely examined two particular Orthodox parishes, one in the Pittsburgh area and the other in Mississippi. While her coverage of conversion is not exhaustive, it provides a valuable snapshot into the process converts experience as they begin

---

[89] See Herbel, *Turning to Tradition*, 120–22.

[90] Amy Slagle, *The Eastern Church in the Spiritual Marketplace: American Conversions to Orthodox Christianity* (DeKalb, IL: Northern Illinois University Press, 2011). For recent demographic shifts in the Orthodox Churches in America, see Alexei Krindatch's illuminating survey report, *The Orthodox Church Today: A National Study of Parishioners and the Realities of Orthodox Parish Life in the USA* (Berkeley, CA: Patriarch Athenagoras Institute, 2010). Krindatch reports that 51 percent of OCA members are converts whereas 29 percent of Greek Orthodox in America are converts.

the process of entering the Orthodox Church.[91] Slagle's definition of the contemporary context is informative as we consider the relevance of the history of the reception of converts today. She defines the present context as a "spiritual marketplace," an acknowledgment of Orthodoxy's position in an increasingly globalized world and pluralized American culture.[92] The notion of a spiritual marketplace is certainly not novel in religious studies, but Slagle shows how it has impacted the process of conversion to Orthodoxy, as the motivations for conversion are often shaped by the situation of religious pluralism. Slagle presents diverse narratives demonstrating that there is no uniform process of conversion, and the motivations for conversion are not monolithic. A married couple, Fred and Mary, came to Orthodoxy after investigating several religious options over twelve years, and attributed at least part of their decision to their disenchantment with a perceived connection between an "American consumerist populist culture" and the so-called "egoism" of Protestant churches.[93] Another convert expressed disappointment in the changes the Second Vatican Council delivered to the Catholic Church, and chose Orthodoxy because of its perceived promise of "offering potential stability, in remaining (in converts' eyes, at least) historically and doctrinally unchanged and unchanging."[94]

These two examples from Slagle's study cohere, at least to some degree, with the perspective expressed by Gillquist, and establish the current situation of conversion to Orthodoxy in America: many converts come to Orthodoxy because of their disenchantment with some aspect of their previous religious or denominational affiliation. Oliver Herbel refers to this phase of the conversion process as "conversions to tradition," a pattern of discerning a sense of ongoing ecclesial tradition in the Orthodox Church to which the convert is drawn.[95]

As for the process engaged by converts in Slagle's study, it is one of selective reading in a sort of independent study. Converts draw

---

[91] Slagle, *The Eastern Church*, 24–37.
[92] Ibid., 8–14.
[93] Ibid., 88–89.
[94] Ibid., 89.
[95] Herbel, *Turning to Tradition*, 151–52.

from a variety of sources in learning about the Eastern church, including print and electronic media, with the internet functioning as an important information source.[96] Some converts study Orthodoxy for over ten years, and the importance of learning about the church has resulted in a type of catechumenate.[97] In some cases, parish clergy provide formal instruction, but the process narrated by the converts is largely self-guided, with clergy offering more coaching and guidance. Interestingly, while converts often viewed Orthodoxy as offering the most traditional manifestation of church in doctrine and worship, their experience of working through these issues seems to represent a sort of intellectual freedom for give and take, which Slagle describes as an "interpretative space."[98] The catechetical process of conversion again underscores the cognitive dimension of contemporary conversion to the Eastern church, where most converts experience a deeper intellectual immersion into its history and theology. The emergence of a *de facto* catechumenate is particularly notable, since the proper provenance for a catechumenate is baptism. The integration of such traditional initiatory language into the mainstream vocabulary of the Orthodox Church reveals its ecclesiological self-identity as *the* holy, catholic, and apostolic church, and also has the capacity to shape how converts reflect upon their own religious heritage.

An interesting exception to the convert experience described above occurs in the narratives of intermarriage converts. For example, Slagle notes that intermarriage converts rarely described their conversions as a "journey," and were much less likely to actively engage in the multifaceted catechetical process of conversion.[99] Many intermarriage converts are already attending their spouses' Orthodox Church and thus depend much more on observation and experience that comes with socialization into the

[96] Slagle, *The Eastern Church in the Spiritual Marketplace*, 48–53. Slagle describes the nature of such contemporary conversions as both "book-driven" and "intellectual" (49).

[97] Ibid., 65–66. Slagle underscores the absence of a uniform catechumenate distinguishing the Orthodox process from Catholic and Protestant ones.

[98] Ibid., 98–103.

[99] Ibid., 58–59.

church.[100] The process of socialization becomes more complicated for well-informed converts who begin their covenantal relationship with the local community and often find themselves at odds with discrepancies between ideal practices they learned in their catechesis and the realities of parish life.[101] Slagle notes that "converts expressed a desire for their churches to conform" to the Orthodoxy encountered in the pages of their theology and history books," and asserts that "converts often saw themselves as informal parish authorities," willing to critique specific liturgical practices or theological attitudes within the parish.[102] Her observation on convert attitudes is provocative, as it underscores the cognitive dimension of the contemporary process of conversion and the potential for conflict that occurs when converts begin the process of belonging to a particular parish community.[103] In such instances, clergy had to mitigate potential conflict by asking converts to respect practices peculiar to parish communities, even if such practices did not cohere with convert perceptions of tradition based on their study. The process of socialization and learning about the Orthodox Church by engaging its life and practices in community emerges as an equal partner in the process of conversion and illuminates the significance of covenant with community.

Slagle's study on conversion contains scant coverage of the actual rite of chrismation, and there is no analysis of the liturgical theology of the rite.[104] The studies of conversion presented by Slagle and Herbel, however, provide crucial information on how converts experienced and interpreted their entrance into the Orthodox Church. A brief review of the salient points of Slagle's study illuminates the general coherence of convert experience with the liturgical theology of the rite, with both subtle and overt discrepancies. First, the rite of receiving converts emphasizes the necessity of re-

---

[100] Ibid., 74–75.

[101] Ibid., 115–21.

[102] Ibid., 115, 117.

[103] Ibid., 119–21. Slagle also discusses the convergence of converts with prevalent Orthodox ethnic cultures in 124–42.

[104] Slagle simply notes that "there is no uniform, churchwide protocol for which rituals should be administered to adult converts," ibid., 14.

jecting false faith and confessing true faith as defined by the Orthodox Church. Slagle's study evidences a tendency among converts to rigorously study Orthodoxy and identify it as an ecclesial repository of true faith, often perceived as unchanging and faithful to apostolic tradition. Convert narratives certainly demonstrate disenchantment and disappointment with perceived errors of some converts' native faith traditions, but such attitudes did not yield overt rejection of one's past. Instead, a sense of relief in discovering the faith expressed by Orthodoxy prevails. It is important to note that some converts were perfectly comfortable embracing Orthodoxy while favoring an ecumenical attitude by occasionally frequenting and participating in the liturgical life of non-Orthodox churches.[105] Perhaps such ecumenical sharing of prayer is a consequence of the contemporary spiritual marketplace, but it underscores the willingness of at least some converts to retain connections with their past or at least sample alternative Christian communities. In terms of theological precision, while some converts became knowledgeable in certain aspects of Christology and trinitarian theology, the catechetical process facilitated a more robust immersion in the history and doctrine of Eastern Christianity. Naturally, the theological interests of today's converts illustrate the current issues debated in the ecumenical arena, which demonstrates that older issues such as the *filioque* and the interpretation of Scripture that converts might confront in renunciation and confession might now be dated.

Second, the rite of receiving converts emphasizes the creation of a covenant with the local community, especially in its theological tenets of faith. The convert narratives strongly suggest that this is the primary emphasis of conversion in the contemporary context, especially for those who were already baptized. Both Gillquist's story and Slagle's narratives show that the process of conversion entails involved encounter with and participation in Orthodox community life, sometimes for long periods of time prior to conversion. The need for study and experience before conversion has resulted in the creation of local catechumenates in Orthodox communities that creates an odd dilemma for the scholar. By

---

[105] Ibid., 121–23.

employing "catechumenate" and "catechumen" as terms describing all converts, the Orthodox are emphasizing their ecclesiology as *the* one, holy, catholic, and apostolic church, and imply that a significant change of life is a prerequisite for entrance into the Orthodox communion. But the degree to which converts actually experience a significant change in their life is somewhat unknown, even though both the liturgical theology of chrismation and the catechetical process suggest inevitable change. The conversion narratives certainly suggest a period of adjustment to community life as converts learn how to navigate the traditions and identities of new communities and their people, but there is no mechanism to assess the degree of change a given convert experiences in the post-conversion period.[106] The most prevalent implication of these studies is that all converts, including those baptized in other Christian faith communities, the unchurched, and intermarriage converts enter Orthodoxy by a desire to satisfy a sense of belonging. In the context of conversion, belonging is multivalent and includes affinities in faith and doctrine, worship, community size, and a sense of fellowship with people. Converts also use other terms and phrases that function as cognates of belonging, such as journey and coming home. In this vein, the anointing with chrism as the rite of receiving converts can be interpreted as something akin to commencement in education. It is the rite that affirms the convert's intellectual readiness not only to enter but to truly belong to a particular community and exercise citizenship in accordance with that community's values. Chrism is a symbol of covenantal belonging to God and God's community, and the rite of anointing with chrism functions as the conclusion to the preparatory process and commencement of new life within that community, which in this case is the Orthodox Church.

CONCLUSION

This chapter has reviewed and analyzed the complicated process of receiving converts in the Orthodox Church. I presented the

---

[106] One potential method is to study converts' lives over an extended period of time and make assessments in increments of five or ten years.

liturgical theology of the rite of receiving converts, and compared it with contemporary narratives of conversion. I will begin this conclusion with a brief review of this chapter's contributions, and will then offer select *desiderata* on the future trajectory of the reception of converts in the Orthodox Church.[107]

Review:
1) The history of the rite of the reception of converts evidences diverse practices governed by the faith community from which the convert hailed. Generally speaking, converts experienced a more detailed and rigorous process of reception corresponding to the church's assessment of the doctrinal deficiency of their native faith community.
2) The core liturgical components that ritualize conversion include renunciation of false teachings, confession of true teaching, and in most cases, anointing with chrism. Participation in the Eucharistic Liturgy is the implied goal of conversion.
3) Interfaith polemics have occasionally caused adjustments to the rite of receiving converts, which resulted in pronounced divergences in ritual practices. Another adjustment occurred when the Orthodox churches of Rus' adapted the postbaptismal rite of chrismation as the liturgical framework for the rite of receiving converts in the seventeenth century.
4) The rite of receiving converts emphasizes the cognitive dimension of changing one's tenets of faith and the creation of a covenant with a community of faith that iterates particular tenets of faith.
5) Chrism emerges as a multivalent symbol because of its function in the reception of converts. While it retains the notion of covenant with the Triune God expressed by the rite of consecrating chrism and the theology of Nicholas Cabasilas and Alexander Schmemann, it also adheres one to correct teaching

---

[107] Readers are urged to consider the excellent pastoral suggestions presented by Alkiviadis Calivas in his recent assessment of the reception of converts in the Greek Orthodox tradition, which includes a revised rite for receiving converts into the Orthodox Church via chrismation. See Calivas, "Receiving Converts," 50–61.

and a sense of belonging to community (Cyril of Jerusalem and Meletios Webber).

6) Contemporary convert narratives demonstrate the context of conversion as religiously pluralistic, with converts preparing for entrance into the church through self-study and community immersion.

7) Convert experience emphasizes a sense of journey and belonging punctuated by their immersion in the teachings and faith of the Orthodox Church, while convert attitudes toward their native faith traditions vary.

Desiderata:

1) Anointing with chrism has proven to be a resilient rite in the liturgical history of initiation and the reception of converts, and its symbolism endures. While respecting liturgical diversity, the Orthodox Church should retain the anointing with chrism as the chief ritual action connoting entrance into the Orthodox Church because of the multivalent symbolism of chrism and its theology of covenant and the prevailing sense of belonging it communicates.

   a. Churches that use confession and Eucharist as the rites of reception for Catholics should continue to follow this practice. Another plausible component offered by Calivas is to require converts to sign a *libellus* professing their Orthodox faith, which would contribute a strong canonical component to what is currently a predominantly liturgical process.[108]

   b. Churches that prefer to use the anointing with chrism as the means of receiving converts should distinguish between postbaptismal chrismation and the anointing with chrism since they communicate different theologies. Chrismation should be employed only for converts who have not experienced chrismation and confirmation. Pastors celebrating the reception of converts with the anointing with chrism should be careful to explain that the anointing with chrism is not equivalent to rebaptism, but a sacra-

---

[108] Ibid., 61.

mental ritualization of the forging of a covenant with God and the community of the Orthodox Church that imparts the spiritual blessings of Orthodox faith, protection, and belonging.

2) The renunciations of false error should emphasize a general sense of renouncing false doctrines and avoid polemical language, while emphasizing an embracing of particular confessions of faith.[109] For renunciations, the general version of renunciation in the Greek rite is preferable. A pastoral acknowledgment that many converts will retain family ties and fellowship with their native communities of faith underpins this pastoral initiative. Also, pastors can emphasize that conversion is part of a larger journey to citizenship in God's kingdom, so converts will not struggle with the pain of rejecting entire faith communities.

3) Pastors should distinguish the catechesis that candidates for conversion engage in from the catechumenate of antiquity, despite the similarities they share. Such a distinction will promote the Orthodox Church's recognition of ecclesial qualities, orders, and teachings present in candidates hailing from a native Christian tradition.

In teaching about chrismation as a rite of conversion, pastors should emphasize the gift of the Holy Spirit as forging a twofold covenant with God and community through Christ. Pastors should also emphasize the notion of the Holy Spirit leading the converts through a journey to entrance into the Orthodox Church. Pastors must explain that God did not abrogate the covenant converts originally received in baptism, but that the anointing with chrism is a solemn entrance into the Orthodox communion where the covenant with the Triune God is renewed through the particular confessions and liturgical life of the Orthodox Church.

---

[109] While not documented, some clergy simply omit words, phrases, or even sections of the liturgical rites that promote polemical labels. Calivas encourages Orthodox to employ terms such as "heretic" and "schismatic" with great discretion.

CHAPTER 3

Orthodox Theologians on Chrismation

The previous chapters examined the liturgical celebration of chrismation in the rites of initiation and the reception of converts. My analysis included a presentation of the liturgical theology of these rites by attending to context, structures, liturgical components, ritual actions, and prayers. Throughout history, theologians have produced a variegated sacramental theology by interpreting the rites of initiation. Among the most salient reflections on the meaning of postbaptismal chrismation is Cyril of Jerusalem's Mystagogical Catechesis number 3, which I referenced in the previous two chapters. The modern liturgical movement restored due attention to the significance of the rites of initiation, especially in their disclosure of ecclesiology. The *ressourcement* movement reinvigorated interest in the ancient initiatory liturgies and sacramental treatises, with one of the fruits being the restoration of the rites of Christian initiation of adults in the Roman Church.[1] The Byzantine liturgical tradition has not implemented a parallel restoration, but several Eastern theologians have taken up a similar interest in the relationship between the rites of initiation and the structure of the church.

In this chapter, I will survey the most influential Eastern Orthodox interpretations of chrismation in order to fill out this theological reflection on chrismation. I will begin by reviewing the accounts of chrismation from the fourteenth-century mystagogue Nicholas Cabasilas and four theologians of the twentieth century: Nicholas Afanasiev, Alexander Schmemann, Boris Bobrinskoy, and

---

[1] For an overview, see Maxwell Johnson, *The Rites of Christian Initiation: Their Evolution and Interpretation*, rev. ed (Collegeville, MN: Liturgical Press, 1999, 2007); and Aidan Kavanagh, *The Shape of Baptism: The Rite of Christian Initiation* (Collegeville, MN: Liturgical Press, 1978; 1991).

Paul Evdokimov. The reader will note my exclusion of the famous fourth-century mystagogue Cyril of Jerusalem.[2] Methodologically, I begin with Nicholas Cabasilas because his fourteenth-century provenance brings us close to the completion of the final synthesis of the Byzantine Rite, whereas Cyril's commentary represents fourth-century hagiopolite liturgy.[3] Cabasilas remarks on chrismation as it is practiced by Byzantine Rite Christians today. Afanasiev, Schmemann, Bobrinskoy, and Evdokimov represent the Eastern theologians whose interest in chrismation and initiation translated into a reinvigorated ecclesiology. My investigation of these five theologians focuses on three chief issues that build on the liturgical theology developed earlier: the repetitive sanctifying activity of the Triune God in the three rites of initiation; the blessing of *theosis* offered by God to liturgical participants in the rites; and the relationship between the anointing with chrism and the imparting of the Christic offices of king, priest, and prophet. My analysis will include reflections on how one can progressively become like God from infancy and what kinds of models might be added to those of king, priest, and prophet in postmodern Christianity.

NICHOLAS CABASILAS

Nicholas Cabasilas was an Orthodox lay theologian of the late fourteenth century who produced prodigious mystagogical works, two of which are particularly noteworthy: *On the Divine Liturgy* and *The Life in Christ*.[4] *The Life in Christ* is a detailed explanation of the

---

[2] I include excerpts from late fourth-century baptismal homilies by John Chrysostom later in the chapter. Chrysostom's appearance occurs late because of Schmemann's references to Chrysostom's theology of king, priest, and prophet. For an analysis of recent scholarship on the rites of initiation in fourth-century Jerusalem, see Maxwell Johnson, "Christian Initiation in Fourth-Century Jerusalem and Recent Developments in the Study of the Sources," *Ecclesia Orans* 26 (2009): 143–61. I am grateful to Professor Johnson for recommending his article.

[3] On the completion of this synthesis, see Robert Taft, "Mount Athos: A Late Chapter in the History of the Byzantine Rite," *Dumbarton Oaks Papers* 42 (1988): 179–94.

[4] For background on Cabasilas and his liturgical output, see Nicholas Denysenko, "*The Life in Christ* by Nicholas Cabasilas: A Mystagogical Work," *Studia Liturgica* 38 (2008): 242–60.

meaning of the mysteries, with particular emphasis on the initiatory rites. Cabasilas begins the work by articulating Christ's salvation of humankind through Pascha and identifying the mysteries as the portal through which humans are restored to the divine community.[5] Cabasilas's explanation of the mystery is a sophisticated exposition of theological anthropology through a review of the sacraments. In his treatise on baptism, Cabasilas describes neophytes as those who have been transformed to an authentic human nature manifested in their behavior: "That which is known of this life, of which we may speak, and which displays its hidden qualities is the courage of the newly initiated, the new character of those who have been baptized and have persevered."[6] The purpose of baptism is to know God, a progressive process which leads to loving God.[7] It is notable that Cabasilas attributes the dynamic of transformation to the Holy Spirit, evidenced by his discussion of the transformation of the apostles. It was when the apostles "received baptism by the descent of the Paraklete" that they became new men capable of leading others to God.[8] Here, Cabasilas is attempting to demon-

---

[5] "The gates of the mysteries are far more august and beneficial than the gates of Paradise. The latter will not be opened to anyone who has not first entered through the gates of the mysteries, but these were opened when the gates of paradise had been closed . . . This is the life which the Lord came to bring, that those who come through these mysteries should be partakers of his death and share in his passion. Apart from this it is impossible to escape death," in Nicholas Cabasilas, *The Life in Christ*, trans. Carmino J. deCatanzaro, intro Boris Bobrinskoy (Crestwood, NY: St. Vladimir's Seminary Press, 1974), 56–57. The critical edition of the text: *La vie en Christ, Livres I–IV*, ed. Marie-Hélène Congourdeau, Sources Chrétiennes 355 (Paris: Cerf, 1989). Congourdeau has also provided the introduction with critical text, translation, annotation, and index in *La vie en Christ, Livres V–VII*, Sources Chrétiennes 361 (Paris: Cerf, 1990).

[6] Cabasilas, *The Life in Christ*, 86–87.

[7] "It is knowing that causes love and gives birth to it. It is not possible to attain love of anything that is beautiful without first learning how beautiful it is . . . the baptismal washing has instilled into men some knowledge and perception of God, so that they have clearly known him who is good and have perceived his beauty and tasted of his goodness. This, I affirm, they are able to know more perfectly by experience than were they merely to learn it by being taught," in Cabasilas, *The Life in Christ*, 89 (treatise on baptism).

[8] Ibid., 91.

strate that learning is not sufficient in itself, since the apostles had received instruction from Jesus himself—the real transformation occurred when they received the gift of the Spirit on Pentecost: "though they had been close to the Sun and shared in his daily life and discourse they had no perception of his ray until they received the spiritual washing."[9] Cabasilas's theology is important here, as he includes the activity of the Holy Spirit in baptism without fragmenting the rites of initiation into mutually exclusive components. He also manifests the activity of the Holy Spirit in baptism when he mentions the head covering given to the neophyte, which he describes as a symbol of the Holy Spirit.[10] Cabasilas's exposition of baptism is instructive for our purposes for three reasons. First, he recognizes the activity of the Holy Spirit in various components of baptism. Second, he describes the transformation that occurs in participants as gradual and progressive, one that God effects and cannot be achieved by learning alone. Third, the purpose of this transformation is restoration to the divine community—the changed Christian is to know God, with love developing together with knowledge.

In his third treatise, Cabasilas presents chrismation as another step in the progression of knowing and loving God in his divine community. Cabasilas focuses on the properties of the chrism itself, and how the anointing with the chrism is an important step in the transformation of the participant. His theological point is sophisticated: transformation is a process, and the human participant needs to be anointed with chrism so that the human has the capacity to attain *theosis*, or become like God. The incarnation of Christ is the theological basis for humanity's capacity to become like God. Cabasilas interprets Jesus' reception of the Holy Spirit as his anointment, and states that Jesus is not only Christ but also chrism.[11]

---

[9] Ibid.

[10] Ibid., 100.

[11] "Christ the Lord was himself anointed, not by receiving chrism poured on the head, but by receiving the Holy Spirit. For the sake of the flesh which he had assumed he became the treasury of all spiritual energy. He is not only Christ (the anointed one) but also chrism (anointing), for it says, 'your name is as ointment poured forth' (canticles 1.3)," ibid., 104.

This association of Christ as the anointing establishes Cabasilas's theology of chrismation. Christ as the anointing is important for the participant, whose transformation into a person growing into God's likeness is patterned after Christ. Cabasilas explains how the neophytes' anointing with chrism represents the fusion of the two natures without division in Christ:

> Since God occupies every place he was not separated from man by place, but by man's variance with him. Our nature separated itself from God by being contrary to him in everything that it possessed and by having nothing in common with him. God remained himself alone; our nature was man, and no more. When, however, flesh was deified and human nature gained possession of God himself by hypostatic union, the former barrier opposed to God became joined to chrism. The difference gave way when God became man, thus removing the separation between Godhead and manhood. So chrism represents Christ as the point of contact between both natures; there could be no point of contact were they still separate.

Cabasilas connects the anointing with chrism with the transformation of the participant. He says that "the chrism brings in the Lord Jesus himself," and "from him we receive the participation in the Holy Spirit and 'through him we have access to the father' (Eph 2:18)."[12] The implications of this statement are profound—the neophyte's growth in Christ's likeness is ritualized by the anointing with chrism, and the effect is twofold. First, the neophyte now has the capacity to live as a Christian by employing the spiritual gifts granted at anointing, including godliness, prayer, love, and mercy.[13] Second, Cabasilas explains the Holy Spirit's gift of Christ as participation in the life of God. The transformation of the participant is a trinitarian action; the Holy Spirit offers the gift of Christ, who brings the participant to the Father. Cabasilas's theology exposes the dynamic interrelationship of Christ and the Spirit: the Spirit brings in Christ, who grants the Spirit's gifts to the participant. In

---

[12] Ibid., 106.
[13] Cabasilas describes the anointing with chrism as an activation of "spiritual energies," ibid., 103, 107.

other words, Cabasilas's sacramental theology enjoys a robust exchange of Christic and pneumatic dimensions.

Cabasilas's exposition of the rites of initiation emphasizes the *telos* of the Christian life: communion with God. The process of becoming like God is tangibly experienced by sacramental participation, and it is crucial to note Cabasilas's sensitivity to the questions of will or intent on the part of the participant. For example, Cabasilas privileges the divine activity in the rites of initiation when he comments on Christians who abandon the faith in favor of the "extremes of impiety and wickedness."[14] Baptism does not "throttle or restrain the will."[15] There is no need to rebaptize lapsed Christians because "they have not lost the infused faculties and do not need a second forming." The chrismation of each Christian capacitates the possibility for a lapsed Christian to return to God, and these gifts do not need to be acquired anew, but are renewed within. Cabasilas's explanation illuminates the notion of a gift that is always present within the Christian, one that can be awakened at any time for the Christian to return to the life of discipleship. Cabasilas's interpretation of the gift of the Spirit pertains to the issue of anointing infants with chrism, an issue he also addresses in his pastoral manner:

> Since this mystery takes place in infancy, they have no perception of its gifts when it is celebrated and they receive them; when they have reached maturity they have turned aside to what they ought not to do and have blinded the eye of the soul. Yet in truth the Spirit imparts his own gifts to those who are being initiated. . . . Nor has the master ceased from doing us good, since he promised to be with us until the end. This sacred rite, then, is not an empty thing.[16]

Cabasilas is consistent in interpreting the gift of the Spirit as something freely given to the neophyte for her salvation. The Spirit capacitates the neophyte to grow in God's likeness, to become a human being counted worthy of the divine community. Cabasilas

---

[14] Ibid., 85.
[15] Ibid.
[16] Ibid., 108.

identifies this imparting of the gift of the Spirit in multiple portions of the rite, transcending baptism and chrismation. An example of Cabasilas's correlation of baptism with the Spirit is in his vocabulary: he defines baptism as not only birth but also "new birth," "creation," and "seal."[17] The seal conforms the participant to the "image of the King and to his blessed form."[18] Cabasilas elaborates its meaning with these words:

> Baptism is called 'anointing' because on those who are initiated it engraves Christ, who was anointed for us. It is a 'seal' which imprints the Savior himself. As the anointing is actually applied to the whole form of the body of him who is anointed, so it imprints on him the Anointed One and displays his form and is really a sealing.[19]

Cabasilas is not blurring the distinction between baptism and chrismation, but is instead faithfully reading the liturgical sources: for him, baptism and chrismation are not mutually exclusive mysteries, but rather constitute one and the same initiatory rite. It is clear that Cabasilas understands baptism as repeatedly imparting the gift of the Holy Spirit to the participant. Most important is Cabasilas's understanding of what the gift of the Holy Spirit communicates: a free gift from God in a trinitarian act, capacitating the recipient to progressively grow in God's likeness and enjoy his community.

NICHOLAS AFANASIEV

Nicholas Afanasiev was a twentieth-century Russian Orthodox scholar and priest who taught at St. Sergius Theological Institute in Paris. Afanasiev is best known for his exposition of eucharistic ecclesiology and was probably Alexander Schmemann's most influential interlocutor. Afanasiev's most important contribution is *The Church of the Holy Spirit*, a detailed examination of the structures and rites of the early church and their shaping of the ecclesiologi-

[17] Ibid., 67.
[18] Ibid.
[19] Ibid., 69.

cal structures and tenets of the Byzantine Church.[20] In this work, Afanasiev includes a chapter devoted to the "ordination of laics."[21] Afanasiev develops a theology of the priesthood of laics by interpreting select passages from liturgical sources of antiquity, especially the Apostolic Tradition attributed to Hippolytus of Rome, and the contemporary Orthodox rites. Afanasiev asserts that the handlaying gesture in the Apostolic Tradition performed by the bishop after the neophyte was baptized denoted the neophyte's ordination to the order of laics. Afanasiev viewed the handlaying gesture described by the Apostolic Tradition as denoting appointment to priestly ministry, both ordained and lay:

> In the ecclesial consciousness of the third century, the laying on of hands at the ordination for ministry signified the ordination for a priestly ministry. In the prayer formula, at the laying of hands on the newly-baptized we find the same verb *servire* (*leitourgein*) used in the prayer formula at the ordination of a bishop. The use of one and the same verb at the laying on of hands in both incidences is not coincidental. Rather this points to one and the same ministry: for one it is a high priestly ministry, for another it is a priestly ministry.[22]

Afanasiev continues to use the Apostolic Tradition as his primary liturgical source for developing a theology of the ordination of laics by referring to the anointing with chrism performed by the bishop.[23] Afanasiev interprets the anointing as conferring both

---

[20] Nicholas Afanasiev, *The Church of the Holy Spirit*, ed. Michael Plekon, trans. Vitaly Permiakov, foreword by Rowan Williams (Notre Dame: University of Notre Dame Press, 2007).

[21] Afanasiev carefully defines "laic": "It is inaccurate to regard laymen as a separate group of the members of the Church. According to modern scholastic teaching, lay people are 'non-consecrated', as opposed to the 'consecrated' which include all those who belong to the priesthood. As 'non-consecrated', lay people do not receive any ordination and therefore the term 'lay ordination' contains in itself a contradiction. This would be accurate if the term 'lay people' is understood as 'laics', i.e., the members of God's people. Therefore, we should speak not of a 'lay' but of a 'laic' ordination," in ibid., 25.

[22] Ibid., 25–26.

[23] Ibid., 26.

a royal and priestly ministry because "in the Old Testament only priests and kings were anointed."[24] It is important to note that the formula for the anointing in the Apostolic Tradition does not mention priests and kings.[25]

Afanasiev turns to the contemporary Orthodox initiatory rites as he develops the theology of the ordination of laics. He infers that the Byzantine Rite once contained a handlaying gesture and points to the prayer recited at the rite of ablution on the eighth day as evidence of the ancient episcopal handlaying since it "speaks of the laying on not of the bishop's but of God's mighty hand."[26] Afanasiev turns to the blessing of baptismal waters and cites one of the blessings requested of God for the neophytes, that they would "receive the prize of his high calling and be numbered with the firstborn."[27] Afanasiev says that the high calling to which the prayer refers is about the neophyte's priestly ministry.[28] The same is true of the anointing with holy oil in the contemporary Orthodox rite of chrismation; this seal likewise signifies belonging to the people of God, or "holy priesthood," as does the donning of the white garment.[29]

At this juncture in his presentation, Afanasiev's pattern of theological development is established. His method is to identify a salient gesture or prayer in the contemporary Orthodox Rite, select a historical antecedent, and interpret the liturgical component in such a way that it contributes to his notion of the ordination of laics and their ministry of royal priesthood. Also present in Afanasiev's exegesis of the initiatory rites is his occasional comparison of initiation with ordination.[30] The method of interritual comparison

---

[24] Ibid.

[25] Afanasiev cites the formulary from the Apostolic Tradition: "I anoint you with holy oil in God the Father Almighty and Christ Jesus and the Holy Spirit" (ibid).

[26] Ibid. Afanasiev cites the text of the prayer in its entirety.

[27] "His" refers to the Holy Spirit; for the text of the blessing of baptismal waters and its context, see the translation by Archimandrite Ephrem Lash, "Baptism," accessed March 25, 2013, http://www.anastasis.org.uk/baptism.htm.

[28] Afanasiev, *The Church of the Holy Spirit*, 27–28.

[29] Ibid.

[30] See William Mills, *Church, World, Kingdom: The Eucharistic Foundation of Alexander Schmemann's Pastoral Theology* (Chicago: Hillenbrand, 2012), 73–75.

emerges most prominently in Afanasiev's interrogation of ordination as an aid to interpreting the tonsuring in the initiatory rites; he describes the purpose of the tonsure in initiation as demonstrating "the complete dedication of the tonsured person to the service of God."[31] Afanasiev asserts that the rites of clerical ordination influenced initiation in the tonsure and in the churching, where the presider escorts the neophyte into the sanctuary to circumambulate the altar.[32] Afanasiev's claim on tonsuring offers no historical evidence, leaving the reader to search for his sources. It appears that he is referring to the practice of setting aside readers ritualized by a tonsure, since the bishop's exhortation to the new reader defines the order of reader as the first step of the priesthood.[33] He summarizes the purpose of his comparison to illustrate the twofold notion of priesthood expressed by the initiatory rites and ordination:

> Tonsuring, laying on of hands, clothing and leading the baptized around the altar—these are acts constituting the sacramental rite of reception into the Church. All these aspects are present even in the contemporary rite of priestly ordination. This affinity is not coincidental. It bears witness to the fact that in liturgical consciousness, the sacrament of entrance into the Church was regarded as the sacrament of ordination for a newly baptized person.[34]

Afanasiev describes this ordination of laics as initiating neophytes into "a nation of kings and priests" who exercise their

---

[31] Afanasiev, *The Church of the Holy Spirit*, 29.

[32] Ibid., 29–30.

[33] The text of the bishop's exhortation to the reader is: "My son(s), the first degree in the priesthood is that of reader. It behooveth thee (you), therefore, to peruse the divine Scriptures daily, to the end that the hearers, regarding you, may receive edification; that you, in nowise shaming your election, may prepare yourself for a higher degree. For by a chaste, holy and upright life you shall gain the favor of the God of lovingkindness, and shall render yourself worthy of a greater ministry, through Jesus Christ our Lord; to whom be glory unto ages of ages. Amen." In *Service Book of the Holy Orthodox-Catholic Apostolic Church*, 6th rev. ed., ed. Isabel Hapgood (Englewood, NJ; Antiochian Archdiocese of America, 1983), 308.

[34] Afanasiev, *The Church of the Holy Spirit*, 30.

ministry alongside those ordained to preside.[35] The ministry laics exercise is legitimate, and Afanasiev insists that "a laic cannot be viewed in opposition to the consecrated," because everyone who belongs to the church has received the pledge of the age to come.

Afanasiev began developing *The Church of the Holy Spirit* in 1947 and had not finished revising it when he died in 1966.[36] The date of his study is important when evaluating it, especially when one considers that the science of liturgical history was still in a state of nascent development at this time. Afanasiev's frequent reference to the Apostolic Tradition should not surprise the reader, because it was widely considered to be a source of precious insight into the third-century Roman liturgy. Afanasiev did not have the benefit of today's liturgical scholarship; his hypothesis on the laying on of hands becomes more plausible when one considers the reference to a laying on of hands with the bestowal of the Spirit, followed by anointing with the oil of holiness, in Macarius's hagiopolite *Letter to the Armenians* (composed circa 335).[37]

While one cannot fault Afanasiev for his veneration of the Apostolic Tradition, the limitations of his method are notable. Afanasiev raises intriguing questions about the Orthodox initiatory rites when he appears to identify a vestige of handlaying in a reference to God's mighty arm in the prayer at the rite of ablution, or recognizes parallels between ordination and initiatory ritual components. As an ecclesiologist, Afanasiev was a product of his environment. His purpose was to develop a theology of the ministry of laics, and he believed that the connections he created between the contemporary

---

[35] Ibid., 30–31. Afanasiev mentions "kings and priests" twice in his summary, manifesting the first foundation of his narrative.

[36] Plekon, "Introduction," in Afanasiev, *The Church of the Holy Spirit*, xiii.

[37] Macarius, referring to the descent of the Spirit on the apostles on Pentecost, says "after the same pattern we also, on the same day, bestow the same Spirit by laying hands on those who are baptized. We fulfill the pattern of this with unfailing care that we may become perfect. And in faith we are anointed with the oil of holiness," in *Letter to the Armenians*, ed. and trans. Terian, 84–87. For a discussion of the potential historical and theological significance of the handlaying gesture and the gift of the Holy Spirit in Macarius's letter, see Johnson, "Christian Initiation in Fourth-century Jerusalem," 153–54.

rites and select antecedents were sufficient.[38] His theology of lay ministry as authentically priestly is interesting, especially since he consults the most salient components of the entire rite of initiation as a whole. Here, Afanasiev's articulation of chrismation is instructive, because his interpretation relies on not only the anointing with chrism and its prayer but also the accompanying initiatory components.

Thus, Afanasiev consults the entire rite of initiation as a unified celebration, and here, his method is sound: no single ritual component monopolizes the meaning of the entire event, but each component shapes the others and is in turn formed by the others, leading to a significant theology of the ordination of laics. One can also appreciate his development of the priesthood of laics as relying heavily upon ritual gestures, especially handlaying. His reference to the parallels between ordination and initiation are suggestive and bolster his theology of the ministry of laics. His interpretation of the sources results in two original contributions: a definition of the laic as a member of God's flock who exercises a priestly ministry and the restoration of the laity to the fullness of the church as consecrated people who exercise their priestly ministry alongside the ministers who preside. With access to the more exacting science of liturgical theology, Afanasiev might have elaborated an even more profound theology of the laic ministry.

ALEXANDER SCHMEMANN

Of Water and the Spirit, Alexander Schmemann's exposition of initiation, is perhaps the most popular theology of baptism in the Orthodox world.[39] Schmemann's contribution is crucial to the task

---

[38] Afanasiev reveals his desire to address the larger ecclesiological issue toward the beginning of this section when he says, "I have no need to examine the history of the rites of baptism and chrismation," as he believed the contemporary rites manifested enough of an older ordo to proceed with his analysis (*Church of the Holy Spirit*, 26).

[39] Alexander Schmemann, *Of Water and the Spirit* (Crestwood, NY: St. Vladimir's Seminary Press, 1974). Schmemann offers a much shorter explanation of chrismation in *For the Life of the World: Sacraments and Orthodoxy* (Crestwood, NY: St. Vladimir's Seminary Press, 1988 printing; originally printed in 1963), 75–76. For a critique of Schmemann's theological exposition of initiation,

of articulating a theology of chrismation not only on account of his continuing influence on contemporary Orthodox theology, but also because his study was offered as a work of liturgical theology. Methodologically, Schmemann walks the reader through the initiatory rites and explains the significance of each major liturgical component. The work is pastoral in genre—Schmemann's references to liturgical history are sporadic, and one does not get a sense of the historical development of initiation in reading the text.

Schmemann's section on the sacrament of the Holy Spirit actually begins with the donning of the white garment. When he attends to chrismation, he briefly discusses the Western influence on an Orthodox theology of chrismation, and implies that his task will be to articulate its positive theology.[40] Schmemann expresses a desire for Orthodox theology to "return to its own essential and genuine source; the liturgical reality which embodies and communicates the faith of the Church."[41] Like Afanasiev, Schmemann respects chrismation as one component in a larger sacramental scheme, yet he opens the door for a theological exposition of chrismation by describing it as a "new act" that gives the initiatory rites a radical new dimension.[42] The remainder of Schmemann's exposition follows two paths: first, he defines chrismation as bestowing the gift of the Holy Spirit himself; then, he explains how the divine gifts grant the threefold ministry of king, priest, and prophet to the neophyte.

Schmemann's explanation of the gifts of the Holy Spirit is problematic because it is quite brief and has limited references to the actual liturgy, but also offers a profound trinitarian theology. Schmemann refers to the anointing with chrism as "this Pentecostal anointment" in which "the Holy Spirit descends on us and abides in us as the personal gift of Christ from his Father, as the gift of his

---

see Peter Galadza, "Schmemann Between Fagerberg and Reality: Towards an Agenda for Byzantine Christian Pastoral Liturgy," *Bolletino della Badia Greca di Grottaferrata* 4 (2007): 7–32. For an assessment of Schmemann's theology of chrismation, see Mills, *Church, World, Kingdom*, 70–76.

[40] Schmemann, *Of Water and the Spirit*, 76.

[41] Ibid., 77. Here, Schmemann endeavors to free chrismation from a typical Western sacramental "reductionism."

[42] Ibid., 78.

life, his sonship, his communion with the Father."[43] Schmemann continues by explaining that the content of the gift is essentially participation in the divine life of the Triune God, or *theosis*. The gift of the Holy Spirit is "the gift and revelation to man of the Triune God himself, the knowledge of him, the communion with him as the kingdom of God and life eternal."[44]

It is notable that Schmemann does not refer to the initiatory rites here: he instead draws from the Byzantine version of the anaphora of St. Basil to support his theology of the Holy Spirit. Schmemann states that the reception of this gift restores the human being's true nature and makes him or her into an anointed one, or christ: "by making him 'christ' in Christ, by anointing him with the anointment of the anointed one, it opens to man the door of *theosis*, of deification."[45] Schmemann sets the stage for the much longer part of his exposition, namely, an explanation of the restored human being's ministry as following Christ's pattern. The neophyte becomes priest, prophet, and king.

Schmemann's motivations for explicating chrismation as bestowing Christ's ministries of priest, prophet, and king are somewhat obscure, though he seems to hint toward the reason when he says that the manuals of systematic theology typically define Christ's ministry according to these categories.[46] He defines the content of each ministry in order—king, priest, and prophet—and the purpose of his exposition becomes clear: it is an exercise in theological anthropology. The gifts of the Spirit make one anointed in Christ's image, and Christ's priestly ministry is imparted to the restored human being, whose mission it is to carry out this threefold ministry in the world.

Schmemann's exposition consists of an essay on the theological anthropology of the rites of initiation and an underlying critique of secular culture. His discussion of the new human being who emerges from the font privileges what he calls "anthropological maximalism."[47] This new human being was once the king of

[43] Ibid., 79.
[44] Ibid., 80.
[45] Ibid.
[46] Ibid., 81.
[47] Ibid., 82.

creation who is now fallen; the human vocation has been restored and humans are now kings again.[48] Later, Schmemann explains that humans exercise this restored vocation through the mystery of the cross.[49] His sources for this discourse are unknown, however. Schmemann attributes the restoration of this gift to humanity to baptism and the postbaptismal anointing with chrism:

> In the eucharistic blessing of water . . . the entire cosmos is revealed again as God's gift to man, as man's kingdom. In the anointment with the "oil of gladness," the new life of the neophyte is announced as power and dominion. He is vested in royal garments, and it is Christ's own kingship that he receives in the "seal" of the Holy chrism.[50]

This quote represents Schmemann's brilliant theology but mystifying method. Schmemann refers to a sequence of ritual components in initiation, namely the blessing of baptismal waters, the prebaptismal anointing of catechumens, and the postbaptismal chrismation. Schmemann's image of the restored human is *positive* (a word he frequently italicizes for emphasis), and seems to be suitable for Christian mission. But Schmemann also appears to have affixed a particular theological anthropology onto the ritual components by ascribing this definition of a Christian to the rite without more direct references to their content. One should also note that Schmemann completes his discussion on the content of kingship imparted to the neophyte by ascribing it solely to the anointing with chrism.[51]

---

[48] Schmemann's distinctions are intriguing, and reveal his task of defining Christianity's theological anthropology in the context of secular culture. For example, he addresses the oft-repeated refrain on the universality of human failure by distinguishing between errors and the innate goodness of vocation when he says, "man misuses his vocation, and in this horrible misuse he mutilates himself and the world; but his vocation is good," ibid., 84.

[49] Ibid., 85, 87.

[50] Ibid., 83.

[51] "Now, and only now, can we answer the question raised at the beginning of this chapter: about the meaning of our kingship bestowed upon us in the sacrament of chrismation. We can answer it because in the Cross of Christ the content of this kingship is revealed and its power is granted. The royal anoint-

Schmemann's exposition on the second and third aspects of the human vocation is likewise attributed to the Holy Spirit. He briefly states that Christ's priesthood is given to the neophyte at chrismation,[52] along with the gift of prophecy.[53] His explanation of the features of these holy gifts follows the pattern he established with kingship: the gifts profoundly change the neophyte. But Schmemann does not establish how the initiatory rites communicate the imparting of these gifts. If Schmemann was well known for his modern articulation of a theological anthropology most Orthodox might recognize as familiar, we might describe his sacramental theology of initiation as a theologumenon, because Schmemann offers only a synthesis, without telling readers how they might identify these particular gifts in the liturgy itself.

Schmemann breaks this pattern in his concluding remarks on the content of the gift of the Holy Spirit by returning to the topic of *theosis*. Schmemann returns to his original thesis that chrismation is the gift of the Holy Spirit himself, who "makes us participants in Christ's life, members of his body, coworkers in his saving work."[54] Schmemann summarizes the gift of the Holy Spirit with two profound statements:

> [The Holy Spirit] seals, makes, reveals, confirms us as members of the Church, the Body of Christ, as citizens of the Kingdom of God, as partakers of the Holy Spirit. And by this seal, it truly makes us into ourselves, "ordains" each one of us to be and to become that which God from all eternity wants us to be, revealing our true personality and thus our only self-fulfillment.[55]

Schmemann has synthesized an Orthodox notion of personhood and attributed it to the postbaptismal anointing with chrism. He explained the meaning of chrismation by making it accessible: a

---

ment truly makes us kings, but it is the crucified kingship of Christ himself—it is the cross as kingship and kingship as cross—that the Holy Spirit bestows on us," ibid., 90.

[52] Ibid., 94, 97.
[53] Ibid., 101, 103.
[54] Ibid., 103.
[55] Ibid., 107.

pastor could use Schmemann's explanation as a way of plainly describing what happens to one's child when she is baptized and chrismated. Schmemann's attempt to explain the relevance of the sacrament to daily life is evidenced by his concluding remarks in this chapter. He stresses that the sacrament is not an abstract theology, but one that embraces "the whole life," since the Holy Spirit capacitates each recipient to "truly transform and transfigure—make whole and holy—the life which God has given to us."[56]

Schmemann's pastoral explanation of the initiation rites is now almost forty years old. While Schmemann does not offer the reader a detailed presentation on the *lex orandi*, his explanation on how receiving the gift of the Spirit makes one into a christ who exercises Christ's ministry in the world remains profound today. It is not my intent to suggest that Schmemann's teaching is passé; indeed, I affirm the continued relevance of his synthetic theological anthropology, and believe it still has the capacity to achieve his original goal: to transform and transfigure Christian life. But it is important to note the inconsistency of Schmemann's presentation. He follows the pattern of Afanasiev, his mentor, in occasionally examining liturgical components in their contexts to illustrate how God blesses the assembly through ritual participation. For our purposes, Schmemann was particularly effective in illustrating the gift of kingship given to the human through the blessing of water, the anointing with the oil of gladness, and chrismation, providing a holistic and integrative reading of the rites of initiation. Similarly, he offered a more robust idea on how the gift of the Spirit imparts a sense of belonging to the holy people of God in his brief references to the anaphora of St. Basil.

That said, one wonders how different Schmemann's presentation might have appeared had he more comprehensively interrogated the rites and their euchology. Schmemann's exposition of the threefold ministry of king, priest, and prophet is popular, but his connection of this ministry to the initiation rites is scant. Ironically, Schmemann appears to violate the very method he consistently espouses in his own liturgical theology. Toward the beginning of

---

[56] Ibid., 108.

his chapter on chrismation, Schmemann claims that Orthodox theology needs to return to its own "essential and genuine source," the liturgy itself.[57] The bulk of his theological explanation discusses the Christian theological anthropology of king, priest, and prophet, which Schmemann attributes to the so-called manuals of systematic theology. He then ascribes this same theology to the rites without presenting them, which one can fairly construe as an imposition of the *lex credendi* on the *lex orandi*. Schmemann's own predecessor and interlocutor, Afanasiev, offered a more effective interrogation of liturgical sources in his discussion of the ordination of laics. It is quite possible that Schmemann articulated his theological anthropology of baptism and chrismation from sources with which he was intimately familiar, and simply neglected to consistently share them with the audience. It is equally possible that Schmemann might have offered an even more profound liturgical theology of initiation had he followed his own method of respecting the *lex orandi* as source and epiphany. Schmemann's exposition of chrismation remains valuable because he respects its position as one component in the larger complex of the rites of initiation, governed by the frequent celebration of the Eucharist, which shapes its meaning for the participants whose liturgical rehearsal is almost exclusively eucharistic. But reading Schmemann is like gazing upon an incomplete work of beauty: while one gains a sense of the profundity of the final product, one simultaneously laments the absence of seeing the whole picture.

BORIS BOBRINSKOY

Boris Bobrinskoy, former dean of St. Sergius Institute, is one of the most prominent Orthodox systematic theologians. Bobrinskoy has written extensively on trinitarian theology and magisterially expounded the development of trinitarian doctrine from the Scriptures through postmodernity. Bobrinskoy offers an intriguing perspective on the rite of the anointing with chrism in his seminal pneumatological work, *Communion de Sainte-Esprit*.[58] Bobrinskoy's

[57] Ibid., 77.
[58] Boris Bobrinskoy, *Communion de Sainte-Esprit* (Abbaye du Bellefountaine, 1992), 161–92.

treatment of chrismation emphasizes the ante-Nicene Syrian liturgical tradition, where the prebaptismal anointing was perhaps the high point of the rites of initiation. Bobrinskoy eschews an exclusive exposition of the actual anointing because he rejects the idea that the Holy Spirit was given to participants in a special rite.[59] Bobrinskoy instead views the gift of the Holy Spirit as imparted through a series of ritual components: prebaptismal anointing, the blessing of waters, the invocation of the Holy Spirit on the water, the baptismal immersion, and participation in the Eucharist.[60] When one embarks on a journey of initiation through this progression of rituals, the Holy Spirit conforms the person to Christ and incorporates her into the glorified body of Christ.[61] Thus, the Holy Spirit is quite active in each part of this process, and each divine activity of the Holy Spirit is oriented toward the transformation of the participant into an anointed one who belongs to the body of Christ.[62] In other words, one cannot separate the pneumatological quality of initiation from its Christology:

> But the whole baptismal initiation has, at the same time, a Christological sense, because the oil inscribes on us the name of Christ himself, the Anointed one; the water makes us participate in his death and his resurrection; the bread and the wine perpetuate this baptismal participation by both strengthening and nourishing us with the heavenly bread of the body of Christ himself, filled with Fire and the Spirit. All disassociation between Christ and the Spirit, between Christology and pneumatology is contrary to the theological vision and the spiritual experience of the most profound and authentic Syrian tradition.[63]

---

[59] Ibid., 188.

[60] Ibid., 189. Bobrinskoy demonstrates this progression by interrogating select patristic sources on pp. 167–87. He also presents an abbreviated version of this presentation in an English translation of a larger work on trinitarian theology titled *The Mystery of the Trinity: Trinitarian Experience and Vision in the Biblical and Patristic Tradition,* trans. Anthony P. Gythiel (Crestwood, NY: St. Vladimir's Seminary Press, 1999), 161–64.

[61] Bobrinskoy, *Communion de Sainte-Esprit,* 189.

[62] Ibid.

[63] Ibid.

Bobrinskoy privileges the Syrian history of initiatory rites because he recognizes the progressive work of the Spirit in conforming participants to Christ and initiating them into Christ's glorified body. Even though he prefers the sequence of the ancient Syrian tradition, he addresses the question of identifying the gift of the Holy Spirit with postbaptismal chrismation in both the Western and Eastern traditions. Bobrinskoy illuminates a parallel progressive action of the Holy Spirit in the current Byzantine Rite according to the following order: baptismal immersion, the anointing with the formula "the seal of the gift of the Holy Spirit," and the threefold procession around the baptismal font accompanied by the Pauline chant, "As many as have been baptized into Christ have put on Christ."[64] Bobrinskoy's presentation of the contemporary sequence as connoting progressive growth and activity in the Holy Spirit demonstrates his recognition that the contemporary rite has retained the theological essence of the ante-Nicene Syrian Rite. His omission of the Eucharist as an essential component of the contemporary rite is somewhat baffling.

Bobrinskoy's analysis of the gift of the Holy Spirit situates the anointing with chrism in the context of the entire sequence of initiatory rites, with the exception of the consecration of chrism, which lies outside the historical scope of his treatment. He views the work of the Holy Spirit as continuing for eternity in the Eucharist. If baptism and anointing conform one to Christ and to his glorified body, the Spirit continues this work in the Eucharist by leading this glorified body into the communion of the Holy Trinity.[65] But Bobrinskoy does not limit the activity of the Spirit to the transformation of people into Christians who share communion with God. The Holy Spirit ushers the kingdom of God into the world, which results in the sanctification of the cosmos; this cosmic transfiguration is tangibly engaged by the liturgical participants in their ritual use of

---

[64] Ibid., 191.

[65] Bobrinskoy reads Irenaeus here by describing this journey as an ascent led by the Spirit to the Son, and through the Son, to the Father. He offers a brief description in *The Mystery of the Trinity*, trans. A. Gythiel, 165. He also accentuates the inseparability of the Spirit from Christ by referring to Irenaeus's notion of the two hands of the Father in *Communion de Sainte-Esprit*, 177.

elements of creation such as water and oil.[66] A cosmic sanctification is necessary because the whole human person is transformed; the change God effects in the person through the rites of initiation is not limited to mental and emotional faculties. Bobrinskoy explains the sanctification of the cosmos accordingly:

> The interior world is inseparable from the corporal, the life of the senses, the bodily condition, the extension of the human body in things, in matter, in time, in space. Here is why the Christian sanctification constitutes the extension, or rather the restoration of the primordial plan of creation, where the six first days found their completion, their fulfillment, their profound sense in the creation of humanity. The latter is consubstantial with the visible world. . . . He is also consubstantial, by vocation, with the Creator, in the creating Trinity, whose image he bears in his entire being, body, soul, intelligence, and person.[67]

Bobrinskoy produces a profound sacramentality located in the rites of initiation and grounded by trinitarian theology. His contribution is immensely valuable to Orthodox theology because he liberates the liturgical theology of chrismation from its scholarly isolation as a sacrament imparting the gift of the Holy Spirit in an identifiable sacrament. Bobrinskoy redefines chrismation as an important component in an organically unified ritual sequence where the progressive and continuous activity of the Holy Spirit is manifold. His methodology respects the entire ritual and sacramental context of initiation, evidenced by the explicit relationships he identifies in ritual components transcending three different "sacraments." Perhaps most significant in Bobrinskoy's presentation is the implication for Christianity: the Holy Spirit continuously conforms the participant to Christ and the church, and through Christ, to the communion of the Holy Trinity. But this experience is quite real and tangible for the participant: her immersion in the water, anointing with chrism, and eating and drinking of the consecrated bread and wine acknowledges her vocation to the world in

---

[66] Bobrinskoy, *Communion de Sainte-Esprit*, 177–78.
[67] Ibid., 177–78.

her daily life. Her vocation of being an anointed one as a member of Christ's glorified body occurs in the daily grind of this life, in this world, and she exercises this vocation as a whole person, body, mind, and soul.

This raises an interesting issue of comparison, because unlike Schmemann, Bobrinskoy does not affix the particular spiritual gifts of kingship, priesthood, and prophecy to his examination of initiation. Such an examination was outside the scope of his particular study. That said, the anthropological type Bobrinskoy establishes through his examination of baptism, anointing, and Eucharist appears to have much in common with Schmemann's theological anthropology.

PAUL EVDOKIMOV

Evdokimov was an important lay Orthodox theologian of the mid-twentieth century. Evdokimov wrote at length on a variety of topics in an ecumenical context. His most important works are *The Sacrament of Love*, his theology of marriage, and *Ages of the Spiritual Life*, his exposition of modern spirituality.[68] One theological idea threads these two different works: an appeal to everyone, men, women and children, to respond to the universal call to priesthood. Evdokimov articulates a particularly Orthodox notion of lay priesthood by offering a potential lifestyle that enfleshes traditional monastic values in the contemporary environment, encapsulated by the now famous notion of interiorized monasticism. Interiorized monasticism allows the Orthodox layperson an opportunity to employ the core values of the Orthodox ascetical tradition and witness to the world. It was important for Evdokimov and other members of the Orthodox Paris school of theology to provide the laity with access to the venerable Orthodox way while fully engaging the world as men and women "on the street."

An important tenet of Evdokimov's universal priesthood of the laity is the theological contribution of the sacrament of

---

[68] Paul Evdokimov, *The Sacrament of Love: The Nuptial Mystery in the Light of the Orthodox Tradition*, trans. Anthony P. Gythiel and Victoria Steadman, foreword by Olivier Clement (Crestwood, NY: St. Vladimir's Seminary Press, 1995).

chrismation.[69] Like Afanasiev, Evdokimov views chrismation as the ordination of the layperson to the priesthood.[70] The layperson's ministry is related to the bishop's: it is an exercise of the priesthood of Christ.[71] The anointing with chrism equips the layperson with the spiritual gifts needed to exercise these ministries. Evdokimov interrogates several select liturgical sources to illuminate these gifts. For example, he refers to the occasional consecration of chrism celebrated by the Orthodox Church and quotes the prayer recited by the bishop, which asks that God would seal the recipients so that they would bear Christ in their hearts.[72] Evdokimov parenthetically elaborates the meaning of "seal" by defining it as making or anointing the participants into "christs."[73] He also views the tonsure that occurs at the rite of ablution as having a parallel to monastic tonsure: "In undergoing the rite of tonsure, every lay person is a monk of interiorized monasticism, subject to all the requirements of the Gospel."[74] Evdokimov carefully distinguishes the priesthood of the laity from the other orders of the church by elaborating their relevance in mission to the world. He cites, *inter alia*, St. Macarius of Egypt and Origen to state, like Schmemann, that the anointing with chrism makes the laity into kings, priests, and prophets.[75]

Evdokimov's definition of the content of this priestly ministry was contextual. Writing in the 1960s as a Russian immigrant forced to flee Bolshevik persecution and take refuge in Paris, Evdokimov

---

[69] Evdokimov expounds his theology of chrismation in an essay titled "L'Esprit saint et l'Église d'après la tradition liturgique," in *L'Esprit Saint et l'Église. Catholiques, orthodoxes et protestants de divers pays confrontent leur science, leur foi et leur tradition: l'Avenir de l'Église et de l'oecuménisme*, ed. Académie internationale des sciences religieuses (Paris: Fanyard, 1969), 85–123; and also *Ages of the Spiritual Life*, trans. Michael Plekon and Alexis Vinogradov (Crestwood, NY: St. Vladimir's Seminary, 1998), 231–39.

[70] Evdokimov, *Ages of the Spiritual Life*, 231.

[71] Ibid., 232.

[72] Ibid., 235. Also see "L'Esprit saint et l'Église d'après la tradition liturgique," 101–2.

[73] Evdokimov, *Ages of the Spiritual Life*, 235.

[74] Ibid., 234–35.

[75] Ibid., 238–39.

lamented the impotence of the Russian Orthodox Church to evangelize within the Soviet Union. He referenced the Russian episcopate's appeal to the laity to exercise their priestly ministry and "become a temple" by living the liturgy in their lives and, consequently, evangelizing those without faith.[76] The universal priesthood of the laity has the capacity to become a "splendid icon of the kingdom of God," a witness to the Gospel "in the immense cathedral . . . the universe."[77] Evdokimov envisioned a priesthood of the laity serving beyond the context of the 1960s, a model of witnessing to the Gospel before the world for all times and places:

> The laity forms an ecclesial dimension that is, at one and the same time, of the world and of the Church. Lay people do not have access to the power of administering the means of grace . . . but, on the other hand, their sphere is 'the life of grace' and 'the state of grace.' By the simple presence of 'sanctified beings,' of 'priests' in their very substance, of 'trinitarian dwellings,' the universal priesthood of the laity bears the power of the sacred in the world, celebrating the liturgy of the entire cosmos therein. Beyond the church walls, lay people continue the liturgy of the Church. By their active presence, they introduce into society and relationships the truth of the dogmas they live, thus dislodging the evil and profane elements of the world.[78]

Evdokimov's exposition of the universal priesthood of the laity, represented by interiorized monasticism and grounded by chrismation, advances the profound theological anthropology commenced by Cabasilas. Like Afanasiev, Evdokimov selectively interrogates the liturgical sources and patristic authors to develop the connection between anointing and the ministry of king, priest, and prophet imparted to each layperson at chrismation. It is important to note that Evdokimov respects the layperson's participation in the divine community, evidenced by his reference to bearing Christ in the consecration of chrism and also the communion of the

---

[76] Ibid., 240.
[77] Ibid., 241.
[78] Ibid., 238.

Holy Spirit that the faithful access at the Eucharist.[79] But his truly original contribution is his presentation of the exercise of the particular priestly ministry in and to the world. For Evdokimov, like Afanasiev and Schmemann, the layperson's liturgical experience grants him or her profound gifts that enable one to serve the world as a legitimate christ. And as Evdokimov soberly demonstrates, the world is in dire need of this ministry.

OTHER VOICES

The theologians I have surveyed above are not the only Orthodox teachers who have commented on the theology of chrismation. I have selected Nicholas Cabasilas, Nicholas Afanasiev, Alexander Schmemann, Boris Bobrinskoy, and Paul Evdokimov because of the authority they have traditionally exercised in articulating Orthodox sacramental theology, and also on account of their theological intersections, which I will analyze below. A comprehensive survey of every Orthodox theological commentary is outside the scope of this study, but I want to mention one more crucial contribution. Peter Galadza has recently articulated a more holistic liturgical pneumatology that identifies long-held but erroneous Orthodox opinions about chrismation, and also explains the manifold activity of the Holy Spirit by drawing from a wide variety of Byzantine liturgical components.[80] For instance, Galadza refers to the following examples from worship as representing pneumatology: the ubiquitous "Heavenly King" prayer and several other texts from the feast of Pentecost; the *anabathmoi*, hymnal refrains accompanying gradual psalms in various offices; the traditionally open arrangement of sacred space, promoting mobility throughout the liturgy; the introit sung at different times by the clergy and choir at a hierarchical liturgy (described by Galadza as "kalophonic cacophony"); and the practice of liturgical fasting.[81]

---

[79] For the eucharistic dimension, see "L'Esprit saint et l'Église d'après la tradition liturgique," 104–5.

[80] Peter Galadza, "The Holy Spirit in Eastern Orthodox Worship: Historical Enfleshments and Contemporary Queries," in *The Spirit in Worship—Worship in the Spirit*, ed. Teresa Berger and Bryan Spinks (Collegeville, MN: Liturgical Press, 2009), 115–40.

[81] Ibid., 135–39.

In other words, Galadza rejects the attribution of the gift of the Holy Spirit to a particular sacrament, namely chrismation. Like Bobrinskoy, Galadza recognizes the divine activity of the Spirit in many aspects of Church life, even outside of the liturgy.

Galadza attends to the explanation of chrismation and suggests that the following assertions require correction: first, the notion that chrismation was universally practiced in Christianity from the second to fifth centuries; second, that in this period, chrismation occurred after baptism and was interpreted as an anamnesis of Jesus' anointing; and third, that "chrismation was everywhere understood to confer the gift of the Holy Spirit as a logical consequence of baptism and its necessary compliment."[82] Galadza expertly addresses most of these issues by demythologizing chrismation as a type of moment of consecration for the Byzantine Rite. He also punctuates the ancient Syrian and Antiochene sequence of baptism, where the prebaptismal anointing is one of the high points of the liturgy. His remarks here are particularly sharp given his references to John Chrysostom, beloved among the Orthodox, as a trustworthy testimony to a prebaptismal pneumatic anointing.[83]

Galadza has thus performed a much-needed service by pointing to the ubiquitous pneumatic aspects of Orthodox ecclesial life, and has also challenged longstanding Orthodox assumptions about chrismation in the context of baptism. That said, his attempt to free postbaptismal chrismation from its isolated position as the sacrament of the Holy Spirit does not completely resolve the issue for the Byzantine Rite, because of two ideas Orthodox theologians tend to express about chrismation: it has a crucial function in granting the participant access to the divine life, and it is the ritual component that transforms participants into anointed ones, or christs, who exercise Jesus Christ's threefold ministry of king, priest, and prophet. These two issues in particular require further exploration to understand how Orthodox theologians developed their *theologumena*, and also to establish some *desiderata* for the next generation of Orthodox reflection on chrismation.

---

[82] Ibid., 120.
[83] Ibid.

The Orthodox theologians surveyed above symbolize independent theological reflection on the meaning of chrismation. For example, one could argue that Cabasilas, Bobrinskoy, and Schmemann constitute a group that interprets chrismation as a rite granting the participant entrance to the life of the Triune God, and capacitating her to embark on the journey to *theosis*. These three theologians even have similar methodological hermeneutics. For example, each of them identifies a ritual sequence transcending the traditional borders of baptism, chrismation, and Eucharist that represents the ongoing gift of the Spirit. Of the authors, Bobrinskoy is perhaps most deliberate in explicating the sequence of ritual components, namely, the consecration and anointing of the font, prebaptismal anointing, immersion, postbaptismal anointing, procession around the font, and participation in the Eucharist. Another group is clustered around the notion that chrismation imparts the Christic gifts of king, priest, and prophet, and that the human's exercise of these gifts symbolizes the universal priesthood of the laity.

THEOSIS AND PARTAKING OF THE LIFE OF GOD

As I surveyed the theologians above, I highlighted the occasional emphasis on the anointing with chrism as providing access to the life of God. The theologians above do not share a monolithic expression of how one might experience such a process. For example, Cabasilas refers to several different ritual moments in which the Spirit descends upon the participant, from the water bath to the donning of the gown and cap. In the postbaptismal anointing, Cabasilas says that the Spirit brings in the Lord Jesus himself, and that Jesus as chrism imparts to the participants new spiritual energies that make them like Christ, human yet ever advancing toward the divine. Schmemann understands the anointing a bit differently, describing it as imparting the Holy Spirit himself.

Bobrinskoy and Evdokimov interpret the Spirit's activity through an Irenaeun lens, wherein the Spirit leads the neophyte to Christ, who then brings the Christian to the Father. Among the theologians, there is no monolithic interpretation, which adds further weight to Galadza's opinion that the Spirit descends on the assembly in manifold ways. There are, however, some consistencies worth noting. First, while the theologians variably accentuate the Christic and pneumatic elements of chrismation, one cannot interpret them as more Christologically oriented, or more pneumatological. The theologians view the ritual sacramental action as consistently trinitarian, and the most important quality of this trinitarian activity is to create communion.

For Cabasilas, the Spirit creates a community between the participants and Christ; for Schmemann, Christ creates a communion of the Holy Spirit. Regardless of the road one chooses, the destination is always the same: life shared with God. One cannot understate the positive theology emerging from these theologumena: God wants to share life with his holy people, and the divine willingness to share results in the transfiguration of the human person, the capacity to know joy and grow in love expressed to others. Bobrinskoy's cosmological perspective is likewise instructive: he reminds the reader that the initiatory rites manifest the world as created by God and thus good, and he defines the human person as consubstantial with the world. This observation leads me to two noteworthy aspects of this theologumenon on chrismation: first, these theologians tended to interpret the sacraments as seamlessly blending with one another. The rituals of baptism, chrismation, and Eucharist are an organic whole, and the boundaries dividing them are manmade. In chapter 1, I suggested that in practice, the Eucharistic Assembly is the source of initiation. The Eucharistic Assembly prepares a bath and consecrates chrism to wash and anoint those who would join the assembly. The *lex orandi* of the consecration of chrism and the prayer of chrismation refer to the Eucharist as the destination of the neophyte. The Eucharist begins and completes the process of initiation and brings the participant to the presence of the Triune God, where he continually renews the gift of the Spirit that capacitates the recipient to love God and his fellow human beings. Perhaps in our contemporary age of increased interest in and awareness of the cosmic dimension of theology and liturgy, we might suggest that the anointed ones of the Eucharistic Assembly receive another new gift of the Spirit, one that equips them with eyes to see the world as beautiful, and to care for it with the divine love with which it was created. Perhaps this reflection might include a reminder courtesy of Bobrinskoy that this is our Christian duty, since we are indeed consubstantial with the world.

ORTHODOX THEOLOGY AND THE NEOPHYTE AS KING, PRIEST, AND PROPHET: AN ECUMENICAL ENDEAVOR

Above, I identified a second cluster of theologians who connect Christ's ministries of king, priest, and prophet with the creation of a universal priesthood fully imparted to the laity. While Schmemann is the most audacious proponent of this theology, it is also present in Afanasiev, who sees the anointing with chrism as a vestige of an ancient ordination of laity.

In assessing this theologumenon, it is clear that Evdokimov was the most effective theologian in connecting this theology to patristic sources, citing, for example, Macarius of Egypt, who interprets the anointing as imparting these gifts. Afanasiev (and Evdokimov to a lesser degree) asserts that an interritual comparison of initiation and ordination demonstrates the imparting of Christ's ministry to neophytes. It also appears that Evdokimov and Schmemann were familiar with the baptismal homilies of John Chrysostom, which the great mystagogue preached when he was a presbyter in Antioch (approximately 388–90).[84] Among the few sources Schmemann cites in his study is Chrysostom's *Third Homily on the Second Letter to the Corinthians*, delivered in the fifth century. In this homily, Chrysostom briefly remarks on how baptism has imparted Christ's offices of king, priest, and prophet to neophytes:

> And what is "anointed," and "sealed"? Gave the Spirit by whom he did both these things, making at once prophets and priests and kings, for in old times these three sorts were anointed. But we have now not one of these dignities, but all three preeminently.[85]

---

[84] For the critical text and French translation of these two collections, see John Chrysostom, *Huit catéchèses baptismales inédites*, ed. and trans. A. Wenger, Sources Chrétiennes 50 (Paris: Cerf, 1957); and John Chrysostom, *Trois catéchèses baptismales*, ed. and trans. A. Piedagnel, Sources Chrétiennes 366 (Paris: Cerf, 1990). The homilies were delivered in Antioch during Lent in the years 388 and 390. Schmemann cites Wenger's edition of the eight baptismal homilies when referring to the white "royal robe," in *Of Water and the Spirit*, 71, n. 2.

[85] Schmemann, *Of Water and the Spirit*, 81, n. 14. The Greek text of Chrysostom's homily appears in J.-P. Migne, ed., *Patrologia Graeca* 61, no. 411 (PG

In the same homily, Chrysostom seems to indicate that he was referring to baptism in its entirety when he says "so also you are yourself made king and priest and prophet in the bath."[86] Schmemann appears to propose an explicit connection between chrismation (since this is the topic of his chapter) and these three offices: the neophyte receives these gifts because she is anointed, which essentially makes her a christ.

It is surprising that Schmemann limited his examination of Chrysostom to the mystagogue's alignment of anointing with the imparting of the Christic offices of king, priest, and prophet. In his baptismal homilies, Chrysostom engages a vast vocabulary to form identity in the neophytes. A close examination of Chrysostom's homilies indicates that this vocabulary was fluid. In his third baptismal homily from the Stavronikita collection (edited by Wenger), Chrysostom uses several titles to form identity in the catechumens:

> Blessed is God, let us say again, who alone has done wonders, who makes and renews all things. Those who were held captive yesterday are now free people and citizens of the Church. Those who yesterday were tarnished by sins are now in boldness and righteousness. For they are not only free, but are holy; they are not only holy, but righteous; they are not only righteous, but are sons; they are not only sons, but are inheritors; they are not only inheritors, but are brothers of Christ; they are not only brothers of Christ, but are also coinheritors; they are not only coinheritors, but are also members; not only members, but also temples; not only temples, but also instruments of the Spirit.[87]

This passage from Chrysostom's third homily presents several titles denoting the identity of those to be baptized. Chrysostom

---

hereafter). English translation taken from Philip Schaff, ed., *Nicene and Post-Nicene Fathers*, vol. 12: *Chrysostom: Homilies on the Epistles of Paul to the Corinthians*, first series, Third homily on 2 Corinthians (NPNF hereafter) (Peabody, MA: Hendrickson Publishers, 1995; originally published in the US by the Christian Literature Publishing Company, 1889), 290.

[86] Chrysostom, *Patrologia Graeca* 61, col. 417; translation adapted from P. Schaff, ed., NPNF vol. 12, 293.

[87] Chrysostom, Baptismal Homily no. 3:5, in *Huit catéchèses baptismales inédites*, 153.

alludes to the covenantal change the catechumens will experience, especially the transition from captivity (to the devil) and freedom in Christ and the church. The titles he employs illustrate the process of formation the catechumens are experiencing: they will become citizens of the church who are free, righteous, and holy. They will also become sons, inheritors, brothers of Christ, coinheritors, members, temples, and instruments of the Spirit.

In baptismal homily number three (from the collection edited by Piedagnel), Chrysostom again explains to catechumens how they gradually experience transformation through identity formation. Chrysostom begins his presentation by drawing deeply from the marital imagery of Ephesians 5: Christ is the Bridegroom who is coming for the church, his bride. Chrysostom carefully explains how the forthcoming participation in the rites of baptism communicates transformation to the catechumen by giving her two kinds of eyes: eyes of the body and eyes of faith:

> God has given you two types of eyes: those of the flesh and those of faith. When you enter the divine mysteries, the eyes of the flesh see water whereas the eyes of faith see the Spirit. The first contemplate an immersed body, the second a man buried in a shroud; the first see the flesh washed, the second see the soul purified; the first see the body coming out of the waters, the second see a new man shining from the divine purification; the first see the priest impose his hand and touch the head, the second contemplate the great high priest of the heavens who invisibly extends his hand and touches the head. For the one who baptizes is not a man, but the only-begotten child of God himself.[88]

Chrysostom's intriguing fusion of ritual and spiritual realities leads to a point: the bodily ritual participation of the catechumens shapes them to become believers—people who, at the conclusion of the process, confess faith.[89] Chrysostom returns to the bridal imagery he introduced in the beginning of the homily to assert that reciting the words of the confession of faith is what creates the covenant

---

[88] Chrysostom, *Trois catéchèses baptismales*, 220–23.
[89] Ibid., 224–25.

between catechumen and Christ.[90] At this point, the catechumen is anointed with holy chrism on the entire front of the body. Chrysostom describes the transformative effect with reference to the preceding covenantal renunciation of Satan and confession of Christ. The devil is furious, but because the catechumen shares a bridal covenant with Christ,[91] the catechumen now bears Christ's light, which the devil cannot bear to behold.[92]

Chrysostom's reference to light has become repetitive at this point. Earlier, he mentioned how the eyes of faith see a shining man emerging from the waters. He also explains why the catechumens make their baptismal promises on Good Friday, at the ninth hour. Christ has dissipated the darkness that ruled between the sixth and the ninth hours when he (who is the sensible and spiritual light) offered a sacrifice on behalf of the universe at this moment.[93]

Chrysostom references Luke 23 when he describes the sun of this world as hiding its rays when it sees the "sun of righteousness shining on high from the cross" while commending his spirit to the Father on behalf of the world. Chrysostom's presentation of light and darkness is not limited to the devil's futile attempts to seize catechumens from God's grasp; he also develops a profound theology of transformation where the bride (the catechumens) becomes like the bridegroom (Christ). The radiant light of Christ, the Son of God and Bridegroom, is the source for the spiritual brilliance given to the bride (the church), a symbol of her transformation.[94]

---

[90] Ibid., 234–35.

[91] Chrysostom explains the mixture of myrrh with oil; myrrh is used because it represents a bride, and oil because it represents an athlete. The matter used for the anointing has both epicletic and apotropaic properties (see ibid., 236–37).

[92] "Because the devil does not dare look on this sight: it is as if he is fixed with the rays of the sun, and he vacates the place; in the same manner, he will be blinded," in ibid., 236–37.

[93] Ibid., 228–29.

[94] Chrysostom summarizes this transformation at the end of Baptismal homily no. 3 (*Trois catéchèses baptismales*): "Having remembered all these things, remain faithful in your whole life, in your attachment, your renunciation, your boldness, for which the Master graces you, and keep yourselves pure and intact so that, crowned in glory, in the meeting with the king of the heavens, you

I have examined these select excerpts from Chrysostom's baptismal homilies at some length to illustrate two larger points. First, Chrysostom clearly views the rites of initiation as a holistic transformative process grounded by salvation history. Read in isolation, the components of the ritual process appear to impart a particular spiritual gift. However, Chrysostom explains the spiritual transformation as gradually occurring throughout the process. The Triune God imparts divine blessings to the participant at each point of the process. The catechumen begins the process of becoming Christ's bride at multiple ritual points, distinct and yet related: at the baptismal promises, the renunciations and confessions, the anointing with chrism, the immersion in the water, the laying on of hands, and by participating in Holy Communion.[95] The anointing with chrism is an important component, yet just one of many in a gradual process of transformation. Second, Chrysostom employs an expansive vocabulary to describe the new Christian identity the catechumens will assume. The selections I have presented from two of his eleven homilies offer a rich spectrum of identity formation. The catechumens are in the process of becoming citizens of the church, righteous, holy, free, sons, inheritors, coinheritors, and temples of the Spirit. The catechumens are also becoming members of the bride of Christ. Chrysostom's marvelous fluidity of terms is particularly evident in his use of "temple": in the first example, catechumens become "temples of the Spirit"; in the second homily, they become "temples of Christ."

I will return to Chrysostom and his potential contributions to updating the spectrum of Christian models presented to neophytes below. For the Orthodox consultation of Chrysostom in developing a theology of chrismation, this examination clearly indicates that Chrysostom did not privilege the models of king, priest, and prophet preferred by Schmemann and Evdokimov. It is not immediately clear why Schmemann and Evdokimov selected and pre-

---

may be accounted worthy to be enraptured in the clouds and manifest as holy ones of the kingdom of heaven," in ibid., 242–43.

[95] Chrysostom informs the catechumens that "the Holy Spirit made you into temples of Christ" when they partake of Eucharistic communion, ibid., 242–43.

sented the models of king, priest, and prophet for lay neophytes. One would expect that the *lex orandi* of the Byzantine Rite would serve as a natural source for gleaning a liturgical theology of the neophyte as king, priest, and prophet. However, an examination of the Byzantine liturgical sources yields surprising results. These theological ideas are not prominent in the Byzantine initiatory *lex orandi*. The prayer for the consecration of chrism includes one such reference in its anamnesis: "with it you anointed priests and high priests, prophets and kings, and through it anointed your holy apostles, and all of those who through the bath of regeneration are born again by them, and continued by the bishops and presbyters up until today."

One could interpret the anamnetic reference to kings, priests, and prophets as assuming that the neophytes would also receive these ministries, but the language of the epiclesis, which states the very blessings the church asks of God for the neophytes, does not retain this language. The epiclesis asks God to grant the neophytes sanctification, so that they would become "a chosen people, a royal priesthood, a holy people."[96] I realize that the absence of lexical equivalence between the anamnesis and epiclesis in this prayer does not rule out the possibility of developing a theology of kings, priests, and prophets. But I want to note that the connection of these offices with the neophytes is not prominent in this prayer, with the exception of its reference to holy priesthood. When we consult the prayer of chrismation, this language of kings, priests, and prophets is altogether absent. The prayer of chrismation itself asks God to grant the following to those who will be anointed: "Keep them in your sanctification; confirm him/her in the Orthodox Faith; deliver them from the evil one and all his devices, and by your saving fear guard their souls in purity and righteousness; so that being in every deed and word well-pleasing to you, they may become sons and heirs of your heavenly Kingdom." The blessing most frequently requested is sanctification, that the neophytes would be holy people. Again, this does not necessarily exclude the

---

[96] See chapter 1 for the texts of the consecration of chrism and the prayer of chrismation.

exercise of kingly, priestly, and prophetic offices. But I believe this brief consultation of the *lex orandi* strongly suggests that our theologians who have suggested that chrismation imparts these offices of Christ to neophytes were reading other sources.

CATHOLIC *RESSOURCEMENT* THEOLOGIANS: KING, PRIEST, PROPHET

If this is true, what sources were the Orthodox theologians reading? This is a difficult question to answer definitively, but I am convinced that Afanasiev, and especially Schmemann and Evdokimov, developed this theology by participating in a type of ecumenical colloquium. The liturgical movement and the twentieth-century theologizing of the laity was a hallmark of Roman Catholic theology. Catholic *ressourcement* theologians tended to trust the Apostolic Tradition as a reliable source representing second- to third-century Roman liturgy. Thus, the Apostolic Tradition inclusion of an instruction for the offering of oil to be used for the anointing of the sick was widely construed to be a precious liturgical source of antiquity. The following translation from the Latin edition of the text for the offering of oil for the sick reads: "as, sanctifying this oil, you give, God, health to those using and receiving it, whence you have anointed kings, priests, and prophets, so also may it afford strengthening to all tasting it and health to all using it."[97] The prayer's text suggests that it was employed for anointing the sick, as it mentions health (twice) and strengthening, and alludes to ritual consumption. There is not enough evidence to suggest that the same oil was used for the postbaptismal anointing that occurred in the rites of initiation. It is worth briefly noting that the liturgical anamnesis of anointing kings, priests, prophets, and martyrs has not been limited to the rites of initiation, but also has been a foundation for the liturgical celebration of anointing the sick.

---

[97] Text and translation taken from Paul Bradshaw, Maxwell Johnson, and L. Edward Phillips, *The Apostolic Tradition: A Commentary*, ed. Harold Attridge (Minneapolis, MN: Fortress Press, 2002), 49–51. It is notable that this prayer is quite similar to one taken from the Monastery of St. Catherine on Mount Sinai of eleventh-twelfth century provenance.

The link between the consecration of chrism and postbaptismal chrismation is more explicit in the seventh-century Gelasian sacramentary, a hybrid prayer book of the Roman tradition.[98] The Gelasian sacramentary emphasizes the imparting of the kingly, priestly, and prophetic offices of Christ to neophytes. The consecratory texts for the blessing of healing oil and chrism of the chrism Mass in the Gelasian sacramentary have a similar anamnesis to the Byzantine version by referring to historical anointing accordingly: "with which you have anointed priests, kings, prophets, and martyrs."[99] The connection between the historical anointing of kings, priests, prophets, and martyrs and the imparting of these ministries to the neophytes is explicated by the preface at the chrism Mass:

> It is indeed meet humbly to ask your clemency to confirm the creature of chrism unto its use in the sacrament of perfect salvation and life for those who are to be renewed in the baptism of the spiritual laver, so that when the unction is poured out to sanctify them and the corruption of their first birth is drawn out, each one may be your holy temple and send up to you the innocent savour of an acceptable life: so that being imbued, as your sacrament shows, with royal and priestly and prophetic honour, they may be clothed with the garment of your perfect gift.[100]

In the contemporary Roman Catholic rite of baptism, the formula recited by the priest when he anoints the neophytes immediately after baptism offers an even stronger connection between the anamnesis of historical anointings and the invocation of God to grant these blessings to today's neophytes:

> The God of power and Father of our Lord Jesus Christ has freed you from sin and brought you to new life through water and the Holy Spirit. He now anoints you with the chrism of salvation, so

---

[98] For the critical edition of this liturgical book, see L. C. Mohlberg, ed., *Liber Sacramentorum*, Rerum Ecclesiaticarum Documenta, vol. 4 (Rome: 1960). I consulted the English translation of this text published in E. C. Whitaker, *Documents of the Baptismal Liturgy*, ed. Maxwell Johnson (Collegeville, MN: Liturgical Press, 2003), 212–43.

[99] Whitaker, *Documents of the Baptismal Liturgy*, 226, 228.

[100] Ibid., 226.

that, united with his people, you may remain forever a member of Christ who is Priest, Prophet, and King.[101]

Given the consistent connection of anointing with the imparting of the kingly, priestly, and prophetic gifts in the Roman Rite, one might assume that Roman Catholic theologians have been at the forefront of developing such a theology, and this is true. The threefold division of Christ's ministry into the kingly, priestly, and prophetic offices has a long and rich history closely associated with the development of a priesthood of all believers.[102] Roman Catholics were hardly the first to explore Christ's ministry as imparted to the laity; Reformation theologians also developed this theology, especially John Calvin.[103] The trilogy of offices continued to develop in the Catholic Reformation and was taken up by John Henry Newman.[104] Perhaps the most significant treatment of the trilogy of Christic offices occurs in Yves Congar's study of the laity in the church.[105]

---

[101] *The Rites*, no. 228 (pp. 160–61).

[102] Several seminal essays break open the historical development of the laity as kings, prophets, and priests in Roman Catholic theology. For the classical overview of the historical development of these offices and their interpretation, see Yves Congar, "Sur la trilogie: prophète-roi-prêtre," *Revues des sciences philosophiques et théologiques* 67 (1983), 97–115. Also see David Power, "Priesthood Revisited: Mission and Ministries in the Royal Priesthood," in *Ordering the Baptismal Priesthood; Theologies of Lay and Ordained Priesthood*, ed. Susan Wood (Collegeville, MN: Liturgical Press, 2003), 97–120; Zeni Fox, "Laity, Ministry, and Secular Character," in *Ordering the Baptismal Priesthood*, ed. Susan Wood, 121–51; and Donald J. Goergen, "Priest, Prophet, King: The Ministry of Jesus Christ," in *The Theology of Priesthood*, eds. Donald Goergen and Ann Garrido (Collegeville, MN: Liturgical Press, 2000), 187–210.

[103] Power, "Priesthood Revisited," 107. For a complete treatment, see Rose Beal, "Priest, Prophet and King: Jesus Christ, the Church and the Christian Person," in *John Calvin's Ecclesiology: Ecumenical Perspectives*, eds. Gerard Mannion and Eddy van der Borght (London, New York: T & T Clark, 2011), 90–106.

[104] See Goergen, "Priest, Prophet, King," 191–92. See John Henry Newman, *Sermons Bearing on Subjects of the Day* (London, New York, Bombay: Longmans, Green, and Co., 1902), 52–62.

[105] Yves Congar, *Lay People in the Church: A Study for the Theology of the Laity*, trans. Donald Attwater (Westminster, MD: Newman Press, 1957, 1963 reprint).

Congar's comprehensive study begins with a definition of the layperson and addresses the question on how the laity exercise Christ's threefold ministry of king, priest, and prophet. Congar offers numerous contributions to lay ministry in the spirit of *ressourcement*, a careful and complete definition of a lay priesthood retrieved from the church's patristic and liturgical heritage. Congar is also keenly aware of the tendency to define the exercise of these offices through a purely hierarchical ecclesial model, and he carefully concludes that the three offices of king, priest, and prophet are not mutually exclusive, but reciprocally shape one another for the building up of the people of God, Christ's body.[106] He defines them as producing a plurality of ministries within the church and is wary of attempting to apply them to the exercise of sacerdotal powers of order and jurisdiction.[107] For Congar, the notion of a plurality of ministries is perhaps best understood when noting that the ordained exercise ministries within the community.[108]

Central to Congar's ecclesiology, and consequently, to his definition of lay ministry, is his cosmology encompassing kingdom, church, and world. After stating that God's purpose is to "bring mankind into fellowship with his divine life,"[109] Congar explains the intersections of kingdom, church, and world through the image of the temple:

> God wills to make the world the temple of his power and glory; he wills to make mankind his temple built of living stones, his body made of free persons, in a word, the temple of his fellowship. This is whither it all tends: that God wills to dwell and to be praised in mankind as in a single temple, but the indwelling and the praise are spiritual, living.[110]

Congar continues by reviewing salvation history and the inauguration of God's kingdom by the incarnation of Christ. He describes the present as a space between the fulfillment of the kingdom and

---

[106] Congar, "Sur la trilogie: prophìte-roi-prêtre," 112.
[107] Ibid.
[108] Fox, "Laity, Ministry, and Secular Character," 140–41.
[109] Congar, *Lay People in the Church*, 53.
[110] Ibid., 53–54.

its inauguration, and describes the church's role in fulfilling God's kingdom accordingly:

> The Church's constitution is in this, that she already has within herself, and as the very things that make her Church, the self-same and decisive causes of that renewal of which the Kingdom will be the consummation: the kingly, priestly, and prophetical power of Christ, and the Holy Spirit. Therefore, the Church cooperates directly in the constitution of the Kingdom, through the exercise of energies that are her own and constitute her reality as Church.[111]

Congar turns to the liturgy for his connecting of the laity and Christ's threefold offices of king, priest, and prophet.[112] In fact, he identifies confirmation as imparting the gift to exercise Christ's ministries of king, prophet, and priest to neophytes.[113] His teaching is quite similar to that of the Benedictine pioneer of the liturgical movement, Virgil Michel, who also understood the rites of initiation as imparting the divine vocation of king, priest, and prophet to neophytes, whose responsibility it is to manifest Christ to the world in which they live.[114] Michel's source for lay ministry was the *theosis* inaugurated by God at baptism. The gift of the indwelling of the Triune God was one for Christians to share with the world, with the priestly goal of transforming it in Christ. Rose Calabretta's description of Michel's last days echoes Congar's theological description of the present as the space between:

---

[111] Ibid., 88.

[112] Congar, "Sur la trilogie: prophìte-roi-prêtre," 99–100. Also see Congar, *I Believe in the Holy Spirit*, 219–20.

[113] Congar, *I Believe in the Holy Spirit*, 219–20. Congar also connects the imparting of these gifts to the anointing in his essay "The Structure of Christian Priesthood," in Congar, *At the Heart of Christian Worship: Liturgical Essays of Yves Congar*, ed. and trans. Paul Philibert (Collegeville, MN: Liturgical Press, 2010), 90, esp. n. 39.

[114] Rose B. Calabretta, *Baptism and Confirmation: The Vocation and Mission of the Laity in the Writings of Virgil Michel*, Tesi gregoriana, Serie Teologia 47 (Rome: Gregorian University Press, 1998), 166–67. For a survey of Michel's background, see Michael Woods, *Cultivating Soil and Soul: Twentieth-Century Catholic Agrarians Embrace the Liturgical Movement* (Collegeville, MN: Liturgical Press, 2009), 66–100.

> The object of this apostolic lifestyle was to obey the mandate of Christ given to his Church in its double commission: a) to announce to all human beings the highest truth about themselves: they were both children of God and members of Christ; and b) to capacitate them for living out their days, soaring even higher towards their sublimest dignity, thus experiencing new frontiers of authentic freedom. They were destined by their Father to enjoy even in time-bound existence the heavenly life that he wished to give them: to share in the eternal love in the inner communion of the Triune God.[115]

A crucial component of Michel's notion of a baptismal priesthood was its accessibility to the people of the laity. Calabretta's notes that Michel translated traditional monastic vocabulary by reintroducing terms such as ascetic and mystical to make it accessible to the layperson, who could truly become fellows of Christ and join the communion of saints.[116] The transfiguration of social structures was a task belonging to the whole people of God, ordained and lay, each exercising the gifts of the Spirit they received in the sacraments.

The robust sacramental theology developed by *ressourcement* theologians like Congar and Michel became official in two documents of the Second Vatican Council. In chapter 4 of *Lumen Gentium*, the constitution on the church, the council defines the laity accordingly:

> The term laity is here understood to mean all the faithful except those in holy orders and those in the state of religious life specially approved by the Church. These faithful are by baptism made one body with Christ and are constituted among the People of God; they are in their own way made sharers in the priestly, prophetical, and kingly functions of Christ; and they carry out for their own part the mission of the whole Christian people in the Church and in the world.[117]

---

[115] Calabretta, *Baptism and Confirmation*, 213.

[116] Ibid., 146–47, 160.

[117] Second Vatican Council, *Lumen Gentium* no. 31, Vatican website, accessed April 8, 2013, http://www.vatican.va/archive/hist_councils/ii_vatican_council/documents/vat-ii_const_19641121_lumen-gentium_en.html.

Lumen Gentium distinguishes the vocation of the laity from that of the ordained priesthood by emphasizing lay ministry and to the world:

> But the laity, by their very vocation, seek the kingdom of God by engaging in temporal affairs and by ordering them according to the plan of God. They live in the world, that is, in each and in all of the secular professions and occupations. They live in the ordinary circumstances of family and social life, from which the very web of their existence is woven. They are called there by God that by exercising their proper function and led by the spirit of the Gospel they may work for the sanctification of the world from within as a leaven. In this way they may make Christ known to others, especially by the testimony of a life resplendent in faith, hope and charity. Therefore, since they are tightly bound up in all types of temporal affairs it is their special task to order and to throw light upon these affairs in such a way that they may come into being and then continually increase according to Christ to the praise of the Creator and the Redeemer.[118]

Vatican II echoes the teaching of theologians like Congar and Michel by placing the ministry of the laity in deliberately worldly terms. The council connects lay ministry to the apostolate in *Apostolicam Actuasitatem*, its decree on the lay apostolate. A strong sacramental theology grounded by the rites of initiation and the ministries of king, priest, and prophet again guides the mission of the laity in the world:

> The laity derive the right and duty to the apostolate from their union with Christ the head; incorporated into Christ's Mystical Body through baptism and strengthened by the power of the Holy Spirit through confirmation, they are assigned to the apostolate by the Lord Himself. They are consecrated for the royal priesthood and the holy people (cf. 1 Pet 2:4-10) not only that they may offer spiritual sacrifices in everything they do but also that they may witness to Christ throughout the world. The sacraments, however,

---

[118] Ibid.

especially the most holy Eucharist, communicate and nourish that charity which is the soul of the entire apostolate.[119]

An emphasis on the legitimacy and power of the universal priesthood of the laity appears in the decree's description of the work of the lay apostolate. *Apostolicam Actuasitatem* describes the laity as "sharers in the role of Christ as priest, prophet, and king," whose work is absolutely essential to the life of the church.[120] The laity's ministry of creating encounters between the world and God's kingdom is essential to the divine will because the laity as the body of Christ is the tangible connection of kingdom, Church, and world.

The teachings of the Second Vatican Council thus officially promulgate Catholic *ressourcement* theology of the twentieth century. This theology is a creative synthesis of theological anthropology and the sacramental theology gleaned from the historical development of the rites of initiation. Catholic theology defines the laity as becoming sharers of Christ and his threefold ministry of king, priest, and prophet through baptism and confirmation, with Congar privileging the latter. The sacramental theology has a salient cosmology—the laity's purpose is to transform and transfigure the world by making Christ present in their daily secular activity. Theologians have assessed the status of this sacramental theology since the Second Vatican Council, but the theological anthropology of the laity as exercising Christ's ministries of king, priest, and prophet continues to hold hegemony in Catholic systematic theology.

This brief survey of the development of a modern Catholic theology of the laity, grounded by sacramental theology, has important implications for modern Orthodox theologies of the meaning of chrismation. Evdokimov and Schmemann in particular promote the idea that chrismation imparts Christ's offices of king, priest, and prophet to the neophyte. The neophyte exercises these offices in ministry to the world as part of the universal priesthood of

---

[119] Second Vatican Council, *Apostolicam Actuasitatem*, Vatican website, accessed April 8, 2013, http://www.vatican.va/archive/hist_councils/ii_vatican_council/documents/vat-ii_decree_19651118_apostolicam-actuositatem_en.html.

[120] Second Vatican Council, *Apostolicam Actuasitatem* no. 10.

Christ, his body in the world. Schmemann offers the most elaborate explanation of the content of the ministry of baptismal priesthood, whereas Afanasiev and Evdokimov present more nuanced models of how lay ministries are grounded by sacramental theology. Of greatest significance is the striking similarity between the models of lay ministry espoused in Catholic magisterial theology and a portion of the Orthodox Paris school. A close reading of the authors illustrates their immersion in *ressourcement*, a careful presentation of historical theology rooted in the testimony of the New Testament and the Fathers. Several patristic and liturgical sources communicate a theological anthropology in the Christic images of king, priest, and prophet. Newman, Congar, Schmemann, and Evdokimov captured this theological thread, retrieved it, and contributed to its restoration in both Catholic and Orthodox theology. This baptismal theological anthropology is, in fact, an ecumenical theological endeavor, as its main artisans used similar methods and sources, and more importantly, held the theological images of king, priest, and prophet in similarly preeminent esteem.

IDENTITY IN POSTMODERN CHRISTIANITY: BECOMING GOD IN THE SPIRIT

While I value the initiatory origins of the theological images of king, priest, and prophet, I believe that more work needs to be done in assessing their baptismal origins and determining their capacity to invigorate baptismal priesthood and lay ministry. A close examination of the relationship between the initiation rites and the theological anthropology of king, priest, and prophet yields a broader spectrum of potential images of identity formation. First, the liturgical evidence suggests that the only direct connection between anointing with chrism and the trilogy of king, priest, and prophet occurs in the Gelasian sacramentary (in the chrism Mass) and the contemporary Roman Catholic consecration of chrism and postbaptismal chrismation. The connection is less clear in the Byzantine Rite, which mentions the trilogy of offices in the consecration of chrism but not in the prayers or anointing formulae of chrismation. Other ancient sources mention the trilogy in connection with the oil, but these sources are not exclusive to initiation.

For example, the blessing of oil in the Apostolic Tradition contains an anamnesis mentioning the trilogy but denoting the ritual use of the oil for anointing the sick. Similarly, Aphraat, a fourth-century Syrian saint, mentions an anamnesis of the trilogy in connection with initiation and the anointing of the sick.[121] The evidence thus informs us that the liturgical anamneses created for blessing oil tended to refer to the historical anointing of kings, priests, and prophets. In the Christian community, the oil is used for diverse purposes to indicate the pouring out of divine grace on its recipient, the giving of the same divine mercy today as yesterday. It does not necessarily mean that the kings, priests, and prophets of old are modular for today.

There is an important methodological lesson to be learned from my review of the Orthodox theologians surveyed here. Some of these theologians identified sequences of ritual celebration that communicate ongoing divine activity. For example, Cabasilas identifies the descent of the Spirit in baptismal immersion and the donning of the head covering, along with chrismation. Bobrinskoy sees divine activity in the blessing of baptismal waters, the immersion, the anointing (either pre or postbaptismal), the procession around the font, and participation in Holy Communion. Schmemann also identifies God's consecrating activity in the blessing of baptismal waters and the postbaptismal anointing with chrism. The theologians demonstrate that God's descent upon the participant transcends superficial divisions between the sacraments and instead reveals them as a united rite with varying ritual components.

But the theologians have made a more significant point with serious implications for participants. They have discerned a pattern of repetitive divine activity within the context of a single ritual celebration revealing a robust sacramentality. The participants encounter God in the materiality of creation—God has entered the waters and revealed them as holy; God has infused the chrism with divine properties as a gift to the participant; God feeds the participants

---

[121] See Paul Meyendorff's citation of Aphraat's *Demonstrations* in Paul Meyendorff, *The Anointing of the Sick* (Crestwood, NY: St. Vladimir's Seminary Press, 2009), 39.

at his table with holy food. The manner of ritual participation varies, but the effect is essentially the same, as God continues to freely offer divine blessings as gifts to the participant at each ritual station. God repeatedly offers these gifts because the participants need them to progressively grow in God's divine image and likeness.

The repetitive activity of God in imparting divine blessings at several points in the ritual celebration is modular for the new life the participant assumes. The ritual pattern is in fact a prolepsis of the participant's Christian life. The participant has been given the spiritual equipment to live the Christian life in baptism, but as a beginner in this life, she needs to learn how to use the equipment. She learns the Christian life by belonging to a eucharistic community where, along with everyone else, she repeatedly receives the gift of the Spirit feeding her through her journey in this life while anticipating the age to come. Perhaps the central reason the participant regularly needs God's gifts can be explored through metaphors like progression, growth, and becoming like God in the Spirit. The process of engaging the rites of initiation involves communication with people of the community and the materiality of the world. Catechumens learn with and from others and are gradually introduced to the church's liturgical life, which employs the divine symbols of creation. The rites of initiation establish the modular pattern of progressive growth in the Spirit. This growth occurs through participation in community and through materiality demanding and receiving blessings from God. Each phase of the Christian life is thus progressive, and the *telos* of the progression is communion with God, finalized in Christ's second coming.

The notion of progressive growth in the Spirit is one frequently offered by Orthodox theologians, but not sufficiently elaborated. Cabasilas states the problem of neglecting God's blessings in his discourse on chrismation:

> Not all, however, have perception of the gifts or eagerness to make use of the riches they have been given. Some are unable to grasp the gifts because of their immature age, others are not eager because they are not prepared or have failed to give effect to their preparation. Some have subsequently repented and bewailed the sins which they have committed and live according to the right

reason, and so have given proof of the grace that has been infused into their souls . . . it does not profit us to have received the gift if we are careless. There is need of effort and vigilance on the part of those who wish to have these things active in their souls.[122]

Cabasilas explores the obvious dilemma of theological anthropology: should humans be entrusted with God's gift? At what point is a Christian ready to receive this gift? Orthodoxy privileges the anthropological maximalism Schmemann mentions in his discourse on chrismation. But the optimism is more theological than anthropological because it offers an image of God as the one who freely and repeatedly gives of himself to humanity. The Orthodox Church accordingly introduces everyone and anyone into the church, including infants who have no experience to guide them on this journey. They are given the divine gift from the very beginning, to establish the pattern of progressing in Christ from infancy. The modular pattern of the rites of initiation facilitates progressive growth, with the expectation of errors and subsequent corrections. Orthodox theologians have grasped for metaphors to explain the process of progressive growth. Perhaps the most frequently mentioned idea is the one attributed to the Russian saint, Seraphim of Sarov, who said that the Christian life entails the acquisition of the Holy Spirit.[123] Christians progress through the journey of the Christian life by growing in the Spirit, whom God freely imparts.

If modern Christian theology drew upon the patristic images of king, priest, and prophet to express the models that Christians were to grow into, perhaps the time has arrived to expand the vocabulary of images that might prove modular for Christians in

---

[122] Cabasilas, *The Life in Christ*, 109.

[123] The following explanation of chrismation by Hilarion Alfeyev effectively exemplifies a reference to Seraphim of Sarov's statement: "The gift of the Holy Spirit, received in chrismation, is not to be passively accepted, but actively assimilated. It was in this sense that St. Seraphim of Sarov said that the goal of a Christian's life is the 'acquisition of the Holy Spirit'. The Divine Spirit is given to us as a pledge, yet we still have to acquire Him, make Him our own," in "Membership of the Body of Christ: Sacraments of Initiation," *Greek Orthodox Theological Review* 43, nos. 1–4 (1998): 570–71.

postmodernity. Postmodern Christians face the challenges of globalization and paradigm shifts in Church demographics. While some aspects of Christian life are familiar, others are new. Parishes are not only multigenerational but now also multiethnic and multilingual. Financial security, employment and school demands, and cultural wars present new challenges to Christian people and families. The economic and cultural landscape is unstable. A versatile vocabulary describing Christian identity is needed to navigate the contemporary turbulent Christian environment. In this vein, John Chrysostom's late fourth-century Antiochene context shares some similarities with contemporary Christianity. Along with the other mystagogues, Chrysostom was preaching to people who lived in a turbulent world of uncertainty. In addition to the models of king, priest, and prophet, Chrysostom offered several other images describing the Christian life, including: free, citizen (of the church), righteous, son, inheritor, coinheritor, temple of Christ, and temple of the Spirit. These images not only draw upon the soteriological nomenclature of post-Nicene Christianity, but they also convey a sense of belonging to Christ. Chrysostom was not alone in developing vocabulary that communicated a sense of identity and belonging for new Christians entering the uncertain waters of Christian life. Cyril of Jerusalem also offered multiple titles denoting a sense of identity and belonging in his mystagogical catecheses, including: photizomenoi, neophytes, christs, Christians, Christ-bearers (christophoroi), heavens, and paradises.[124] Like Chrysostom, Cyril attempted to communicate to the neophytes that they had become recipients of the blessings of the salvation history underpinning their participation in the rites of initiation. The titles are multifunctional: they define the ethics required to fulfill the requirements of the Christian life, but they also remind the Christian of the promise of the age to come that now belongs to them, namely life in communion with God. The titles challenge the Christian to fulfill the expectations borne by the titles: no Christian has earned paradise

---

[124] Donna Hawk-Reinhard, "From Χριστιανοί to Χριστοφόροι: the Role of the Eucharist in Christian Identity Formation according to Cyril of Jerusalem" (PhD diss., St. Louis University, 2011), 303–34.

or is worthy of being a temple of the Spirit or Christ; but because God wants the Christian to share life with the Trinity, the Christian is given divine faculties to grow in the Spirit and become like God. These faculties are given in baptism and the anointing with chrism and renewed whenever the Christian participates in the Eucharistic Assembly.

Christians of postmodernity have a treasury of tools at their disposal. I am neither calling for an abandonment of pastorally applying the images of king, priest, and prophet, nor am I calling for a mere expansion of a list of potential models for progressive Christian growth. I am suggesting that Christians today retrieve the divinely endowed method employed by mystagogues like Chrysostom and Cyril and carefully develop a new vocabulary of images and models for Christian life that can be recognized and captured by local cultures and capacitate their people to progressively become the people God has called them to be in the Spirit. All of the liturgies comprising the rites of initiation suggest diverse models of becoming like God. Ultimately, they point to one common underlying fact: every human being is called to be a holy member of the body of Christ. It is not only possible but also even desirable for the unity underpinning God's people to be expressed in diverse images and models.

CONCLUSION

This chapter has provided a select survey of Orthodox theological analyses of chrismation. The survey yields fascinating facts on the diverse ways Orthodox theologians have interpreted the meaning of chrismation. The methods and theologies are plurivocal, and it is neither possible nor desirable to create an Orthodox theological synthesis of chrismation. In conclusion, I will summarize the main points and suggestions contributed by the study.

Most Orthodox theologians have viewed chrismation as one crucial component of the rites of initiation. Most of the theologians observe a recurring pattern of divine activity that transcends superficial divisions of the mysteries. The pattern of divine activity follows this general sequence of events: the blessing of baptismal waters; prebaptismal anointing with chrism; immersion in the font;

postbaptismal anointing (beginning in the fourth century); procession around the font; donning of the hat; and Holy Communion. The Holy Spirit performs a transformative act at each station of the rite. Chrismation, then, is crucial, but one component in a larger sequence.

Cabasilas, Bobrinskoy, and Schmemann view the divine activity as works of the Triune God. Their description of the blessings participants receive is not univocal. Cabasilas says that the Spirit brings in Christ himself; Schmemann says that the Spirit is himself given; Bobrinskoy says that the recipient is granted access to the life of God.

Bobrinskoy and Schmemann develop a robust sacramentality from chrismation. Both situate the human person as serving the world, which Bobrinskoy describes as consubstantial with God and the world. The innate goodness of creation emerges as an important motif from this sacramentality.

Afanasiev, Evdokimov, and Schmemann suggest that the rites of initiation are similar to ordination and appoint all neophytes to the universal priesthood. The three theologians (especially Schmemann) connect chrismation to the imparting of the Christic gifts of king, priest, and prophet. Orthodox theology developed in tandem with Catholic magisterial theology in the *ressourcement* movement, with Congar and Michel key contributors to the human vocation of king, priest, and prophet. The imagery of king, priest, and prophet is pre-eminent in baptismal theological anthropology and is an endeavor of ecumenical theology.

I have suggested that the sequence of ritual patterns where the Triune God transforms participants is modular. The gifts of the Spirit are given repeatedly through the material things of the world. The repetitive activity of God promotes the notion of the progressive growth to become like God in the Spirit.

I have also suggested that the contemporary conditions of Christianity occasion the development of new modular images that Christians can recognize and readily adopt as their own in progressing toward God. The development of new images should not be limited to populating a list of titles in addition to king, priest, and prophet, but actually requires employing the patristic method of drawing from the liturgical sources to creatively develop a vocabulary coherent with the culture and Christian identity. One might begin with the communion of saints, an inexhaustible source of identity formation for men, women, and children. The twentieth and twenty-first centuries have witnessed to an ecumenical appeal to all to embrace the Christian life of holiness. Initially, I suggest two additional titles to accompany king, priest, and prophet: "saint" and "laic." Integrating "saint" into the euchology of initiation reinforces the *telos* of baptism, chrismation, and Eucharist: each and every human being is called to become holy, a saint, regardless of gender, ethnicity, and age. Adding "laic" to this list of titles strengthens the laity as the original and legitimate order of the church. Each laic joins Christ in the work he performs at the right hand of the Father. These two terms are compatible with the rites of initiation, and adding them to the church's liturgy will enable ordinary Christians to gradually recognize the holy vocation that is given to them.

In summary, Orthodox theology views the anointing with chrism to be a crucial ritual experience where the gift of the Spirit is freely given. The Spirit capacitates the participant to progressively become like God with the rest of her eucharistic community while navigating the conditions of this world and enjoying its holy materiality.

CHAPTER 4

Chrismation and Catholic Confirmation

The purpose of this chapter is to examine the Roman Catholic rite of confirmation from an Eastern Orthodox perspective. This exercise presumes that the Roman and Byzantine traditions have something valuable to offer one another. The bulk of this chapter surveys the history and contemporary situation of Roman confirmation to identify the prevailing theological issues. Attentive readers will note that I do not address each issue raised by scholars who have studied confirmation in the Roman tradition. My hermeneutic for selecting issues to address is the ability for Byzantine chrismation to engage Catholics in meaningful dialogue on addressing the theological and pastoral issues of confirmation.

I begin by reviewing scholarship on the liturgical history of Roman confirmation to establish the difficulty in reconstructing its origins, especially the bishop's role in handlaying and anointing neophytes with chrism a second time, after an initial postbaptismal presbyteral anointing. I then address the following topics: the position of confirmation in the sequence of the rites of initiation; pneumatology in confirmation; and the question of a minimum age for confirmation. The chapter includes a proposal for reconfiguring Roman confirmation by adding a blessing of oil at the chrism Mass designated for a solemn anointing of adolescents. This proposal attempts to restore confirmation to its native home and illuminate its unique sacramental character as the ritual bestowing the free gift of the Spirit upon all recipients, who renew their baptismal vows and grow in the Spirit through frequent participation in the Eucharist.

REVIEW OF CATHOLIC SCHOLARSHIP: HISTORY

In the introduction to this book, I stated that Catholics tend to describe confirmation as a sacrament in search of a theology. A review of confirmation's turbulent and elusive liturgical history appears to inevitably result in this conclusion. Numerous liturgical historians have rigorously interrogated the extant evidence communicating the origins and theology of confirmation. Maxwell Johnson's seminal study on the history of Christian initiation comprehensively tells confirmation's story in all liturgical traditions.[1] Other scholars have attempted to reconstruct the particular Roman tradition of confirmation as originally a sacrament with a ritual celebration of episcopal handlaying and postbaptismal anointing with chrism. Students of liturgy and sacramental theology are indebted to the seminal work of Aidan Kavanagh on episcopal handlaying and anointing with chrism in the Apostolic Tradition church order long attributed to St. Hippolytus of Rome.[2] Kavanagh employed the comparative liturgical method by studying episcopal handlaying in the Apostolic Tradition and comparing it to other contemporaneous dismissal rites of Christian antiquity. The results of his research yielded a hypothesis that the handlaying and anointing with chrism in the Apostolic Tradition was actually a rite of dismissal. In an early response to Kavanagh, Paul Turner examined the historical evidence and cautioned readers that there is not enough evidence to advance Kavanagh's theory beyond the realm of hypothesis.[3] Frank Quinn suggested that the episcopal postbaptismal anointing with chrism in the Apostolic Tradition functioned as a continuation of the presbyteral anointing.[4] Johnson also addressed the historical issue by exploring other contemporaneous sources, namely the fifth-century letter of Pope Innocent to Decentius of Gubbio and Ambrose of Milan's mystagogical catechesis,

---

[1] Maxwell Johnson, *The Rites of Christian Initiation: Their Evolution and Interpretation*, rev. ed (Collegeville, MN: Liturgical Press, 1999, 2007), 254–66.

[2] Aidan Kavanagh, *Confirmation: Origins and Reform* (New York, NY: Pueblo Publishing Company, 1988). Also see Kavanagh, "Confirmation: A Suggestion from Structure," in *Living Water, Sealing Spirit: Readings on Christian Initiation*, ed. Maxwell Johnson (Collegeville, MN: Liturgical Press, 1995), 148–58.

[3] Paul Turner, "The Origins of Confirmation: An Analysis of Aidan Kavanagh's Hypothesis (with Response by Aidan Kavanagh)," in *Living Water, Sealing Spirit*, ed. Johnson, 238–58.

[4] Frank Quinn, "Confirmation Reconsidered: Rite and Meaning," in *Living Water, Sealing Spirit*, ed. Johnson, 219–37.

De Sacramentiis.[5] Johnson noted similarities between Ambrose's testimony and the Apostolic Tradition and offered three possible models for a fourth-century Roman Rite.[6] But Johnson's assessment of the first two possibilities cast them as spurious, due to the conjectural nature of the evidence. The only possibility he found reasonably plausible (based on Ambrose's testimony) is that Rome's theology of the handlaying had become pneumatic, but that it had either not yet adopted a second episcopal anointing by the fourth century, or had done so only recently.[7] These studies demonstrated the difficulty in attempting to reconstruct the ancient Roman rites of chrismation; the absence of evidence permits only hypotheses on the early Roman rites of anointing with chrism and handlaying that became more widely known as confirmation after the fifth century.

The absence of historical testimony on the Roman rite of confirmation is frustrating to liturgical scholars and pastors. The lack of evidence has not impeded an attempt to explain how confirmation eventually separated from baptism. Frank Quinn suggests that the episcopal anointing was probably "a continuation and completion of the presbyteral anointing of the body."[8] Dominic Serra agrees, asserting that the episcopal rite of handlaying and anointing with chrism should not be separated from the brief postbaptismal anointing with chrism performed by presbyters.[9] Serra argues that the fragmentation of what is now confirmation from its initiatory context caused the pneumatic element to be removed from initiation:

> Even the Roman separation of episcopal chrismation from baptism did not leave the water-bath isolated from the ritual action that

[5] See Maxwell Johnson, "The Postchrismational Structure of Apostolic Tradition 21, the Witness of Ambrose of Milan, and a Tentative Hypothesis Regarding the Current Reform of Confirmation in the Roman Rite," *Worship* 70 (1996): 16–34.

[6] Ibid., 26–27.

[7] Ibid., 27–28.

[8] Frank Quinn, "Confirmation Reconsidered: Rite and Meaning," in *Living Water, Sealing Spirit*, ed. Johnson, 224.

[9] Dominic Serra, "Baptism and Confirmation: Distinct Sacraments, One Liturgy," *Liturgical Ministry* 9 (Spring 2000): 69.

makes its meaning explicit, the messianic anointing by a presbyter. This anointing is theologically pneumatic while effectively christic . . . the separation of the episcopal chrismation and handlaying did not separate confirmation from baptism, but separated the constitutive elements of confirmation itself. Confirmation is the messianic anointing with the Holy Spirit that specifies the very meaning of the baptismal bath by conforming the initiate to the image of the Anointed one. It is pneumatic because it is christic, yet its pneumatic quality is not explicit without the prayer that accompanies the episcopal handlaying and specifies the meaning of the chrismation done by the bishop. This suggests that confirmation in the Roman rite begins with the presbyteral chrismation immediately after baptism and is completed by the episcopal handlaying and signing with chrism.[10]

Serra's discussion of the historical separation of the presbyteral anointing from the episcopal handlaying and anointing sets the stage for both a historical and theological discussion reflecting the dilemma Catholics confront in confirmation. First, the separation of episcopal handlaying and anointing from the postbaptismal presbyteral anointing became both permanent and pronounced. The main cause of this separation was the restriction of handlaying and anointing to bishops. As episcopal ministry became more centralized in urban centers, the faithful generally had infrequent contact with their bishop, and confirmation came to be separated from infant baptism by at least three or more years.[11] The episcopal component of confirmation became increasingly remote from the rites of baptism and as a consequence, more illuminated as being a separate and distinct sacrament. In attempting to explain its significance, medieval theologians described confirmation as a sacrament increasing the grace given at baptism, and strengthening the Christian in this life, perhaps best exemplified by Thomas Aquinas.[12] In a sharp critique of the scholastics, Martin Luther denounced confirmation as a sacrament, claiming that it merely provided tasks to

---

[10] Ibid.

[11] Johnson, *The Rites of Christian Initiation*, 247.

[12] Thomas Aquinas, *Summa Theologiae*, as cited by Johnson, *The Rites of Christian Initiation*, 254.

keep bishops busy.[13] Reformers significantly modified confirmation, essentially reshaping it into a sacrament of faith affirmation to be bolstered by sober catechesis.

Having evolved from a baptismal ritual environment with a pregnant Christic-pneumatic dynamic to a separate and distinct rite associated with bishops and maturity, confirmation became permanently alienated from its origins by the seventeenth century. The seventeenth century is crucial because the Roman Church's adoption of the Gelasian sacramentary's rite of baptism for a sick catechumen significantly impacted the sequence of the order of initiation.[14] The editors of the seventh-century Gelasian sacramentary deferred confirmation for sick catechumens. The editors presumably knew that any given catechumen might die before she was able to receive confirmation from her bishop. So the initiation sequence started with baptism, followed by postbaptismal chrismation by a presbyter, and concluded with the reception of communion. If the catechumen survived, she would receive confirmation from the bishop in due course. This Gelasian rite was meant to be exceptional, for sick catechumens, but it became the norm by the seventeenth century as the basis for infant baptism in the Roman Rituale of 1614. By this time, Catholic confirmation was completely remote from baptism and the presbyteral anointing; it followed first communion, and was denounced and substantively reformed by Protestants. During the course of its evolution, theologies developed to validate confirmation as a legitimate sacrament. Confirmation thus became a sacrament of maturity since it was conferred upon older children or adolescents, a rite of passage into maturity bolstered by catechesis. It was also described as conferring strength to recipients, a sacrament designed to ignite baptism anew.

In the twentieth century, during the course of the ecumenical movement, the search for the origins of Christian worship and the historical method emerged as important factors in updating the life of the church. A historical-critical examination of confirma-

---

[13] Johnson, *The Rites of Christian Initiation*, 353.
[14] Ibid., 229–31.

tion unveiled its complex journey as an essential initiation rite that came to be exiled from its native home. After the Second Vatican Council, confirmation experienced a sober liturgical reform in the Catholic Church. Recognizing the need to return confirmation to its baptismal provenance, the Catholic Church took important steps in reconnecting confirmation to baptism. Several steps are particularly noteworthy.

First, the apostolic constitution on the sacrament of confirmation by Pope Paul VI addresses the isolation of confirmation from baptism by calling for its revision so that "the intimate connection of this sacrament with the whole of Christian initiation may stand out more clearly."[15] The revision of the confirmation rite sought to grow closer to initiation by adding the renewal of baptismal promises to the rite, which includes a renunciation of Satan, a threefold confession of faith in each person of the Trinity, and a confession of faith in the church.[16] The constitution called for the bolstering of pneumatology in the rite of confirmation as well. The Roman Church strengthened confirmation's pneumatic quality in two ways. First, the pope explicitly aligned confirmation with the outpouring of the Holy Spirit on Pentecost. He explicated this intention, stating "it has been our wish also to include in this revision what concerns the very essence of the rite of confirmation, through which the faithful receive the Holy Spirit as gift."[17] Paul VI presents several foundational New Testament texts as the cornerstones for imparting the gift of the Holy Spirit at confirmation. These New Testament texts include Mark 1:10, Luke 4:17-21, Luke 12:12, John 15:26, Acts 1:8, and several passages from Acts 2.[18] Two episodes from these texts

---

[15] Pope Paul VI, "Apostolic Constitution on the Sacrament of Confirmation." I used the English translation published in *The Rites of the Catholic Church*, vol. 1, study ed. (Collegeville, MN: Liturgical Press, 1990), 472–78. Paul VI is not the originator of the call for the reform of confirmation, however. Paul VI was executing the mandate of the fathers of Vatican II, as *Sacrosanctum Concilium* 71 had originally called for restoring confirmation to initiation.

[16] See "The Rite of Confirmation Outside Mass," no. 40, in *The Rites*, 498–99.

[17] Pope Paul VI, "Apostolic Constitution on the Sacrament of Confirmation," in *The Rites*, 473.

[18] Ibid.

are of special importance: the descent of the Spirit upon Jesus at his baptism in the Jordan, and the coming down of the Spirit on the apostles on the feast of Pentecost. Paul VI used these New Testament models as the foundations for imparting the gift of the Spirit at confirmation: "The laying on of hands is rightly recognized by reason of Catholic tradition as the beginning of the sacrament of confirmation, which in a certain way perpetuates the grace of Pentecost in the Church."[19]

While venerating the antiquity of the Roman laying on of hands, Paul VI revised the rite of confirmation by adopting the Byzantine formula for anointing, the "seal of the gift of the Holy Spirit." The purpose of adopting the Byzantine formula, "almost word for word," was its apt expression of the gift of the Holy Spirit, cohering with the outpouring of the Spirit on the day of Pentecost.[20] The ritual change in the Roman rite of confirmation mandated by Paul VI was a deliberate attempt to bolster the sacrament's pneumatology, and consequently prioritized the ritual gesture of anointing with chrism over the episcopal handlaying.[21] This reform of confirmation was significant in reshaping its structure and form and highlighting the sacrament as imparting the gift of the Holy Spirit.

If we assume that the pastoral implementation of this reform of confirmation was significant, we can ask if the people of the church noticed the implementation of the reform. It is fair to assert that, in many ways, the experience of confirmation was largely unchanged. The church's revision of confirmation retained the practice of administering the sacrament to children who have attained the age of reason, while allowing conferences of bishops to adjust the target

---

[19] Ibid., 474.

[20] Ibid., 477. For an intriguing assessment of this adaptation, see Anne McGowan, "Eastern Christian Insights and Western Liturgical Reforms: Travelers, Texts, and Liturgical Luggage," in *Liturgy in Migration: From the Upper Room to Cyberspace*, ed. Teresa Berger, foreword by Martin Jean (Collegeville, MN: Liturgical Press, 2012), 200–203.

[21] "But the laying on of hands on the elect, carried out with the prescribed prayer before the anointing, is still to be regarded as very important, even if it is not of the essence of the sacramental rite," ibid. This attempt to explain the significance of the laying on of hands betrays its subordination to the anointing with chrism in the reformed rite.

age.[22] Thus, confirmation came to be delayed for baptized infants, and the gap between postbaptismal anointing by a presbyter and the completion of confirmation by the bishop remained in force. Notably, the revision of confirmation impacted the experience of adults, who receive confirmation immediately after baptism. The only oddity in this practice is that the postbaptismal presbyteral anointing is omitted when adults are baptized and confirmed in the same ceremony. Aidan Kavanagh accurately assessed the situation in his dated but seminal study:[23]

> It must be pointed out that in the whole strategy of the postconciliar reform, an initiatory sequence which does not end regularly and ordinarily in first communion is severely abnormal, a *ritus interruptus* which cannot but cause serious warps in theology and pastoral practice. Thus the relatively recent custom of delaying confirmation to later years has led to admitting young children to the eucharist prior to their confirmation. This in turn has led to making the sacrament of penance, instead of confirmation, the standard overture to first communion for children, a practice not without its critics among theologians and religious educators. The practice is sacramentally most abnormal, which makes it unlikely that satisfactory rationales for it will be forthcoming.[23]

Kavanagh's hope for restraint in justifying the sequence of confirmation turned out to be futile. The limited revision of confirmation resulted in the emergence of creative theologies that justified the diverse practices of confirmation. In his excellent pastoral explanation of confirmation, Paul Turner presents seven different models of confirmation to illuminate the increasing polarity of their respective theologies.[24] Catholics can receive confirmation according to the following contexts: adults receive confirmation with baptism in

---

[22] See "Introduction to the Rite of Confirmation," nos. 11–12, in *The Rites*, 482–83. In adjusting the age for admittance to confirmation, the introduction infers that it may be more suitable to raise the age to allow for sufficient formation in preparation for the sacrament.

[23] Kavanagh, *Confirmation: Origins and Reform*, 88.

[24] Paul Turner, *Confirmation: The Baby in Solomon's Court*, rev. and updated (Chicago: Hillenbrand, 1993, 2006).

the RCIA (without the postbaptismal presbyteral anointing); unconfirmed and baptized Christians who are entering the Catholic Church receive confirmation as the rite of passage into the church;[25] children and adolescents receive confirmation between the ages of seven and eighteen, and Turner has distinguished them by creating two models; and Byzantine Catholics receive postbaptismal chrismation in accordance with their tradition.[26] Turner's models represent the diverse ways in which confirmation is celebrated in contemporary Roman liturgy, and it is certainly plausible to conclude that most Catholics belong to the children or adolescent models, since most Catholics receive baptism as infants. For children and adolescents, confirmation is a rite of passage denoting either a sense of deeper belonging to the church or a mechanism one must engage to remain nominally Catholic.[27]

Allow me to elaborate further through a collective anecdote. As a liturgist, I have been teaching the theology of confirmation to Catholic students from the perspective of its history and hypothetical reconstruction, assuming that it belongs to the baptismal milieu. As a rule, the vast majority of my students, both undergraduate and graduate, have fiercely resisted the idea that confirmation should immediately follow baptism. Instead, they vehemently and emotionally defend confirmation as a rite of passage into firm commitment to Jesus Christ, a sacrament of maturity safeguarded by sufficient catechesis and the surety of young people who voluntarily confess their faith in Christ. In other words, they are staunch defenders of Turner's models of confirmation for children and especially adolescents.

The rite of receiving baptized Christians into the full communion of the Catholic Church is another important model of confirma-

---

[25] On the history and meaning of this rite, see Turner's comprehensive study, *When Other Christians Become Catholic* (Collegeville, MN: Liturgical Press, 2007).

[26] Turner also presents a model for Protestant-Anglican Churches in *Confirmation*, 38–60.

[27] For a humorous yet sober reminder of this tension in belonging, see Turner's account of a letter written by a teenager in the Diocese of Kansas City–St. Joseph in "The Origins of Confirmation," in *Living Water, Sealing Spirit*, ed. Johnson, 255, n. 64.

tion.[28] The rite of confirmation plays an important role in the process of receiving other Christians into the Catholic Church. Paul Turner's seminal presentation of the development of the reformed process for receiving baptized Christians into the Catholic Church illuminates the sensitive ecumenical issues involved when other Christians decide to become Catholic. Turner concludes that the new rite for reception represents significant progress in Catholic theology on acknowledging the validity of baptism in other churches and ecclesial communities. The process for reception is complex, depending on the native tradition from which the candidate hails.

For example, baptized Christians from reformed communities who become Catholic receive confirmation because the Catholic Church does not recognize the sacramentality of their rites of confirmation.[29] The liturgy used for Orthodox Christians is profoundly simple, as the Catholic Church accepts the sacramentality of Orthodox postbaptismal chrismation.[30] Turner explains why confirmation is a suitable component in the rites of receiving other Christians by emphasizing it as the sacrament bestowing the gift of the Holy Spirit, not as a ceremony of commitment to Christ.[31] But Turner is also quite forthcoming on the ecumenical challenges caused by the Catholic Church's rite for receiving other Christians, stating that confirmation "carries the joy of the gift of the Holy Spirit" on the one hand, but also "lays bare the disparity of Christian churches yearning to be one" on the other.[32] The rite of reception emphasizes ecclesial fullness: the Catholic reform exhibited ecumenical progress by recognizing qualities of churchliness in other ecclesial communities, but a solemn sacramental ritual was needed to establish that one entered the fullness of the church when becoming Catholic. Confirmation's role in promoting this ecclesial fullness

---

[28] Comprehensively treated by Turner, *When Other Christians Become Catholic*. This section follows Turner's exposition of the rite of receiving baptized Christians.

[29] Turner, *When Other Christians Become Catholic*, 147–48.

[30] Ibid., 141.

[31] Ibid., 148–49.

[32] Ibid., 148.

is crucial, as it ushers one into the eucharistic communion of the Catholic Church.

Clearly, the multiple models of confirmation serve diverse purposes, united by the bestowal of the gift of the Holy Spirit. It can be difficult to reconcile the differences emerging from the multiple purposes of confirmation: a teenager who receives the anointing with chrism after completing a program of religious education views confirmation differently from someone who has recently become Catholic. Many Catholic scholars and pastors understand the implications of allowing the tensions between these models to remain unreconciled. In his introduction, Turner perhaps articulates the tension most effectively: "It seems to me that each model influences the others, and this leakage causes inconsistencies within each form and for confirmation as a whole."[33] I sympathize with Turner and other Catholics struggling to reconcile the inconsistencies of the various models of confirmation in the Catholic Church, but would also like to suggest that these diverse models might actually illuminate a path to reshaping the theology of confirmation, since each model apparently provides a precious ministry to Church. In the following sections, I will address the central issues contributing to these inconsistencies as a student and practitioner of the Byzantine Rite and then propose a new hypothetical model accommodating the various rites involving anointing with oils under the parent eucharistic celebration of the chrism Mass.

CONFIRMATION: WHEN?

In addressing central issues of confirmation for Roman Catholics, perhaps the most vexing issue is the timing of its celebration. Above, I briefly introduced the historical hypothesis that the Apostolic Tradition presented the following sequence of initiatory rites: baptism, postbaptismal chrismation by a presbyter, episcopal handlaying and anointing with chrism, and the Eucharist. The presbyteral postbaptismal anointing always remained connected to the rite of baptism, whereas the episcopal handlaying and anoint-

---

[33] Turner, *Confirmation*, XII.

ing became associated with imparting the gift of the Holy Spirit. Johnson asserts that the Roman Rite "encountered in Gaul, primarily, the terminology of 'confirmation'" as Charlemagne imposed the Roman liturgical rites throughout western Europe.[34] In the process of liturgical development, confirmation was identified with not only the handlaying gesture but also the chrismation performed by the bishop.[35] Thus, confirmation seems to have been established as the title describing this postbaptismal handlaying and anointing with chrism for the Roman Catholic Church by the eighth century.

The reservation of confirmation to bishops alone in the Roman Rite contributed to its separation from baptism, given that most neophytes were not in close proximity to a bishop at the time of their baptism.[36] In the seventeenth century, when the rite of baptism of a sick catechumen became the norm in the Roman Church, First Communion preceded confirmation as the latter was delayed indefinitely. Confirmation's complex history resulted in the odd practice of unconfirmed children participating in the fullness of church life by receiving the Eucharist before they had been confirmed, although the order of the sacraments varied according to circumstances.[37] The practice of allowing children to receive Holy Communion before they were confirmed was punctuated by the decree of the Sacred Congregation for the Sacraments, *Quam Singulari* (issued in 1910), which encouraged children to fully participate in the Eucharistic Liturgy once they had reached the age of reason.[38]

Confirmation's position in the sequence of the rites of initiation changed after Vatican II for adults and children of a catechetical age

---

[34] Johnson, *The Rites of Christian Initiation*, 248.

[35] Quinn, "Confirmation Reconsidered," 230.

[36] Geoffrey Robinson remarks that "the bishop confirmed as he rode around his diocese on horseback, with parents holding up their children to him to be confirmed," in Geoffrey Robinson, "Confirmation: A Bishop's Dilemma," *Worship* 78 (2004): 51.

[37] Liam Walsh, *Sacraments of Initiation: A Theology of Life, Word, and Rite*, 2nd ed. (Chicago: Liturgy Training Publications, 2011), 152–53.

[38] Ibid.

who were being baptized. In these instances, confirmation immediately follows baptism and the neophytes also partake of the Eucharist in the same liturgical context.[39] When adults and children of a catechetical age are confirmed immediately after baptism, they do not receive the presbyteral postbaptismal anointing with chrism.[40] The restoration of confirmation to the liturgical celebration of baptism raises the question of who can impart the sacrament, since the Roman tradition has reserved this privilege to bishops. The reform allows for priests to assist with the anointing when there are large numbers of candidates.[41] Necessity allows for bishops to authorize certain priests to administer confirmation if the diocesan bishop or another bishop is unavailable to celebrate the sacrament.[42] Presumably, permitting certain priests to administer the sacrament of confirmation in the absence of the diocesan bishop allows for large numbers of people to receive confirmation immediately after baptism by employing the ecclesiological principle of subsidiarity.

The post–Vatican II reforms applied to the rites of initiation and confirmation resulted in different orders of sequence in the celebration of the sacrament, depending on the age and status of the candidate, as illustrated by table 4.1:

---

[39] "Adult catechumens and children who are baptized at an age when they are old enough for catechesis should ordinarily be admitted to confirmation and the Eucharist at the same time as they receive baptism," in "Introduction to the Rite of Confirmation," no. 11, *The Rites*, 482.

[40] "Accordingly, confirmation is conferred after the explanatory rites of baptism, the anointing after baptism being omitted," in "Introduction to RCIA," no. 216, in *The Rites*, 147. Also see "Celebration of the Sacraments of Initiation," no. 228, in *The Rites*, 160–61.

[41] "Celebration of the Sacraments of Initiation," no. 228, *The Rites*, 160. Note also that "priests associated as ministers of the sacrament also hold their hands outstretched over the candidates" at the gesture of the laying on of hands in confirmation, "Celebration of the Sacraments of Initiation," no. 234, in *The Rites*, 163.

[42] *The Rites*, "Introduction to the Rite of Confirmation," no. 8, in *The Rites*, 481.

Table 4:1: Sequence of Initiation Rites Compared

Sequence of Initiation Rites: Adults and Children of Catechetical Age	Sequence of Initiation Rites: Children and Adolescents[43]
baptism confirmation eucharist	baptism Postbaptismal chrismation (presbyteral) penance eucharist confirmation

Many adults and children of catechetical age experience the sacraments in their historical order, in one seamless liturgical context: baptism, confirmation, and Eucharist. Clearly, the Roman Church prefers to retain its tradition that the diocesan bishop preside at the sacrament. In practice, it is possible that a priest might be authorized to confirm. The comparison of sequences allows us to note two glaring differences a confirmand would experience: adults and children who are immediately confirmed do not receive the first component of confirmation, the postbaptismal presbyteral anointing with chrism along with its prayer. Children and adolescents have essentially experienced the beginning of confirmation with the postbaptismal anointing, and then are admitted to the Eucharistic Assembly before they receive the remainder of the confirmation rite at a later time. Children customarily receive the sacrament of penance before admittance to First Communion, leaving confirmation to conclude the sequence of initiatory rites.[44]

One could assert that the Vatican II reform of confirmation was incomplete. For adults and older children, the messianic postbaptismal chrismation was omitted from the process. The neophytes still receive the laying on of hands and are anointed with chrism with the accompanying prayer, but the omission of the postbaptismal

---

[43] The "Introduction to the Rite of Confirmation," no. 11, defines this age as seven (*The Rites*, 482).

[44] See Kavanagh, *Confirmation: Origins and Reform*, 88.

anointing prayer removes the language defining adhesion to Christ as connoting the gifts of priesthood, prophecy, and kingship.[45] Younger children experience a fragmented confirmation, with participation in the Eucharist typically interrupting the second phase of confirmation celebrated by the bishop.

Liturgical theologians have noted the discrepancies in these practices. Dominic Serra notes that the separation of the presbyteral and episcopal components of confirmation represents a fragmentation of confirmation itself.[46] He suggests that restoring the episcopal handlaying and anointing to its original position bolsters the theology of the whole event, as the handlaying and second anointing provide the pneumatic element and complete the Christic element of the postbaptismal anointing with chrism. Serra argues that returning confirmation to the rite of baptism provides the Christianizing action, which he describes as "making a Christian."[47] Serra describes confirmation, in its fullest form (both presbyteral and episcopal), as establishing the neophyte into the holy people of God, the final pneumatic rite of baptism that welcomes the neophyte into the eucharistic community.[48] The implications of introduction into this eucharistic life are not to be taken lightly: Serra suggests that the neophyte now participates in God's life, perhaps more commonly described as deification, or *theosis*.[49] Perhaps most significantly, restoring the full confirmation rite to its initiatory provenance no longer requires one to "seek a new significance for confirmation."[50] Serra also suggests that the separation and isolation of confirmation allows for one to create distinct classes of membership in the church. Serra's proposal for restoring confirma-

---

[45] "The God of power and Father of our Lord Jesus Christ has freed you from sin and brought you to new life through water and the Holy Spirit. He now anoints you with the chrism of salvation, so that, united with his people, you may remain for ever a member of Christ who is priest, Prophet, and King," "Celebration of the Sacraments of Initiation," no. 228, in *The Rites*, 160–61.

[46] Serra, "Baptism and Confirmation," 67.

[47] Ibid., 70.

[48] Ibid., 71.

[49] Ibid., 68.

[50] Ibid., 70.

tion to its initiatory provenance is grounded by the fruits of historical scholarship, and bolstered by the potential theological fruits such a restoration might contribute to the church.

In his study of the ancient history of confirmation and assessment of the post–Vatican II liturgical reforms, Maxwell Johnson suggests that the Roman reform compromised the rich theology offered by the episcopal handlaying, and overemphasized the pneumatic content of the anointing with chrism.[51] Johnson's remarks on the relationship between the presbyteral and episcopal anointing are worth repeating here:

> The imposition of hands and the prayer for the seven-fold gift of the Spirit should have been restored theologically as constituting confirmation's matter and form. Such a reform or restoration of the essential nature of the handlaying prayer would have allowed the traditional presbyteral anointing in baptism to remain an integral component of all baptisms and not just those of infants or others unfortunate enough not to be confirmed in the same celebration. . . . A true "reform" of confirmation would have simply restored it to its ancient Western location immediately following baptism in all cases, as, indeed, the final pneumatic blessing and ecclesial ratification of Christian initiation and public welcome to the Eucharistic communion of the Church.[52]

Johnson critiques the reform's preference for emphasizing the anointing with chrism, and its consequent subordination of the handlaying gesture to the anointing.[53] His assessment of the rite and his suggestion for restoring confirmation does not address the practical question of the availability of bishops to regularly celebrate the sacrament.

The Dominican scholar Liam Walsh systematically addresses the history and theology of confirmation in his analysis of the sacraments of initiation. An important segment of his treatment

---

[51] Johnson, "The Postchrismational Structure of Apostolic Tradition 21," 33–34.

[52] Ibid.

[53] See Paul VI, "Apostolic Constitution on the Sacrament of Confirmation," in *The Rites*, 472–78, for a fuller background of the Catholic reform's preference for the anointing with chrism as the preferred form over the laying on of hands.

concerns a suitable age for confirmation, a topic I will address with some detail below. For Walsh, the question of the sequence of sacraments is impacted by age. He recognizes that many children are admitted to the Eucharist before they are confirmed, which he describes as a "major theological difficulty."[54] Walsh argues that admitting children to the Eucharist prior to confirmation compromises the sacramentality of all the sacraments of initiation. He lauds the practices of some dioceses of the Latin Rite that call for the confirmation of children before First Communion, as confirmation is the authentic preparation for participation in the eucharistic banquet. Walsh even suggests that the preferred path for the Roman Church would be to "return to the practice that was common before Pope Pius X opened the way to First Communion for children reaching the age of reason: confirmation was given to young people in their teens and their First Communion was delayed until they had been confirmed."[55]

Walsh's theological premise about the integrity of the sequence of sacraments differs from Serra's and Johnson's. Walsh firmly believes in the preparatory quality of confirmation, and suggests that the Eucharist is the "food of the strong, not of the childish."[56] Walsh's position is unique in his comfort with delaying confirmation and Eucharist as long as is necessary, to ensure that participants are truly prepared for the messianic banquet.

Tension shapes the crucial question of when confirmation should be celebrated in the Roman Rite. Historical research demonstrates that confirmation's native home is adjacent to baptism, regardless of age. Multiple developments in the life of the Roman Church caused confirmation to separate from baptism. Its separation isolated it as an individual rite, and a new theology came to shape the isolated rite. Liturgical historians seem to favor the restoration of confirmation to its original home, immediately following baptism, whereas other influential voices see it as having organically developed into the initiatory rite of passage that provides a portal into the full communion

---

[54] Walsh, *Sacraments of Initiation*, 213.

[55] Ibid., 213–74. Walsh admits, however, that this proposition is "unthinkable today."

[56] Ibid., 213.

of the Catholic Church for young people. The Roman Church's provision for pastoral discretion on determining the age of confirmation appears to function as a type of compromise, as models exist for diverse celebrations of confirmation. The pastoral compromise has not, however, resolved the pastoral and theological tensions concerning the appropriate time for celebrating confirmation.

THE AGE FACTOR IN CONFIRMATION

In surveying the history of confirmation in the Roman tradition, I have presented multiple factors that caused the separation of confirmation from baptism. Perhaps the most important of these is that confirmation is traditionally conceived as a sacrament with the bishop as presider. Theologically, this is both consistent and significant. The diocesan bishop presides over the chrism Mass celebrated on Holy Thursday and recites the prayer consecrating the diverse oils and chrism that will be used in the church's sacramental ministries. The bishop's presidency at confirmation, culminated by the laying on of hands and anointing with chrism, appears to be a theologically organic continuation of the consecration of chrism. The bishop, whose sacramental ministry to the diocese is one of faith and order, personally completes the initiation of neophytes, whose admittance to the body of Christ is akin to the order of the laity. The bishop's handlaying gesture has apostolic precedent in the New Testament, a salient demonstration of the antiquity and authority vested in this particularly episcopal ministry.

The antiquity of this model is informative. As far as we know, the ancient models presume the bishop's frequent presence in and interaction with the faithful of his diocese when Christianity was a minority religion in the Roman Empire. As the Christian populace grew in the fourth century, each bishop presided over a larger regional church, and the delegation of ministries evolved alongside ecclesial demographic development. Presbyters began to preside at the Eucharist by the fourth century, and eventually exercised most of the ministries once belonging to the episcopacy, with the exception of ordination.[57] The resilient reservation of confirmation for the

---

[57] See John Zizioulas, *Eucharist, Bishop, Church: The Unity of the Church in the Divine Eucharist and the Bishop During the First Three Centuries* (Brookline,

bishop is notable for Roman Catholics; perhaps the prohibition of presbyteral celebration of confirmation illuminates the perceived solemnity of confirmation in late antiquity and the medieval period. In reality, the bishops continued to celebrate confirmation, but many neophytes had to wait for confirmation until the bishop visited, sometimes for a period of several years.

It is clear, though, that this delay was not originally caused by pastoral concern about the absence of a requisite maturity for receiving the sacrament. In fact, the medieval evidence suggests that bishops and councils established age ranges in an attempt to urge parents to have their children confirmed.[58] A theology of spiritual combat and maturity affixed itself to confirmation in this period, so that the gift imparted by the Spirit in its celebration was "strength for battle" and "strength to preach to others."[59] Gerard Austin notes that "this interpretation was reinforced popularly by the gesture of the confirming bishop being changed from a welcoming kiss of peace into a symbol of spiritual combat—the bishop striking the candidate's cheek."[60] Johnson describes the fusion of this theology of combat and maturity with the age of reason as the new norm for confirmation accordingly: "with this the door is thrown wide open for the popular understanding that confirmation is the special sacrament for adolescents!"[61]

The practice of confirming children evolved from the labyrinthian history described in survey form above. As for the actual age at which Catholic children are confirmed, practices vary from one diocese to another. The revised rite of confirmation allows national

---

MA: Holy Cross Orthodox Press, 2001), 205–8. For more recent scholarship on when presbyters were deputized to preside at the Eucharist in Rome, see John Baldovin, "The Fermentum at Rome in the Fifth Century: A Reconsideration," *Worship* 79 (2005): 38–53.

[58] "Equally important is that this legislation also demonstrates that a concern for the age at which confirmation is to be administered has its origins in these various conciliar attempts to set not a minimal age for its reception but a maximal age (varying from age one, three, seven, or even ten) by which confirmation was to have been received already!" in Johnson, *The Rites of Christian Initiation*, 212.

[59] Austin, *Anointing with the Spirit: The Rite of Confirmation*, 19–20.

[60] Ibid., 20.

[61] Johnson, *The Rites of Christian Initiation*, 213.

conferences of bishops to establish an appropriate age of confirmation based on pastoral discretion.[62] Paul Turner describes the age range for confirmation as a "broad spectrum," but it is clear that the emergent model for contemporary Catholicism is adolescent confirmation.[63] Catholic people naturally interpret their sacramental participation on the basis of their experience, which either occurred in adolescence or was shared with adolescents.

Turner develops adolescent confirmation as emerging, describing it as an innovative model that is still evolving.[64] Its popularity is understandable because it enjoys support from people who witness to its benefits in contemporary practice; historical niceties are not the key criterion for confirmation's shaping of Catholic youth.[65] Turner asserts that adolescent confirmation found fertile ground in the United States due to the prevailing environment of religious formation.[66] A paradigm shift in catechetical theory, privileging personal experience, provided a series of formative experiences that shaped the growth of faith in adolescents preparing for confirmation. Ironically, Turner asserts that confirmation ritualizes the phenomenon of progressive faith formation.[67] If Turner is correct, then the historical evolution of confirmation finds itself at a crossroad, since its past history represented the phenomenon of the theologizing of a ritual. Turner offers a clear description of what adolescent confirmation confers to the participant, namely commitment, maturity, and witness:[68]

---

[62] "Introduction to the Rite of Confirmation," no. 9, in *The Rites*, 482–83.

[63] Turner, *Confirmation*, 78, and Austin, *Anointing with the Spirit: The Rite of Confirmation*, 53. A resource offering several perspectives on adolescent confirmation is James Wilde, ed., *Confirmed as Children, Affirmed as Teens: The Order of Initiation* (Chicago: Liturgy Training Publications, 1990). Another resource offering proposals, models, and perspectives for confirmation is James Wilde, ed., *The Order of Initiation: When Should We Confirm?* (Chicago: Liturgy Training Publications, 1989).

[64] Turner, *Confirmation*, 106. Here, I follow Turner's exposition of adolescent confirmation in 97–131.

[65] Ibid., 117.

[66] Ibid., 101.

[67] Ibid.

[68] Ibid., 102. Note also that Turner establishes the popularity of adolescent confirmation across Catholic cultures. The practice becomes popular even

> Adolescent confirmation . . . works from the assumption that children reach a point where faith becomes their own, not another's, and then they make a free choice to belong to the community that holds that same faith. . . . A free choice shows that they have appropriated faith for themselves. This self-appropriation, then, is ritualized in a sacrament of the Church.

Turner continues by critically analyzing adolescent confirmation through the hermeneutic of confirmation's history, sacramental theology, and diverse practices within the Roman Rite. Briefly, Turner identifies the following issues illuminated by the popularity of adolescent confirmation: it has the capacity to diminish baptism;[69] it has a tendency to stratify the church into classes through a sacramental rite of commitment;[70] and its relationship with the conferral of the gift of the Holy Spirit is not clear.[71] Despite these problems, adolescent confirmation has enjoyed support from influential theologians such as Karl Rahner and Yves Congar, who value the maturity required to express commitment.[72] Turner's most insightful assertion is his identification of adolescent confirmation as symbolizing the Roman problem with the sacrament, given the apparent incoherence of adolescent confirmation with its historical connection with baptism. Turner muses that its popularity may have increased as a result of the Catholic Church's reform of the rites of initiation, where those baptized in infancy longed for a rich process of catechesis that could be ritualized.[73]

Adolescent confirmation thus appears to be a vibrant symbol of the evolution of the sacrament, regardless of how one assesses the historical conditions that paved its road to the present. This model represents a complex historical process where a ritual, removed from its native context, develops a theology explaining its relevance. Adolescent confirmation finds a convenient home in the modern milieu,

---

among immigrant people who practice infant confirmation in their native countries.

[69] Ibid., 103–4.
[70] Ibid., 123.
[71] Ibid., 124.
[72] Rahner and Congar, quoted in Turner, *Confirmation*, 115–16.
[73] Turner, *Confirmation*, 130–31.

providing a meaningful rite of passage for adolescents who develop and articulate their faith with maturity and commitment. Despite his concerns, Turner poses the obvious question: has confirmation's evolution reached a point of becoming a new species altogether?[74]

Adolescent confirmation is an instance of a contemporary church problem. On the one hand, it offers several attractive blessings: adolescents engage a process of interiorizing tenets of faith that equip them to live the Christian life more deeply as members of the body of Christ. As a rite, confirmation ritualizes a much larger and more elongated process, one that many view as quite meaningful, especially as churches continue to seek innovative ways of ministering to youth. On the other hand, adolescent confirmation illuminates alarming fissures in the practice of Catholic initiation. In this model, confirmation is privileged as the culminating rite of initiation, with the Eucharist as one of many rites preparing one for it. More alarming are the potential divisions it can create within an assembly, especially diverse multicultural parishes. How does adolescent confirmation compare with the practice of infant confirmation in the rites of Eastern Churches and other ethnic groups? What is the meaning of baptism for children whose confirmation is delayed for an elongated period? Are these children incapable of receiving the gift of the Holy Spirit, which is imparted to them when they receive Holy Communion, or are they even unworthy of it? Perhaps most relevant is the cognitive dimension. Does engaging a process of faith formation ritualized by confirmation make one a better and more reliable Christian? What if a young person has a learning disability and does not have the cognitive capacity to understand and interiorize particular tenets of faith? Finally, how might one assess the effectiveness of adolescent confirmation?

This question particularly pertains to the nature of the gift of the Spirit imparted at the sacrament. Confirmation does not guarantee retention of youth in the church; this fact should motivate scholars and pastors to return to the question of how God acts in confirmation, with the pastoral task emphasizing equipping all the holy people to respond.[75]

---

[74] Ibid., 131.

[75] Kevin Seasoltz offers a sober assessment of confirmation: "Unfortunately, those who are confirmed as adolescents often discontinue the practice of religion,

CONFIRMATION AND THE GIFT OF THE HOLY SPIRIT

The reform of confirmation emphasized the sacrament as one of the Holy Spirit, rooted in the feast of Pentecost, and imparting the gift of the Holy Spirit. Above, I surveyed the theological issues illuminated by the fruits of historical research on confirmation. These issues include the question of a missing pneumatic element in confirmation, the Christic-pneumatic tension in the two anointing with chrism, and Johnson's assertion that confirmation is a sacrament enacted by the Trinity. In attempting to recover the elusive theology of confirmation, theologians have accentuated its pneumatic quality. That confirmation confers the gift of the Spirit in the Roman tradition is evidenced by the euchological witness of the prayer of confirmation in the seventh-century Gelasian sacramentary, which mentions the sevenfold gift of the Spirit. The Roman reform of confirmation strengthened its pneumatic aspect, favoring the anointing with chrism as the core ritual gesture and adopting the Byzantine formula of anointing, referring to the seal of the gift of the Holy Spirit. These ritual changes, supported by Paul VI's emphasis on confirmation as recalling the descent of the Spirit on Pentecost, clearly identified confirmation as the sacrament imparting the gift of the Holy Spirit to participants. In this vein, the Roman Church bolstered the expression of pneumatology in its liturgical practice and sacramental theology.

Select references to confirmation in the teachings of the Second Vatican Council explicate the relationship of the gift of the Holy Spirit to mission. For example, *Lumen Gentium*, Vatican II's dogmatic constitution on the church, states that the Holy Spirit bestows the following special gifts on the laity through confirmation: "They are more perfectly bound to the Church by the sacrament of confirmation, and the Holy Spirit endows them with special strength so that they are more strictly obliged to spread and defend the faith, both by word and by deed, as true witnesses of Christ."[76] Both

---

so the rite becomes in a sense a graduation rite." *A Virtuous Church; Catholic Theology, Ethics, and Liturgy for the 21st Century* (Maryknoll, NY: Orbis Books, 2012), 177.

[76] Second Vatican Council, *Lumen Gentium* no. 11, Vatican website, accessed March 18, 2013, http://www.vatican.va/archive/hist_councils/ii_vatican_council/documents/vat-ii_const_19641121_lumen-gentium_en.html.

Lumen Gentium and *Apostolicam Actuositatem* (Vatican II's official teaching on the lay apostolate) directly identify confirmation as the gift of the Holy Spirit equipping recipients with the strength needed for mission, as illustrated by this quote from *Apostolicam Actuositatem*:

> The laity derive the right and duty to the apostolate from their union with Christ the head; incorporated into Christ's Mystical Body through baptism and strengthened by the power of the Holy Spirit through confirmation, they are assigned to the apostolate by the Lord Himself.[77]

The explicit identification of confirmation as the sacrament of the Holy Spirit raised questions old and new concerning confirmation in the life of the Roman Catholic Church, even after the reform of confirmation. Bishop Geoffrey Robinson described the theological problem as "implying some defect in baptism," an old issue in the Catholic theology of confirmation.[78] Robinson proposes that aligning baptism with the theology of Easter and confirmation with the theology of Pentecost is an adequate pastoral approach to resolving the problem, literally referring to baptism as the "sacrament of Easter and confirmation as the "sacrament of Pentecost."[79] Robinson attempts to explain how his proposal might contribute to resolving the problem of the theology of confirmation:

> At confirmation what happens to the candidates is what happened to the apostles at Pentecost. At Pentecost the apostles received the gifts of the Holy Spirit and were then immediately sent out into the world to carry with them the message of God's love in Jesus Christ.

---

[77] Second Vatican Council, *Apostolicam Actuositatem* no. 3, Vatican website, accessed March 18, 2013, http://www.vatican.va/archive/hist_councils/ii_vatican_council/documents/vat-ii_decree_19651118_apostolicam-actuositatem_en.html. See *Lumen Gentium* no. 33 for a similar linking of confirmation and the lay apostolate.

[78] Robinson, "Confirmation: A Bishop's Dilemma," 53.

[79] Ibid., 59. For more on Pascha and Pentecost as the theological foundations for baptism and confirmation, see Yves Congar, *I Believe in the Holy Spirit*, vol. 3, trans. David Smith (New York, NY: Crossroad Publishing), 219.

It could hardly be argued that the Holy Spirit had not come near the apostles until that moment. We must argue that the Spirit had constantly been with them and filled them with all the gifts they needed. Now, at Pentecost, they were given the special gifts that they needed for what was being asked of them at that moment, that is, their mission . . . in a similar way, candidates for confirmation have already received many gifts of the spirit at baptism and throughout their lives. At confirmation, their personal day of Pentecost, they are given the special gifts they will need for their mission and then sent on that mission. Confirmation recognizes that they are growing up and are ready to begin to take on a new role and a new responsibility within the community.[80]

I have quoted Robinson at length here because his proposal is a creative attempt to fuse the pneumatological emphasis of confirmation with the practice of confirming children who have attained catechetical age. First, he honors both baptism and confirmation by identifying them with the core events of salvation history, namely Easter and Pentecost. He continues to honor the fullness of baptism in analyzing Pentecost as an event that is not the sole source of the Holy Spirit. His distinction is clear: baptism imparts the gift of the Holy Spirit; confirmation is different in imparting particular gifts of the Spirit equipping the recipient for mission. Robinson's explanation is a pastoral compromise because he assumes that the recipients of confirmation are children when he refers to the process of "growing up." Robinson's explanation is useful for this discussion because he acknowledges that the gift of the Spirit is not limited to confirmation, but that particular gifts are imparted through the sacrament that enables mission. Speaking as a pastor who must honor baptism and confirmation without diminishing either sacrament, Robinson's explanation is sensible for families who will bring their infants to baptism and their children of varying ages to confirmation. Robinson's analysis illuminates the reality Catholics face with confirmation: in reforming confirmation, the need to explain the dignity of both baptism and confirmation is still present, and the activity of the Holy Spirit in each sacrament is perhaps the most elusive theological dynamic.

[80] Robinson, "Confirmation: A Bishop's Dilemma," 59–60.

Thus, it appears that the Roman Church succeeded in establishing confirmation as the sacrament that imparts the gift of the Holy Spirit to participants. However, this reform raised new questions about the presence and descent of the Holy Spirit in the other sacraments of initiation. The enrichment of the pneumatic aspect of confirmation appears to have relied on a medieval tenet of Catholic theology: the notion of a moment of consecration. The need to explain how the gift of the Holy Spirit can be given in baptism and in confirmation in a special way illustrates that some have interpreted confirmation as the sacrament of the Spirit, where the gift of the Spirit is imparted in an identifiable ritual action: the anointing with chrism. Robinson's attempt to address this issue is laudable, but also cautionary, since his discussion allows the complicated question of the Holy Spirit to surface for all to see.

RECONFIGURING CONFIRMATION: AN EASTERN ORTHODOX PROPOSAL

Byzantine postbaptismal chrismation has not experienced the turbulence of Roman confirmation. Chrismation was always performed by a presbyter after baptism, with no eminent handlaying gesture included as a core sacramental component. In fact, without the Western influence of categorizing the sacraments and numbering them as seven, chrismation would probably be completely unnoticed in the Byzantine rites of initiation. The two traditions are similar in three ritual components: the consecration of chrism, anointing the neophytes with chrism after baptism, and the reception of Christians into the full communion of the church via anointing with chrism. While one could suggest that Byzantine chrismation is the Eastern equivalent of confirmation, I tend to agree with Johnson, who casts the equivalence of the two sacraments as spurious.[81] The Byzantine Rite lacks the second episcopal anointing and the theologically rich gesture of episcopal handlaying.

Given the theological capacity of a fully restored confirmation rite, I will assess the Roman situation with dispassion, but not

[81] Johnson, ""The Postchrismational Structure of Apostolic Tradition 21," n. 36, p. 31.

indifference. One of the greatest gifts modern and postmodern Western liturgists have bestowed upon Byzantine Rite communities is reverence for their fidelity to their native tradition.[82] So any assessment of the Roman tradition should begin with encouragement to Romans to be their best selves, and to be comfortable in their own skin.[83] In the following paragraphs, I comment on the Roman Catholic sacrament of confirmation in the spirit of an ecumenical gift exchange.

OPTIONS FOR RITES OF PASSAGE

My survey of Catholic confirmation revealed a collection of tensions. The tensions concern the place of confirmation in the sequence of the rites of initiation, the appropriate age for confirmation, and how the Triune God acts in confirmation and the other sacraments. In reflecting on how to assess the Roman situation, it seemed to be sensible to begin with the problem of the order of the rites of initiation, but the preeminence of adolescent confirmation in contemporary practice complicated the question for me. In my estimation, the popularity of adolescent confirmation and its vigorous defense by its proponents necessitated a more creative approach. This creative approach seeks to honor both history and the contemporary ministerial challenges posed to pastors and leaders. In other words, perhaps the Roman Church could propose a reconfiguration of confirmation that would acknowledge the history and sacramental integrity of confirmation in antiquity and the need to provide a meaningful rite of passage to children of varying ages.

I argued earlier that confirmation begins with the consecration of chrism, which occurs at the chrism Mass on Holy Thursday in the Roman Church. The chrism Mass begins the confirmation process as the church anticipates baptism at the Easter Vigil. The Eu-

---

[82] See John Baldovin, *Reforming the Liturgy: A Response to the Critics* (Collegeville, MN: Liturgical Press, 2008), 150.

[83] See Robert F. Taft, "Between Progress and Nostalgia: Liturgical Reform and the Western Romance with the Christian East; Strategies and Realities," in *A Living Tradition: On the Intersection of Liturgical History and Pastoral Practice; Essays in Honor of Maxwell E. Johnson*, ed. David Pitt, Stefanos Alexopoulos, and Christian McConnell (Collegeville, MN: Liturgical Press, 2012), 37–38.

charistic Assembly gathered for the chrism Mass petitions God to create the chrism needed for the anointing at the rites of initiation. Other oils are also blessed at this Mass, namely those for anointing the sick and the catechumens. The blessing of multiple oils for diverse pastoral needs reveals the church's recognition that anointing with oil can address multiple pastoral needs. If we attend only to the consecration of chrism, we see that chrism is used for several pastoral purposes, as illustrated by figure 4.1:

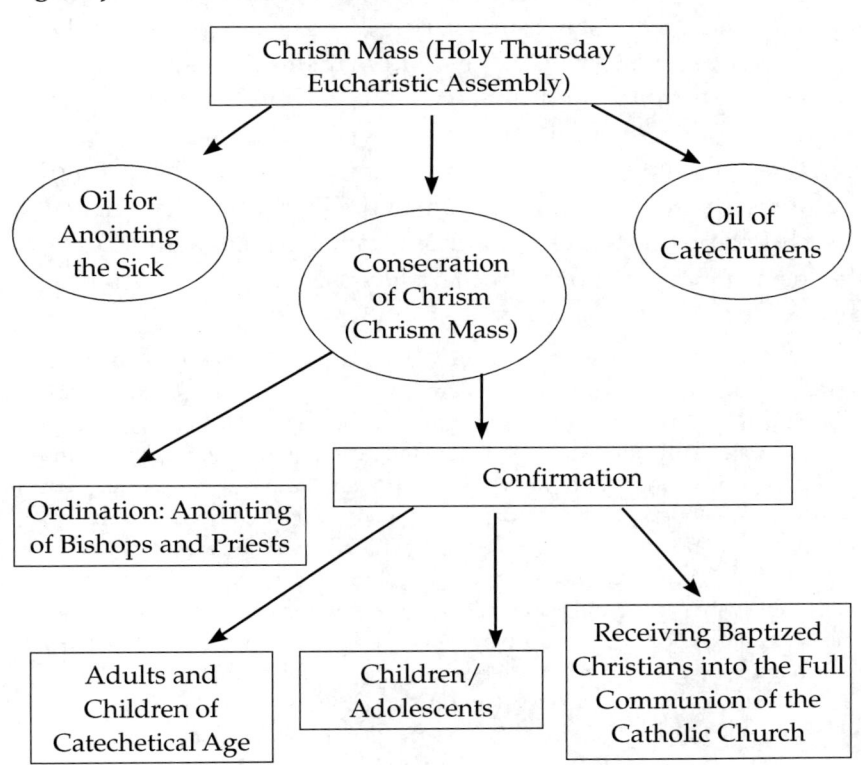

Figure 4.1: Chrism Mass and Chrism

```
                  Chrism Mass (Holy Thursday
                    Eucharistic Assembly)
         ↙                  ↓                    ↘
  Oil for                                              Oil of
  Anointing              Consecration              Catechumens
  the Sick                of Chrism
                         (Chrism Mass)
         ↙                  ↓
                        Confirmation
         ↙                  ↓                    ↘
  Ordination: Anointing                     Receiving Baptized
  of Bishops and Priests                    Christians into the Full
                                            Communion of the
    Adults and         Children/            Catholic Church
    Children of       Adolescents
  Catechetical Age
```

Figure 4.1 depicts how the Eucharistic Assembly petitions God to provide the oils that all contribute to the building up of the body of Christ in different ways. Each function of anointing serves a distinct ecclesiological purpose, where the assembled church attends to specifically defined groups within the body of Christ that warrant divine mercy—namely, catechumens, the sick, prospective neophytes, and candidates for the episcopacy and ordained priesthood.[84] The group of prospective neophytes is narrowly defined by differences in the rites used to receive them into the church: this group is segmented into adults and infants who are presented for baptism, baptized children and adolescents who are presented for confirmation, and Christians who are joining the Catholic Church.[85]

Perhaps the best point to be gleaned from this limited illustration is that the Eucharist serves as the source and origin of the rituals celebrated to create the oils, which are then used to attend to these groups. The consistent theological and liturgical dynamic occurs between the Eucharist and the church. The Eucharistic Assembly acknowledges the various stages of human life experienced by each of these groups, and creates a variety of oils that build them up for the purpose of full participation in the Eucharistic Assembly. The church provides anointing of the sick so that they would be strengthened to fully participate in the Eucharistic Assembly; the church provides oil for catechumens to be strengthened for baptism and entry into the Eucharistic Assembly; the church pro-

---

[84] See *Rites of Ordination of a Bishop, of Priests, and of Deacons*, 2nd typical ed. (Washington, DC: United States Conference of Catholic Bishops, 2000, 2002). The Roman rite performs an anointing with chrism at the ordinations of bishops and priests. Bishops are anointed on the head after the laying on of hands and prayer of ordination, followed by this prayer: "May God, who made you a sharer of the High priesthood of Christ, himself pour out upon you the oil of mystical anointing and make you fruitful with an abundance of spiritual blessings" (*Rites of Ordination*, no. 49, pp. 30–31). Priests are anointed on the hands after the laying on of hands and prayer of ordination, with the accompanying prayer: "The Lord Jesus Christ, whom the Father anointed with the Holy Spirit and power, guard and preserve you that you may sanctify the Christian people and offer sacrifice to God," in *Rites of Ordination*, no. 161 (p. 110). Also see James F. Puglisi, *The Process of Admission to Ordained Ministry*, vol. 1: *Epistemological Principles and Roman Catholic Rites* (Collegeville, MN: Liturgical Press, 1996), 155–57; and Susan K. Wood, *Sacramental Orders*, ed. John D. Laurance, Lex Orandi (Collegeville, MN: Liturgical Press, 200), 52–53, 106.

[85] A detailed analysis of the Catholic process for receiving Christians into the full communion of the Catholic Church is beyond the scope of this study. For the seminal history and theology of this work, see Turner, *When Other Christians Become Catholic*.

vides chrism to receive other baptized Christians into the full communion of the Catholic Church, ritually experienced, again, in the Eucharistic Assembly.

Confirmation complicates this illustration because it has become a sacramental end as opposed to a means. The top portion of figure 4.1 illustrates a Eucharistic Assembly building up groups of people who are either already in the assembly (the sick or candidates for the priesthood) or those on the periphery of the assembly seeking to join it (catechumens). The bottom portion, headed by the confirmation triangle, represents a tremendously diverse fragmentation of the church, including: unbaptized people of all ages; baptized and unconfirmed children and adolescents who participate in the Eucharistic Assembly; baptized, but non-Catholic, Christians. We are quite familiar with the cause of such a stratified ecclesial structure from our examination of confirmation's history, but perhaps a missing element in this discussion is, why does a sacrament of initiation serve so many purposes? I believe it is possible to reconstruct the model above by employing three principles gleaned from confirmation's structure: first, the source and origin of anointing with any oil is the Eucharistic Assembly; second, the purpose of anointing is to build up the body of Christ by attending to the needs of various parts of the body; and third, the practice of anointing has proved to be both elastic and preferential as an expression of belonging and adherence in rites of passages.

Figure 4.2 provides a reconfigured chrism Mass that accomplishes two pastoral objectives. First, it restores the natural process of initiation by providing the same rite to everyone who has just been baptized: confirmation, with the reminder that in the Roman tradition, the handlaying gesture deserves prominence alongside the anointing with chrism. This reconfiguration respects the solemnity and sacramentality of confirmation and prevents its dilution by renewing its consistency, since everyone who has been baptized will be immediately confirmed, regardless of his or her age. Restoring the original order of confirmation also illuminates the Eucharist as the source and summit for everyone who receives anointing with chrism. The Eucharist addresses the question of repeating the sacrament for strength because it occupies the position as the sacrament that is repeated (on a daily basis for some Catholics) imparting blessings to each participant.

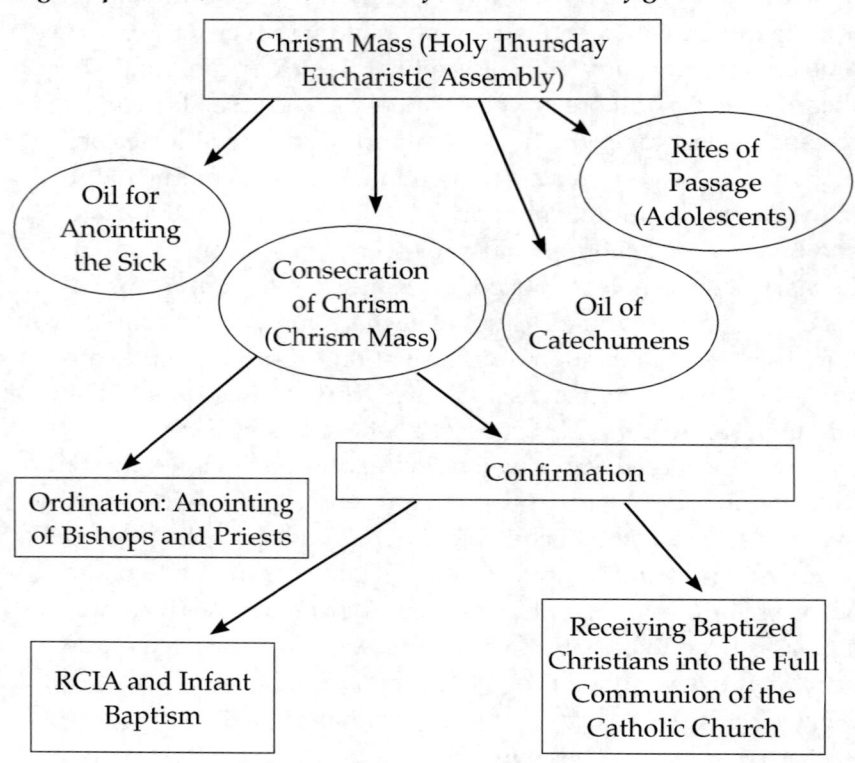

Figure 4.2: Oils, Chrism, and Confirmation Reconfigured

```
                    Chrism Mass (Holy Thursday
                      Eucharistic Assembly)
              ↙              ↓         ↘
    Oil for                              Rites of
    Anointing                            Passage
    the Sick      Consecration          (Adolescents)
                   of Chrism
                  (Chrism Mass)          Oil of
                                         Catechumens
              ↙              ↘
                          Confirmation
    Ordination: Anointing
    of Bishops and Priests
              ↙              ↘
                                    Receiving Baptized
    RCIA and Infant                 Christians into the Full
    Baptism                         Communion of the
                                    Catholic Church
```

This reconfiguration has the capacity to address the valid concerns of pastors and other church ministers who value confirmation as a rite of passage for children and adolescents. The setting aside of a new oil used for rites of passage, particularly for adolescents, acknowledges the church's concern for members of the body of Christ who are experiencing a particularly intense period of life involving transition. Dioceses and parishes could sustain their programs of religious education and ritualize the completion of this program with a ceremonial rite of passage including an anointing with oil. Such a rite coheres with Catholic liturgical tradition in many ways, especially since the church's setting aside of multiple oils for diverse needs represents its theological elasticity. Given the popularity of adolescent formation in contemporary Catholicism, creating a rite with anointing of oil ritualizing the process's completion contributes to the building up of the body of Christ. This reconfigured rite would no longer be confused with the imparting of the gift of the Holy Spirit, which adolescents would have received at baptism and confirmation, and receive anew each time they participate in the Eucharistic Assembly. An anointing with oil for a rite of passage in adolescence would detach from confirmation as an initiatory rite, because the process of strengthening during the course of a lifelong journey of faith need not be described as one of initiation, but one of sustaining.

My proposed reconfiguration of confirmation amidst a larger framework of processes involving anointing with oils is designed to create further discussion. As an Orthodox scholar observing an issue in Catholic sacramental theology, I am motivated by a desire to see Catholics be their best selves in the contemporary milieu, and I believe this proposal has the capacity to meet this need. This proposed model privileges a kind of eucharistic ecclesiology favored by Orthodox and admired by some Catholics.[86] Also, rituals of anointing with oil are rooted in liturgical history and seem to become easily adopted in rites of passage in both the Orthodox and Catholic traditions.[87] However, there may be better alternatives.

---

[86] The three classical works of Orthodox eucharistic ecclesiology are by Nicholas Afanasiev, *Trapeza Gospodnia* (Kiev: Khram Prepodobnogo Agapita Pecherskogo, 2003); Afanasiev, *The Church of the Holy Spirit*, ed. Michael Plekon, trans. Vitaly Permiakov (Notre Dame, IN: University of Notre Dame Press, 2007); and John Zizoulas, *Being as Communion: Studies in Personhood and the Church*, foreword by John Meyendorff (Crestwood, NY: St. Vladimir's Seminary Press, 1985; 2002 reprint). Also see Paul McPartlan, *Sacrament of Salvation: An Introduction to Eucharistic Ecclesiology* (Edinburgh: T & T Clark, 1995).

[87] An abundance of evidence supports this fact, particularly in the Orthodox tradition. I have surveyed and analyzed the preference for anointing with chrism as the method for receiving all converts in Orthodoxy in chapter 2 above. However, a similar tendency prevails in the mystery of the anointing of the sick. Many Orthodox parishes celebrate this sacrament on Holy Wednesday, where each participant is granted the forgiveness of sins. The history of the emergence of this parish celebration in Orthodox has largely eluded

Paul Turner offers some possibilities in his book: "Opportunities for ritual commitment already abound: the renewal of baptismal promises at Easter, Liturgies of the Word, celebrations of penance in its many forms, blessings, and popular devotions."[88] The search for a meaningful rite of passage is not difficult for Byzantine Rite Christians, as countless variants of the *molieben* (literally "prayer service") cover every imaginable occasion in life, from inaugurating a major event to celebrating wedding anniversaries. Ultimately, only faithful Roman Catholics can affirm that a particular rite adequately lifts up and offers a particular event in life to God in a spirit of thanksgiving.

EXPLORING PNEUMATOLOGY IN CATHOLIC LITURGY

The reconfiguration of confirmation is not complete with the creation of a separate rite of anointing for adolescents who have completed a religious education program. Veterans of a contemporary adolescent confirmation might protest that the completion of the program, ritualized by confirmation, is a pneumatic moment warranting sacramental status.[89] In this survey, it appears that the Roman Church has succeeded in heightening the pneumatic quality of confirmation as the sacrament of the Holy Spirit, and I suggested that one of the consequences of this reform is that confirmation is now construed as the only sacrament in which one receives the unique gift of the Holy Spirit. I also hypothesized that the tendency in Catholic sacramental theology to identify a particular ritual action as denoting a moment of consecration embellishes the sense that confirmation is the sacrament of Pentecost. The implications of identifying confirmation as the sacrament of the Holy Spirit are serious. Such a pneumatic investment in con-

---

scholars to this point, but it is likely a consequence of the decay of annual sacramental penance among many Orthodox populations in the world. That such communities found the sacrament of anointing to be a suitable replacement for penance is a phenomenon worthy of further study and analysis. For Catholics, that confirmation emerged as an enthusiastic suitor for the rite of passage into adolescence is telling. It appears that the ritual of anointing with oil or chrism conveys a sacramental sense of belonging, return, and reconciliation.

[88] Turner, *Confirmation*, 118.
[89] Ibid.

firmation fuels the debate on one's readiness to receive it. If this is the singular ritual at which one receives the Spirit, shouldn't one's preparation be thorough and foolproof?[90]

The tendency for some Catholics to allow confirmation to be repeated as a sacrament of commitment is informative on how participants perceive the imparting of the gift of the Holy Spirit.[91] A rigorous process of forming, shaping, and rehearsing commitment that is solemnly ritualized by the anointing with chrism is, indeed, meaningful. As an Orthodox Christian, I am struck by the sharp contrast between this perception of confirmation and Roman Catholic eucharistic piety. Roman Catholics differ significantly from Orthodox in the frequency with which they celebrate Mass. In Catholic practice, the Eucharist is the repeated sacrament *par excellence*, with many Catholics throughout the world attending Mass and receiving Holy Communion daily.[92] I would expect a sense of receiving the Holy Spirit to be organically emanating from frequent eucharistic participation.

The situation among Byzantine Rite communities is quite different. Even small Byzantine Rite communities are at least vaguely familiar with the structures of the liturgy of the Hours, especially Vespers and Orthros, and other liturgical offices.[93] A typical Byzantine Rite parish celebrates Eucharist once a week, on Sunday

---

[90] Liam Walsh appears to imply such readiness as a prerequisite: "what confirmation sacramentalizes is the coming of age of the history of salvation, the arrival of the age of grace, with the gift of the Pentecostal spirit, rather than the becoming adult of individual Christians. However, it is true that the kind of behavior proper to the adult age of grace can normally be exercised only by adults. On that ground one can make a theological case for delaying confirmation until children are entering adult age. There can be a real gain in doing so." Walsh, *Sacraments of Initiation*, 211.

[91] Turner, *Confirmation*, 127–29.

[92] A former undergraduate student of mine from the Catholic University of America in Washington, DC, informed me that he would not have the spiritual strength to endure a whole week without receiving Holy Communion each day.

[93] In Orthodox liturgical piety, the *panikhida*, a non-eucharistic requiem for the dead, is the most popular liturgical service. See Alexander Schmemann, *Introduction to Liturgical Theology*, trans. Asheleigh E. Moorhouse (Crestwood, NY: St. Vladimir's Seminary Press, 1986), 36.

mornings. But Byzantine Rite Christians seem to have acquired a strong awareness of receiving the Holy Spirit in the course of the Eucharistic Liturgy. The Byzantine Eucharistic Liturgy has a reputation for being pneumatically rich, with several epicleses occurring during the course of a single liturgy.[94] In addition to the invocation for the Holy Spirit to sanctify the gifts and people in the anaphoras of Basil and John Chrysostom, the liturgy has other pneumatic episodes. The contemporary versions of the anaphoras of Basil and John Chrysostom request that God grant communicants the "communion of the Holy Spirit," a phrase taken from the beginning of each anaphora that quotes St. Paul ("The grace of our Lord Jesus Christ, the love of God the Father, and the communion of the Holy Spirit be with you all," 2 Cor 13:14).[95] This phrase appears again in the synapte immediately preceding the Lord's Prayer before Holy Communion, as the deacon leads the people in petitioning God to grant to them "the communion of the Holy Spirit," a petition repeated in the collect preceding the Lord's Prayer.[96] Two of these episodes occur during the commixture of the consecrated bread and wine in the chalice. When the presider places the consecrated bread into the chalice of mixed wine and water, he exclaims, "the fullness of the Holy Spirit."[97] Then, in a gesture called the *Zeon*, the deacon pours hot water into the chalice and exclaims, "the warmth of faith, filled with the Holy Spirit."[98] These gestures have a rich and complicated ritual and mystagogical history, and they testify to multiple pneumatic moments associated with the preparation, distribution

---

[94] Boris Bobrinskoy attests to the numerous epicleses in the Byzantine Eucharistic Liturgy in *The Mystery of the Trinity: Trinitarian Experience and Vision in the Biblical and Patristic Tradition*, trans. Anthony P. Gythiel (Crestwood, NY: St. Vladimir's Seminary Press, 1999), 191.

[95] For the contemporary texts, see "The Divine Liturgy of St. Basil the Great" and "The Divine Liturgy of St. John Chrysostomos" at the Greek Orthodox Archdiocese of America website, accessed June 26, 2013, http://www.goarch.org/chapel/liturgical_texts.

[96] For the history and theology of these petitions, see Robert F. Taft, *A History of the Liturgy of St. John Chrysostom*, Vol. 5: *The Precommunion Rites*, Orientalia christiana analecta 261 (Rome: Pontifical Oriental Institute, 2000), 83–128.

[97] Ibid., 381–439.

[98] Ibid., 441–526.

and reception of Holy Communion in the Byzantine Eucharistic Liturgy. Furthermore, the first hymn sung during the elongated post-Communion dismissal of the liturgy is taken directly from the festal hymnography of the Pentecost feast, "We have seen the true light! We have received the heavenly Spirit!" Regardless of its history, the Byzantine liturgy clearly communicates a pneumatically rich environment, one from which even the most casual observer can attest to the reception of the gift of the Spirit via participation.

Given that Roman Catholic liturgical piety heavily emphasizes frequent participation in the Eucharist, a deeper exploration of the pneumatic gifts imparted through the Eucharist can clarify the meaning of confirmation for Catholics. Catholics receive the gift of the Spirit at each Eucharist, and the blessings imparted by the Spirit cohere with those of confirmation: building up the body of Christ, going out as missionaries into the world, and receiving spiritual strength all occur at the Eucharist.[99] The common recitation of the Nicene-Constantinopolitan Creed at Mass functions as the repeatable renewing of baptismal vows, one each Catholic regularly rehearses. The Eucharist, then, is the source of life in the Spirit, where God imparts the divine gifts anew to the assembly of the holy people of God, and in practice, it is the repeatable and repeated sacrament. The original sequence of the order of rites of initiation renders this solution sensible. Once God freely blesses the neophyte with spiritual gifts, he or she regularly receives the blessings anew in the Eucharistic Assembly. The gifts are imparted to capacitate the participant to become a eucharistic being, which is why they are unrepeatable—God gives them only once because they do not die, they can only be ignored by the participant.

---

[99] Numerous studies explore the reinvigoration of pneumatology in the Catholic celebration of the Eucharist. Two of the best resources are Jerome Hall, *We Have the Mind of Christ: The Holy Spirit and Liturgical Memory in the Thought of Edward J. Kilmartin* (Collegeville, MN: Liturgical Press, 2001); and Kevin W. Irwin, *Models of the Eucharist* (Mahwah, NJ: Paulist Press, 2005), esp. Model no. 10, the Eucharist as the work of the Holy Spirit, 263–89. Also see Paul Bradshaw, "The Rediscovery of the Holy Spirit in Modern Eucharistic Theology and Practice," in *The Spirit in Worship—Worship in the Spirit*, eds. Teresa Berger and Bryan Spinks (Collegeville, MN: Liturgical Press, 2009), 79–98.

From a certain perspective, this emphasis on the Eucharist as the culmination of the rites of initiation for Catholics is not at all original; it is, in fact, an oft-repeated refrain. What I believe is original in this proposal is the juxtapositioning of confirmation as a pneumatically rich but unrepeatable sacrament to the Eucharist, another pneumatically rich but repeatable sacrament. The Roman Mass has its own native lexicon and gestures communicating the giving of the Spirit, and it is not its content that is so different from its Byzantine cousin, but rather the frequency and emphasis of explicating the giving of the Spirit. For Catholics, a deeper exploration of the Eucharist and its blessings might yield a sacramental pneumatology that has the capacity to clarify the relationship between confirmation and Eucharist. The core of this dynamic relationship is that God imparts the Holy Spirit and grants the neophyte entry into the Eucharistic Assembly as a citizen of God's kingdom. The neophyte continues to freely receive the gift of the Spirit who nourishes her through the course of her Christian journey and vocation at each Eucharistic Assembly. The Catholic's desire to continually receive the Spirit is, in fact, satiated at each Eucharist. Perhaps a more concentrated exploration of the pneumatic element of the Eucharist, not only in catechesis but also in euchology and ritual gesture, might elucidate the outpouring of the Spirit in the Mass to Catholics.

ACCEPTING THE CHURCH AS AN ICON OF THE KINGDOM

This proposal leads us to the final point, the question of the appropriate age for confirmation. Those who sympathize with my proposal must note that infants are by definition confirmed. This final section will attempt to engage the question of age by demonstrating how confirmation is an essential sacrament that builds up the church by making God's Spirit available to everyone.

I will begin by briefly repeating a personal anecdote to set the stage for addressing the issue of the appropriate age of confirmation. In 2011, a member of the Christian initiation seminar of the North American Academy of Liturgy meeting expressed pastoral frustration over the difficulty in retaining young people who have completed confirmation programs. Many members of the seminar shared his angst, which generated a discussion on the lessons of liturgical history. These lessons ultimately pointed to the Byzantine practice of immediately chrismating infants as a possible model for the West, but the frustrated pastor finished the session by asking me a sober question: if chrismating infants is the ideal model for the sequence of initiatory rites, shouldn't the churches of the Byzantine Rite be filled with people who have grown in the image and likeness of God since infancy? The most direct response to his query is that the Byzantine Rite churches face the same challenges of retention that frustrate our friends in the Roman and Reformed traditions. However, in this section I propose that the Roman Church should restore its ancient practice of confirming infants for *theological* reasons.

While this survey has established the justification for delaying confirmation until the age of reason (at minimum), two issues stand out. First, the proponents of adolescent confirmation argue that confirmation effectively ritualizes and sacramentalizes the adolescent passage into maturity and thus fulfills a real pastoral need. I attempted to address this issue above by proposing the creation of a new rite containing an anointing with blessed oil for adolescents. The other argument concerns catechesis and maturity: given the sobriety needed for navigating the Christian life, how can a young child voluntarily promise to live in accordance with her baptism and then fulfill that promise? It seems reasonable to catechize children so that they are capable of "assuming the apostolic responsibilities of Christian life."[100] The Catechism of the Catholic Church establishes that confirmation can be granted to children who have been adequately catechized by distinguishing between "adult faith" and "the adult age of natural growth."[101] The rite of confirmation states that "those possessing the use of reason must be in a state of grace, properly instructed, and capable of renewing the baptismal promises."[102] The prevailing idea is that the child has attained an age where she can voluntarily proclaim her baptismal

---

[100] *Catechism of the Catholic Church* (CCC), 2nd ed. (Rome: Libreria Editrice Vaticana, 1994, 1997), no. 1309.

[101] Ibid., no. 1308.

[102] "Introduction to the Rite of Confirmation," no. 12, in *The Rites*, 483.

promises and then daily live them. Both the Catechism and the rite of confirmation permit the confirmation of infants as an exception, if the danger of death is present.[103]

The Byzantine Church's practice of chrismating infants stands in contradistinction to the practice of the Roman Church. Infants receive the postbaptismal anointing with chrism as part of the rite of baptism, followed immediately by Holy Communion. The anointing with chrism occurs as an important component that seamlessly follows the order of baptism, as demonstrated by the presentation of the Euchologion in chapter 1 above. The difference between the two rites results in a set of two parallel pastoral and theological implications. Pastorally, most Roman Catholic children participate in a religious education program preparing them for First Communion and then confirmation. Children will be baptized as infants, receive instruction, receive the sacrament of penance, partake of First Communion, receive additional instruction, and then receive confirmation. Most children will actively proclaim their baptismal promises at confirmation and will remember the experiences of penance, communion, and confirmation. Children of the Byzantine Rite will typically receive baptism, chrismation, and Eucharist as infants.[104] Children will receive the sacrament of penance around the age of seven, though there is no official designation for this age. As a rule, children will not remember the events of baptism, chrismation, and Eucharist, though children will be full liturgical participants beginning with their baptism.

The theological differences between the Roman and Byzantine sequence of initiatory rites are stark in contrast. Roman Catholic children receive cleansing from original sin and are initiated into the holy people of God with the presbyteral postbaptismal cleans-

---

[103] CCC, no. 1307; "Introduction to the Rite of Confirmation," no. 11, in *The Rites*, 483.

[104] Most children will receive their First Communion at the next celebration of the Eucharistic Liturgy. Occasionally, children are baptized as part of a baptismal liturgy fused together with the Sunday Eucharist. For more on the contemporary restoration of this ancient Constantinopolitan practice, see Mark Morozowich, "Liturgical Changes in Russia and the Christian East? A Case Study: The Mysteries (Sacraments) of Initiation with the Eucharistic Liturgy," *Worship* 83 (2009): 30–47.

ing. They receive the Holy Spirit in baptism, and again upon becoming frequent communicants in the Eucharistic Liturgy. Children then receive the particular gift of the Spirit equipping them for mission through confirmation. Perhaps most significant is that the Spirit is imparted to children once they have completed the requirements of their religious education program: again, the Spirit is given as a ritual of completion. Conversely, children in the Byzantine Rite receive the full gift of the Spirit from the very beginning. Absent from a typical Byzantine process is a sense of completing a program and receiving the gift of the Spirit. In short, for the Byzantine Church, the Spirit is given at the very beginning of the process; for the Roman Church, the Spirit is given at the end of the process.

Many difficult adjustments would inevitably result from a hypothetical restoration of Roman confirmation to the original sequence of initiatory rites. Several generations of people who had experienced the process of adolescent confirmation would have to receive and affirm the new order. Religious education programs and content would need fine-tuning. The cognitive priority that shapes contemporary confirmation would be diminished. The salient theologies of maturity and mission that accompany adolescent confirmation would become secondary or even tertiary to an ancient, but largely unknown theological cornerstone of the sacrament. Canonically, the Roman See would have to implement yet another adaptation of the rite by permanently granting presbyters the authority to impart confirmation.[105] However, I believe that this restoration would be manifest as a blessing and assist in recovering the Roman Church's theology of confirmation, for reasons I will briefly explain below.

INFANT CONFIRMATION IS THE AUTHENTIC ROMAN TRADITION

Liturgical historians who specialize in Roman liturgy have established that infants received confirmation for over one thousand years in the history of the Catholic Church.[106] Our historical

---

[105] Skeptics might view this as yet another unnecessary Byzantinization of the Roman liturgy.

[106] For example, see Austin, *Anointing with the Spirit: The Rite of Confirmation*, 145–46.

survey presents the specific causes of confirmation's separation from baptism and the theologies that emerged alongside the innovative practice of delaying confirmation. Restoring confirmation to its native position in the order of initiatory rites would not be an innovation, but a pastoral reform that reinvigorates the authentic Roman Catholic tradition. Most important, implementing this renewed model would clearly show how each sacrament shapes the life of a Catholic Christian from its beginning.[107]

THE HOLY SPIRIT IS GIVEN FREELY

One of the difficulties in the current order of Catholic rites is the notion that the Holy Spirit can be earned by completing a religious education program. Above, I discussed how Catholics constantly receive the gift of the Holy Spirit anew by frequently participating in the Eucharist. Catholic theology has always privileged God's gratuity in pouring out blessings and gifts to the church. Pastors have traditionally navigated the tension between approaching such gifts without sufficient preparation and freely receiving them by providing pastoral instruction that coaches participants through a process. The discovery and reinvigoration of the fourth-century mystagogical tradition through the RCIA demonstrates the Catholic value for adequate preparation. However, the practice of delaying the imparting of the gift of the Spirit until children have demonstrated sufficient readiness to receive the Spirit violates the spirit of divine gratuity. No canonical decree can impede God from acting, and older children who partake of the Eucharist before they are confirmed are already receiving the gift of the Spirit. Church leaders are responsible for developing programmatic materials that sufficiently equip people to navigate Christian life.

Here is an opportunity for the Byzantines to share a vision of full participation for everyone who engages the liturgy, regardless of age, gender, or ethnicity. From the Byzantine perspective, each person is granted access to the fullness of divine life, through the mediation of the Holy Spirit, by receiving the gift of the Spirit as infants. When infants receive the gift of the Spirit, they have the

---

[107] For a Catholic perspective favoring this restoration, see Austin, *Anointing with the Spirit: The Rite of Confirmation*, 125–46.

capacity to grow into the holy people defined by the church's euchology: to paraphrase the Roman Catholic consecration of chrism, infants now have the capacity to become "priests and kings, prophets and martyrs."[108] Infants' initiation is like everyone else's: they participate fully in the church's liturgy, and by definition, in the life of the Triune God. This participation regularly introduces them to who they might become: holy people. The assumption is that regular liturgical participation will shape and form the infant into a holy person, with the process of imprinting in progress from infancy. The infant participates in a Eucharistic Assembly and hears the word of God, praises God, professes faith in God, and receives God's gift. James Purves, in presenting the pneumatology of Irenaeus of Lyons, describes the process of growing into God's likeness through the gift of the Spirit as "becomingness."[109] For the Byzantines, "becomingness" begins at infancy and thus encompasses the entire human life.

The capacity of infants not only to participate but also to receive the blessings of liturgical engagement is well established in Catholic sacramental theology. Mark Searle underscores the ecclesiological significance of an environment of faith in infant baptism:[110]

> This grace, this gift of faith, comes through hearing, through the Word of God addressed to the child. But the Word here is not the written Word, as yet unavailable to the infant, so much as the biblical *dabar*, the revelatory and salvific event of God's presence, mediated in this instance by the community of faith and especially the believing family. Thus it is not so much that baptism infuses faith into a child as that baptism is the deliberate and conscious insertion of the child into the environment of faith, which faith is the faith of the Church, which in turn is the faith of Christ himself.

---

[108] *The Rites*, vol. 2 (Collegeville, MN: Liturgical Press, 1991), 336.

[109] James Purves, "The Spirit and the Imago Dei: Reviewing the Anthropology of Irenaeus of Lyons," *Evangelical Quarterly* 68 (1996): 99–120.

[110] Mark Searle, "Infant Baptism Reconsidered," in *Alternative Futures for Worship*, Vol. 2: *Baptism and Confirmation*, ed. Mark Searle (Collegeville, MN: Liturgical Press, 1987), 43.

The ecclesial environment of faith is what shapes the faith of the participant. Searle punctuates his baptismal ecclesiology by emphasizing the sacramentality of the family's commitment in infant baptism, which he describes as "a domestic household of faith within the communion of the local assembly."[111] In other words, Searle views the family as an icon of the church, and the infant's belonging to the family allows her to participate fully in church through the mediation of family. In a recent interdisciplinary analysis of infant baptism, Kimberly Belcher demonstrates the infant's capacity to engage symbols and participate fully in the liturgy.[112] The benefit of such participation is initiation into the life of the Triune God through ecclesial mediation.

Searle and Belcher developed their arguments to demonstrate the theological potency of infant baptism. I suggest that this train of thought bolsters the argument in favor of confirming infants as part of a single initiatory rite because the infant is defined as a full liturgical participant. Searle's description of an environment of faith that shapes and forms participants is valid, but it does not only shape infants—in fact, the process of shaping and forming is circular, transcending divisions of gender, ethnicity, and age.[113] In other words, the church's adults need to engage the participation of infants to enter more deeply into the mystery of divine-human communion imparted through the sacraments of initiation. The alternative is a fragmented church rooted in an intellectually elite cohort, a model of church that has no footing in Christian tradition. Granted, the environment of faith is also one of failure and deficiency. Infants will also learn disappointment and find that many adults, if not most, provide inadequate modeling of the Christian life, not to mention deficient explanations of faith. But this is exactly why infants should be fully initiated into the church from

---

[111] Ibid., 48.

[112] Kimberly Belcher, *Efficacious Engagement: Sacramental Participation in the Trinitarian Mystery* (Collegeville, MN: Liturgical Press, 2011).

[113] Searle suggests that the Church gains a type of self-understanding by participating in infant baptism in "Infant Baptism Reconsidered," *Alternative Futures for Worship*, Vol. 2: *Baptism and Confirmation*, ed. Mark Searle (Collegeville, MN: Liturgical Press, 1987), 49.

the beginning. The infant is an icon of both human limitation and potential. No Christian can see her as deficient because the infant is a complete human being. However imperfect her faith, she joins the church in professing the Catholic faith, alongside men, women, and children of varying intellectual and motor capacities. Affirming infant confirmation likewise acknowledges the gift of the Spirit God freely grants to people with mental disabilities who may never completely understand every detail of faith, but are essential organs of a vibrant ecclesial organism.

A ROMAN GIFT TO THE BYZANTINE RITE

After a lengthy exposition on what the Byzantine Rite can contribute to the Roman tradition, we now turn to the Roman gift to the Byzantines. The treasures of Roman confirmation are apparent in the unicity of the history and theology of Roman confirmation. Here are some staples of Roman confirmation that have the capacity to enrich the Byzantine perspective.

The Bishop and the Handlaying Gesture

The Roman rite of confirmation contains an ecclesiological tradition unique to its heritage and history. Among the most notable differences between the two rites are two elements: the handlaying gesture and the designation of the sacrament as episcopal. The handlaying gesture has not remained unnoticed by Orthodox theologians: Nicholas Afanasiev speculated that the Byzantines once also employed the laying on of hands, and states that a reference to the imposition of God's hand in the ablution rite on the eighth day is a vestige of this gesture.[114] Afanasiev's point is well taken: the episcopal handlaying contains an ecclesiological significance from which Byzantine Rite Christians can learn. The rite expresses a sense of being church in its fullness that the Byzantine Rite cannot quite capture. The Catholic and Eastern Orthodox Churches have much in common, particularly in the areas of ecclesiology and sacramental theology. Both churches are conciliar and hierarchical,

---

[114] Afanasiev, *The Church of the Holy Spirit*, 26. Macarius's hagiopolite Letter to the Armenians mentions the handlaying gesture, a potential antecedent for the Byzantine Rite.

ecclesiological tenets grounded by the apostles and sacraments. The role of the bishop in Roman confirmation brings the bishop into intimate contact with the laity of the diocese. Confirmands gain a sense of how the church works, and families who participate in the sacrament experience the hierarchical structure of the church.

It's absolutely true that the reconfiguration of confirmation I proposed for Catholics above would diminish the role of the bishop. There is another layer of ritual celebration in confirmation that purely preserves the role of the local bishop, though, and that is the annual celebration of the chrism Mass on Holy Thursday. Orthodox also consecrate chrism on Holy Thursday, but the ecclesiological motif expressed by the Orthodox celebration of this rite is complex, at best. First, the Orthodox schedule the rite only when a need for additional chrism is ascertained, which hardly expresses confidence in the missionary imperative of the church. Second, the rite privileges the Orthodox ecclesiological notion of synodality, as only the first hierarch of an autocephalous church can preside at the rite. The Catholic celebration of an annual chrism Mass in the diocesan cathedral accentuates the potency of sacramental celebration in what Catholics define as the local church. In an unlikely reversal of roles, the Roman tradition of consecrating chrism more effectively promotes an ecclesiology of a local church than that of Orthodoxy. In this vein, contemporary Orthodoxy could learn from Catholics how to promote a potent baptismal ecclesiology and missiology by adopting the Roman model for consecrating chrism. Orthodox can also attain a stronger admiration for the Catholic tradition of episcopal handlaying as conveying a liturgically robust notion of ritualizing belonging in the dual covenant of community and God.

Deepening Faith and Commitment

From the late medieval period until now, Roman confirmation was customarily delayed, which differentiated it from the Byzantine practice. With the confirmation of children and adolescents established as a norm, Catholics developed a sense of commitment in preparing for and celebrating the sacrament. Above, I argued that Catholics should restore the original sequence of sacraments and confirm infants. When communities implement reforms, it is tempting to dispose of many good things along the way, believing that they will now be useless in the new model. The process of confirmation has traditionally valued the process of developing faith and rehearsing commitment by seriously attending to the educational needs of younger people. In so doing, the Roman tradition has illuminated the dynamic of ecclesial faith expressed in the sacraments. Maintaining the proper balance between terse, objective expressions of faith in the liturgy and the more elaborate examinations of specific aspects of doctrine in religious education is a challenging task. Promoting faith in dialogue with the liturgy always carries the risk of imposing particular theologumena on the liturgy, or conversely, completely ignoring elaboration of faith by referring to the liturgy as its only source of expression. Pastoral finesse is needed to promote effective learning through the liturgy, and avoid turning a process of growth into a study course.[115]

Catholics are still negotiating the challenge of promoting faith through and in the liturgy, and confirmation manifests the process's benefits and difficulties. The Romans offer a commitment to a process of deepening faith and commitment in confirmation to communities of the Byzantine Rite. Byzantine communities do not need to concern themselves with reforming chrismation so that it becomes a catechetical moment. The Byzantine synergy of euchology, architecture, the liturgical arts, and ritual gesture communicates a theology of belonging to participants. What is often absent from Byzantine Rite communities is a program of religious education that effectively communicates to people how the sacraments enable participants to enter the process of *theosis* through sacramental celebration. Models for such programs exist, and I have often observed parish clergy using an English translation of a mystagogical text (such as St. Cyril of Jerusalem's *Mystagogical Catecheses*) as a way to demonstrate to the parish the relevance of liturgical celebration to Christian life. Perhaps the best such model is the more elaborate

---

[115] See Ron Lewinski, "A Pioneer and Pastor: Reflections on the Pastoral Implementation of the RCIA," in *The Impact of the RCIA: Stories, Reflections, Challenges*, ed. Jerry Galipeau (Franklin Park, IL: World Library Publications, 2008), 24–27.

discourse on the sacraments written by Nicholas Cabasilas in the fourteenth century, a mystagogical treatise accessible to contemporary laity.[116] Unfortunately, there is no real verifiable consistency among Byzantine Rite churches in committing to introducing the laity to the potency of the sacraments. The Roman tradition of aligning catechesis with liturgy can contribute to a renewed mystagogy within contemporary Byzantine Rite churches. In the same vein, a commitment to authentic and sustained postbaptismal mystagogy would greatly benefit the Roman Church, were she to embrace the proposal for a reconfigured sequence of initiatory rites.

Ecumenical Sensitivity in Receiving Other Christians

The process for receiving other Christians into the communion of the Catholic Church was inspired by the ecumenical movement. Turner's study indicates that the authors of the reformed rite wanted to abandon the antiquated and negative language of heresy and schism in shaping a new process for joining the Catholic Church. Turner also acknowledges that many problems remain, especially the popular practice of receiving other Christians at the Easter Vigil, which blurs the distinction between catechumens and candidates.[117] Turner's study affirms the progress represented by the reformed rite, and expresses hope that progress might continue.

The Orthodox Church's rites of reception are similar to the Roman practice, especially in identifying anointing with chrism as a ritual expressing belonging and adhesion to a community. Given that the faithful of both churches recognize the ritual act of anointing with chrism as expressing a profound passage from one ecclesial body to another, there is no reason to adopt a new practice. However, the Catholic rite of reception is grounded in an ecumenical sensitivity freed from the polemics of antiquity that could enrich the Orthodox practice. For example, Orthodox Christians are not anointed with chrism when they become Catholic.[118] Since the

---

[116] See Nicholas Denysenko, "*The Life in Christ* by Nicholas Cabasilas," 242–60.

[117] Turner, *When Other Christians Become Catholic*, 167.

[118] Orthodox automatically become Eastern Catholic, a canonical act that deserves careful ecumenical study.

majority of Orthodox Christians recognize Roman Catholic baptism, Orthodox should receive Roman Catholics who have received anointing with holy chrism by admitting them to eucharistic communion. There is no need for the Orthodox Church to repeat an unrepeatable act of God, since baptized Catholics have been anointed with holy chrism. A universal Orthodox adoption of this practice would verify the important ecumenical progress accomplished in Orthodox-Catholic interfaith dialogue. Furthermore, the adoption of such a practice should reinvigorate ecumenical discourse on the final step: the removal of obstacles toward full eucharistic communion.

An important derivative of adopting this practice is the abandonment of antiquated language. The Catholic rite of reception correctly distinguishes the process of conversion to Christianity from moving from one ecclesial body into the Roman Catholic communion. This is why Christians who become Catholic are candidates, not catechumens. The word "catechumen" should be restored to its proper provenance: that of preparation for baptism, not for joining a particular ecclesial community. Progress in this area is sure to be slow; Turner acknowledges that the word "convert" as applied to Catholics who used to belong to other Christian communities remains popular in Catholic parish life. The same applies to Orthodox Church life, but distinguishing conversion from a journey to a new community would be a healthy pastoral initiative for Orthodox, who would then affirm the goodness of the candidate's native church home. Such a shift would also give credibility to Orthodox participation in ecumenical discourse.

CONCLUSION

This chapter has explored the Roman Catholic rite of confirmation and identified the chief theological questions surrounding its future. My review of the Catholic rite of confirmation was essentially a survey, and I urge readers to engage the history of confirmation through the historical and theological studies of Maxwell Johnson, Aidan Kavanagh, Gerard Austin, and Paul Turner. This chapter focused on three primary issues impacting Catholic sacramental theology: confirmation's place in the sequence of the rites of initiation; pneumatology in the reformed rites of Catholic confirmation; and the question of the appropriate age of confirmation. My chapter proposes that examining confirmation in the context of the entire ritual process helps one see that the source and origin of the sacrament is the Eucharistic Assembly. I suggest that a new rite of anointing with holy oil blessed and set aside during the chrism Mass for adolescents would allow a reconfiguration of confirmation, with everyone being confirmed immediately after baptism—children and adults of all ages. I proposed that this reconfiguration would clarify the proper place of the Eucharist not only in the rites of initiation, but also as the proper sacrament of spiritual and baptismal renewal in the daily lives of Catholics. I suggested that this reconfiguration might motivate Catholics to thoroughly explore the Eucharist as the Catholic sacrament that creates communion of the Holy Spirit. I asserted that infant confirmation would not only restore the traditional order of confirmation in the sequence of initiatory rites, but also illuminate the church as an environment where all people contribute to a mutual sharing of faith formation. Finally, I suggested that the Roman tradition of confirmation could enrich the Byzantine Church in two ways: by promoting a healthy hierarchical ecclesiology through learning about the episcopal handlaying and adopting the Roman pattern of the chrism Mass, and by retrieving the Roman commitment to dialogue between catechesis and liturgy in the contemporary confirmation process.

My reflection is offered in the spirit of ecumenical gift exchange, and I believe that its greatest potential lies in its capacity to reveal the church as an icon of the kingdom, God's sacred space that has a place for everyone to enjoy the divine community as the holy people of God.

Conclusion

In conclusion, I would like to reflect on four elements of this study. First, I will briefly review the main contributions of this study. Second, I will identify items emerging from this study of chrismation that would benefit from further academic exploration. Third, I will delineate specific pastoral recommendations for the Orthodox celebration of chrismation. Then, I will conclude by reflecting on the goal I iterated at the beginning of this study, that Christians who value chrismation would receive it as a sacrament that produces divine energy in the liturgical assembly, an energy one can perceive even in an empty church building.

CHRISMATION IN THE BYZANTINE ORTHODOX TRADITION

The primary goal of this study was to glean the theology of chrismation as it is practiced by Christians of the Byzantine Rite. The ritual celebration of chrismation is manifold: its native home is in baptism, and its position in the context of the rites of baptism has moved in history. The contemporary postbaptismal anointing with chrism is typically described as one of the seven sacraments, but this study demonstrates that chrismation cannot be interpreted in isolation from baptism or Eucharist. The Byzantine practice of consecrating chrism as part of the Vesperal Liturgy of Holy Thursday shows that chrism originates in the Eucharistic Assembly, which petitions God to bless it for people who will be baptized. The prayer recited for the consecration of chrism is a precious source of its theology. It asks God to bless the chrism, and to make those who will be anointed with it into his holy people who are freed from sin and live in communion with the Triune God, with Christ dwelling in their hearts.

The study of the actual anointing with chrism in the sequence of the order of baptism confirms that chrismation belongs to a unified rite of initiation beginning with baptism and concluding with the Eucharist. The rubrics of chrismation do not identify it as separate from baptism, and it occurs as a natural component of initiation in the sequence of ritual events and prayers. The historical development of texts accompanying the anointing with chrism evidences an attempt to express the theology of a ritual gesture. The theology of anointing is described as a protection against temptation that imparts the gift of sanctification to the participant. If one could summarize the meaning of chrismation in one short phrase, it could be this: chrismation equips the neophyte to *become holy*. The larger purpose of becoming holy must also be noted: God capacitates the participant to become holy so that the Christian, who now belongs to the communion of the Triune God, would introduce and share God's community with the world. God's sanctification is not merely anthropological, but also cosmological: the entire universe is filled with God's glory when Christians joyfully serve the world and seek to build it up into an icon of the kingdom.

Chrismation is also the rite used for receiving other Christians into the communion of the Orthodox Church. This study shows how chrismation as a rite of reception has been fine tuned to correspond to the context of entering the Orthodox communion. More noteworthy is how those who have entered Orthodoxy via chrismation have described the process. Preparing to become Orthodox is a matter of not only heart and spirit but also one of mind. The liturgical rite of chrismation accentuates the cognitive dimension, where the participant not only learns but rehearses the faith of the community she hopes to join. A selective reading of Orthodox people who were previously baptized in a different Christian community confirms the rite of reception via chrismation as largely cognitive. My examination of this section defines the anointing of chrism as sealing the new Orthodox Christian in the twofold covenant in the Triune God and local community. Those who have entered the Orthodox communion renew their covenant of belonging to God, and live this covenant within the human community of the Orthodox Church.

The next sections of the book examined the most prevalent Orthodox interpretations of chrismation. My study summarizes the contributions of Nicholas Cabasilas, Nicholas Afanasiev, Alexander Schmemann, Boris Bobrinskoy, and Paul Evdokimov, while liberally drawing from John Chrysostom and Peter Galadza. This portion of the study attended to several important contributions. First, Orthodox theologians have interpreted chrismation as a crucial component belonging to a larger sequence of ritual actions in baptism. In each liturgical component, the Triune God acts, with the Spirit descending on the materials used (water, chrism, bread, and wine) and through them, creating communion between the participants and God. I suggested that this pneumatology discloses a liturgical trinitarian theology. Also, the repetitive action of God is modular: God continues to bless the Christian, over and over again, so she can draw from the divine energy to become holy in the divine image and likeness. Thus, the anointing with chrism contributes to *theosis*, a gradual process of acquiring the Spirit. This section also explored the Orthodox interpretation of chrismation as creating a baptismal priesthood of the laity, where the holy people of God exercises Christ's offices of king, priest, and prophet in, to, and for the life of the world. The development of this theology by Orthodox thinkers shares a strong parallel with the Roman Catholic adoption of this theology in documents of the Second Vatican Council. I concluded that this theology is ecumenical in nature.

The final chapter was written as a gift exchange between Orthodox and Roman Catholics. In this chapter, I summarized the problem of confirmation as a sacrament in search of a theology for Catholics. The chapter focuses on the theological issues of the place of confirmation in the sequence of sacraments, the question of age, and the meaning of the gift of the Holy Spirit. The actual sequence of sacraments in Catholic liturgy begins with the eucharistic chrism Mass, which asks God to create the chrism required for baptisms at the Easter Vigil. I attempted to resolve the question of the sequence of sacraments and the issues raised by the ascent of adolescent confirmation as the prevailing model by reconfiguring the order of sacraments and calling for the blessing of a fourth oil to anoint adolescents at the chrism Mass, which would restore the ancient Roman tradition of confirming infants. I also suggested that Catholic eucharistic theology has a formidable pneumatology, and that the frequency of eucharistic participation among Catholics reveals the Eucharist as the repeatable sacrament imparting the gift of the Spirit. I suggested that the Catholic practice of the annual chrism Mass celebrated as the diocesan model might be worthy of consideration by the Orthodox Church, which only consecrates chrism as it is needed. I also suggested that Catholics have seriously attended to the relationship between right faith and sacramental participation and offer models that could be instructive to Orthodox.

RECOMMENDATIONS FOR THE ORTHODOX PASTORAL PRACTICE OF ANOINTING WITH CHRISM

Academic works of liturgical theology are designed to inform, not reform, and the scholars leading the field of liturgical studies have traditionally allotted the task of reforming to Church hierarchy. The following initiatives for revising the Orthodox celebration of anointing with chrism are offered in this spirit; they are potential models for revision bishops might consider, given the liturgical evidence.

Celebrate an Annual Diocesan Consecration of Chrism

I offered this recommendation in chapter 4. The current Orthodox practice of consecrating chrism as needed on Holy Thursday privileges the Orthodox ecclesiological tenet of synodality, with the first hierarch having the authority to consecrate and then distribute to his brother bishops. The problem with this model is that it limits exposure to the original Eucharistic Liturgy where chrism is consecrated. If diocesan bishops consecrated chrism in their cathedrals every year, more people would be exposed to the context, text, and structures of the *lex orandi*. Adopting an annual model of consecrating chrism at the diocesan level would provide parish priests, deacons, and laity access to the innate liturgical theology underpinning the consecration of chrism. The residual effect would have the potential to introduce the purpose and power of chrism to a broader audience. Orthodox churches could preserve the synodal accent of this practice by having the first bishop of a synod consecrate chrism either bi-annually, or every fourth year. The new model would also provide one way to introduce the innate goodness of oil as an instrument of healing, covenant, and belonging to people in the parishes.

Integrate Baptism and Anointing with Chrism into the Sunday Assembly

The predominant time for celebrating baptism and chrismation in the Orthodox world is privately arranged between parents and the priest. Schmemann introduced a model for integrating baptism into the Eucharistic Assembly, but he recommended Saturday instead of Sunday, as Saturday would serve as a mimesis of the current position of the original Paschal Vigil, now the Vesperal Liturgy of Holy Saturday.[1] However, the Moscow Patriarchate both authorized and implemented a model for celebrating baptisms with the Eucharist on Sundays. As above, this model can introduce the liturgical theology of baptism and chrismation to more people when it is celebrated with the Eucharist on Sundays. The model also demonstrates the inner reciprocity of the three sacraments as an integrated whole, transcending their artificial divisions.

Create an Initiative for Revising the Rite of Receiving Converts

The current rites of receiving converts into the communion of the Orthodox Church have retained an antique nomenclature describing people who belong to another church body as heretics or schismatics. The liturgical texts also refer to their previous way of error, and often call upon converts to refute particular tenets they have held as heretical or erroneous. The language retains the weight of tragic ecclesial history by expressing a bitter sense of separation and promoting Orthodoxy as triumphant over other Christian groups. There is no doubt that some Orthodox bishops and priests hold this view and regard other Christians with disdain. However, many Orthodox have embraced the ecumenical movement and actively seek constructive ways to unify Christians into one eucharistic community. The current situation for ecumenical relations in Orthodoxy is mixed. Orthodox find themselves living in the same neighborhoods as other Christians and face the same pastoral challenges. While tensions between Orthodox and other Christians still exist in some places of the world, the Orthodox do not need to vivify the hyperbolic polemics infused into the language of the rites of conversion. Orthodox bishops should consider revising the

---

[1] Alexander Schmemann, *Of Water and the Spirit* (Crestwood, NY: St. Vladimir's Seminary Press, 1974), 169–70.

language of renunciations so that they do not present a harsh caricature of a particular Christian church or community. This proposed initiative would require Orthodox to adopt a more ecumenically sensitive approach in general, and concurrently develop a vocabulary that supports interfaith dialogue. One obvious consequence of revising the rite for receiving converts is to adopt a new vocabulary for receiving converts that acknowledges current ecclesial conditions. One example is to find a suitable replacement for "catechumen" when describing one who is preparing to enter the Orthodox Church, as "catechumen" really belongs to the provenance of baptism. The Roman term "candidate" aptly expresses the status of one preparing to enter the communion of the Orthodox Church.

Place the Need for Rituals Marking Rites of Passage on the Agendas of Synods

Creating a ritual that commemorates an important threshold of life is natural for communities and cultures. While baptism, marriage, and funerals all constitute threshold rites, contemporary culture celebrates occasions such as adolescence, graduation, wedding anniversaries, middle age, and retirement. In Orthodox ecclesial culture, the *molieben* has proven to be a reliable liturgical commemoration of all these events, as it is a readily adaptable liturgical rite that can offer multiple combinations of Scripture lessons and hymns expressing particular themes. Orthodox bishops should consider updating such liturgical commemorations with the use of appropriate symbols, and encouraging pastors to celebrate them. The growing popularity of the *quinceañera* and the rapid emergence of confirmation as a rite of passage for adolescents witness to the natural demand for liturgical rites commemorating central episodes in life. The inseparability of chrismation, baptism, and Eucharist does not allow for the adoption of anointing with chrism as a liturgy suitable for threshold rites such as those described above. Bishops should create initiatives calling for the study of appropriate threshold rites that commemorate life events. These hypothetical rites might be grounded by the theology of initiation, but should be distinct from the initiatory rites so as to prevent their dilution.

CHRISMATION AS *THEOSIS* AND IDENTITY FORMATION

Orthodox theology explains chrismation as the gift and seal of the Holy Spirit given to newly baptized people. In our review of the liturgical theology of chrismation and Orthodox explanations of its meaning, we have discovered a profound and multivalent meaning. It is ironic that the Vatican II reform of confirmation used the Byzantine Rite as its chief source. Catholic confirmation emphasizes the pneumatological aspect of chrismation and pastorally explains its meaning as receiving the gift of the Spirit imparted at Pentecost, with the assumption that the neophyte experienced Pascha at baptism. Orthodox theology has largely followed this theological trajectory, perhaps exemplified by Alexander Schmemann's definition of chrismation as imparting the gift of the Holy Spirit. The parallel between Catholic and Orthodox theology is strikingly close in explaining chrismation as imparting the Christic offices of king, priest, and prophet to the participant. These three offices, which Congar described as a trilogy, constitute the foundation of the baptismal priesthood of the laity. For Catholics, this trilogy belongs to magisterial theology and marks an important achievement of Vatican II, since the priesthood of the laity is now firmly rooted in baptismal sacramental theology. The laity's primary exercise of this priesthood is in and to the world, which distinguishes the lay priesthood from the ordained.

Contemporary Orthodox theologians have also underpinned the universal priesthood of the laity with baptism. The most vocal exponents of this theology, where chrismation is the sacrament imparting these Christic gifts to the laity, are Afanasiev, Schmemann, and Evdokimov. Like Catholics, this Christic ministry is exercised in and to the world, and as Schmemann famously said, for the life of the world. It is worth repeating that the retrieval of this theology of the lay priesthood from select patristic and liturgical texts of antiquity was a remarkable achievement of ecumenical *ressourcement*. The promotion of the laity's exercises of king, priest, and prophet, and the connection of these offices to baptism, is an instance of identity formation. Laypeople view themselves as formulating their daily activities in accordance with Christ's exercises of these offices. Christ is the exemplar for the exercising of the offices, and the laity is called to imitate his action.

The privileging of the trilogy for the lay priesthood does not exhaust the possibilities offered by the rites of initiation for models and metaphors of identity formation. The prayer for the consecration of chrism asks that God make those who are anointed with it holy and chosen people who keep Christ in their hearts and dwell with God. Cyril of Jerusalem interprets the rite of baptism as marking the people with several titles forming their identity, including Christs, Christians, Christ-bearers, paradises, and heavens, among others. John Chrysostom also offered multiple titles for the neophytes: holy, righteous, sons, inheritors, temples of the Spirit, and temples of Christ, among others. The rites and the fathers presented multiple titles connoting identity to the neophytes as a way of inscribing them into the divine narrative written by God. The biblical narratives offer numerous models for Christian men and women to adopt, as do the hagiographical narratives of the universal church. The trilogy of king, priest, and prophet will continue to enjoy hegemony in pastoral application, especially in the Roman Catholic communion, since it is now attached to magisterial teaching. Pastors should be encouraged, however, to offer new models exemplifying holiness to the laity in the spirit of Cyril of Jerusalem and John Chrysostom. Some laity might find it difficult to relate to the trilogy, given the attachment of the nomenclature to gender, specifically male versions of governance and priestly service. Society has evolved since the second half of the twentieth century, and the laity now engages a more complex and professionalized daily life with fewer clearly delineated gender roles. The mission of the laity remains the same, and each layperson can and should exercise the priestly ministry in, to, and for the world. The churches need to develop and promote a more diversified and fluid list of models exemplifying holiness that the laity can easily capture and adopt. I offer "saint" and "laic" as initial terms denoting the identities richly informed by chrismation.

The church should populate a rich list of models communicating identity formation to laity for the exercising of the baptismal priesthood. This list begins with the trilogy of king, priest, and prophet, and might include Cyril of Jerusalem's and John Chrysostom's lists as well. The point of the exercise is not necessarily to capture the exact language used by the venerable fourth-century mystagogues. Rather, the point is to capture their pastoral spirit of fluidity and employ their genius in developing a theological vocabulary that promotes a holy life that laity will find relevant and accessible in their current environments. This list should not be burdened by antiquated gender roles or functions.

In addition to developing a robust vocabulary of identity formation, the rites suggest that God acts to gradually form people into becoming holy people. Baptism inaugurates this gradual process and the Triune God acts repeatedly, imparting the gift of the Spirit who promotes the gifts that allow one to grow in God. Baptism and chrismation are sacraments that inaugurate *theosis*, and the Eucharist sustains it. The process of becoming like God has no measurable end; the sacraments demonstrate that the participants keep returning to God and receive spiritual blessings that empower them to bear Christ in their service in, to, and for the world. The rites and their genius interpretation by Cabasilas, Schmemann, and Bobrinskoy expose a pattern of trinitarian action. The Spirit descends upon the water in which the neophytes are baptized to join the community of God. The Spirit descends upon the oil with which the neophytes are anointed to make them one with Christ. The Spirit descends upon the bread and cup of which the neophytes partake to make them bearers of Christ and communicants of the Spirit. The pattern of divine activity is always trinitarian, communal, and covenantal. Bobrinskoy began a potential process of profound theological reflection by describing the neophytes as being consubstantial with God and consubstantial with the world through sacramental participation.

While Bobrinskoy referred to the specific ritual components of the blessing of waters, baptismal immersion, procession around the font, anointing with chrism, and Holy Communion as communicating a human encounter with the Triune God through material items, I would suggest that these examples can be more liberally applied to the rites of the church.[2] The pattern discloses a profound

[2] My idea is inspired in part by Msgr. Kevin Irwin's definition of sacramentality in "A Sacramental World—Sacramentality as the Primary Language for Sacraments," *Worship* 76 (2002): 97–111.

sacramentality of *theosis* in which the community encounters the Triune God through the material things of the world used in daily life. We can glean three important principles from this synthesis. First, although it has become customary to describe chrismation as a pneumatological sacrament, its pneumatology illuminates the activity of the three persons of the Trinity. The Spirit's descent manifests Christ and grants the participants access to God through Christ. Perhaps the greater purpose of the Spirit's work is to bring the community into God's presence in continuing the process of *theosis*. Second, the rites are modular in their repetition. God repeatedly blesses participants in initiation and continues to bless them as they participate in the Eucharistic Assembly. This repetition promotes a sense of gradual transformation. Christians are always in the process of acquiring the Spirit, working out their salvation, becoming like God, and growing in faith, and the sacraments provide the spiritual sustenance needed to nourish Christians through this journey. Third, the *theosis* experienced by Christians through the sacraments and other spiritual practices supports their exercise of baptismal priesthood in, to, and for the life of the world. It is only through regular contact with the life-giving God who imparts the gifts of the Spirit that Christians have the power to bear Christ to the world for its transfiguration. Christians can offer Christ in, to, and for the world only if they actually bear Christ, a privilege which one receives in the Eucharistic Assembly.

In addition to the conclusions I have drawn above, my examination of chrismation has yielded theological issues worthy of further exploration, a task outside of the scope of this study. I briefly outline these areas below to encourage readers to immerse themselves in these issues.

THE LITURGICAL USE OF OIL AND ITS MANIFOLD SYMBOLISM

One of the more intriguing trends I discovered in this study is the tendency for Christians and communities to be drawn to the practice of anointing with chrism as imparting multiple gifts and being suitable for numerous occasions. History shows us that the anointing with chrism became the preferred method for receiving other Christians in the Orthodox community because it completed baptism and healed theological deficiencies. In contemporary practice, those who have become Orthodox look upon chrismation as completing a process of journey to a new home, a rite not only of reception but also of entrance into parishes of people who share the same values and beliefs. Our examination also shows that the process accents the cognitive dimension, not only of learning facts, but of rehearsing the particular confessions of faith that form a key pillar in the community's foundation. The ecumenical gift exchange between Catholics and Orthodox yields a similar result, as adolescents graduate from a program of faith formation, and culminate the process with confirmation and the anointing with chrism. Thus, we have an interesting relational dynamic involving chrism, learning and rehearsing, and belonging. The notion of chrism correcting and perfecting orthodox faith is important, especially given its mystagogical roots in Cyril of Jerusalem, who interprets chrism as imparting true faith.

Our examination also showed that chrism is one of many oils used in the liturgy. There is some historical evidence suggesting that an anamnesis of the anointing of kings, priests, and prophets was included for the consecration of the oils for healing, in the Apostolic Tradition and in Aphraat's *Demonstrations*. The task of developing a potent sacramentality of chrismation occasions a renewed opportunity to explore how the oils of anointing the sick, catechumens, neophytes, Christians entering a new community, and adolescents relate to one another and communicate theology. On the surface, the corrective and healing properties of oil might point to a healthy theological anthropology, promoting the good health of a Christian in body, mind, soul, spirit, and emotion.

PASTORAL LITURGY AND RITES OF PASSAGE

Our elongated discussion of the development of adolescent confirmation as a preeminent model in the Roman Catholic communion has introduced us to the pastoral question surrounding rites of passage. In chapter 4, I recommended the restoration of infant confirmation as the prevailing model for Catholics while adding an anointing with oil blessed during the chrism Mass for adolescents.

Most Christians in the world celebrate sacraments that have endured development in complex interaction with politics, socioeconomic conditions, and other phenomena of the world. Liturgical history has provided precious contributions illustrating that the modern celebration of sacraments retains the inner core of its origins. The liturgical *ressourcement* movement retrieved crucial elements that served to illuminate the inner core, vivify liturgical celebration, and update the life of the church. That said, one might suggest that sacraments retain antiquated elements and interpretations. Life expectancy, parenting, learning, employment, technology, and living conditions (to name a few!) have significantly evolved since antiquity. Baptism and chrismation mark the entrance of a person into a new community and covenant. The church provides new clothing for the neophyte. In antiquity, the number of years one might expect to live after joining a eucharistic community would be considerably smaller than one would expect today. Communities also celebrate other life occasions as thresholds to new stages of community involvement or status: adolescence, high school and college graduation, retirements, and anniversaries are shared community events. Adolescence carries a special significance in modern Western culture, evidenced not only by the establishment of confirmation as the suitable liturgical rite marking this stage, but also by similar rites such as the *quinceañera* in Latino communities and *B'nai Mitzvah* in Jewish communities.[3] Paul Turner, *inter alia*, has challenged the claim that adolescent confirmation should not only remain the norm for adolescents but also become a repeatable sacrament.

I agree with Turner, but also believe that the church should seriously weigh the demands of its assembly. The most likely justification for the emergence of confirmation as the most suitable rite of passage for adolescence is that the assembly had no other rite that effectively communicated this reality. The question of how to ritualize rites of passage is problematic. For example, while the creation of the order for the blessing on the fifteenth birthday presents a beautiful theological model for young women, it is limited by gender. This is an issue demanding further careful research and deliberation, a pro-

---

[3] I am grateful to my graduate student, David Savage, who suggested the parallels shared by the three rites to me.

cess that must include a consultation of the existing liturgical tradition before inaugurating the process of creating new liturgies.

TOWARD AN ECUMENICAL PNEUMATOLOGY AND COMMUNION ECCLESIOLOGY

This study employs the method of liturgical theology and analyzes its results. The twentieth century witnessed a bold attempt to retrieve the shape and foundational theology of baptism in the patristic era. For Catholics, liturgical study shaped a reform of confirmation professing a strong pneumatology. Many Orthodox theologians turned to ancient liturgical and patristic texts in demonstrating how baptism and chrismation express *theosis* and create a lay priesthood exercising the trilogy of Christic offices. These endeavors were ecumenical, with theologians representing both churches interrogating their sources and scrutinizing the liturgical structures to show how God has empowered his people to represent him in this world. The endeavor punctuates the relevance of the sacraments of initiation.

In this study, I have attempted to carefully illustrate how the pneumatology of chrismation points to a twofold covenant with the Triune God and the church. My hypothesis that the anointing with chrism is a crucial component in a larger complex of rites is modular; God repeatedly bestows grace upon the Christian to equip her to live in accordance with both covenants. In serving God, the Christian serves the world, and in serving the world, she serves God. By implication, if not definition, this model suggests that communion ecclesiology contains the twofold covenant, and communion means living in community with fellow humans in the world and with the Triune God. The communion of the Holy Spirit received in baptism and chrismation and repeatedly received in the Eucharist is a communion of belonging. The Christian belongs to the Triune God and also to a faith community that worships God with particular confessions of faith. It is my conviction that this notion of belonging is intimate. It has the capacity to transform a world afflicted by polarization and deepening divisions between nations and classes of people. A theology of belonging rooted in baptism, chrismation, and Eucharist accentuates the realized eschatology of having the privilege of being a citizen of God's kingdom in the circumscribed conditions of contemporary life.

Despite the many steps taken toward the eucharistic reunion of the Catholic and Orthodox Churches, some theological obstacles have proven too formidable to overcome, at least for now. That said, when theologians of both traditions interrogate the same resources and espouse compatible variants of sacramental theology, the impact has the capacity to be similar: together, by God's grace, Catholics and Orthodox have the power to achieve Congar's goal and bring the world into the eschaton, the age to come of God's reign. I believe that elements of the pneumatology and communion ecclesiology I have initially proposed here are present in both traditions. These areas are fertile ground for a joint ecumenical research venture.

In the introduction to this book, I shared anecdotes of my experience in empty churches that communicated communal sacramental events filled with divine energy. These events spoke to the senses: the smell of incense, wax drippings, bread crumbs, spilled water, and icons communicated an encounter of God with his people. I drew upon an intangible, unquantifiable assertion as an invitation to take a closer look: you could feel the energy of what happened in the air. In the nonliturgical events that parallel sacramental celebration, we remember select moments of conversations with loved ones over a hot meal, the sound of laughter at a picnic; we feel the intensity of these moments after they have concluded. Sometimes we can express them, like humming the tune to a hymn sung in church earlier in the morning several hours after the fact. I suggested that even an imperfect symbol like an empty church has the power to communicate the divine-human encounter that occurred because the energy in the air unveils the mystery. It is my hope that the gift of the Holy Spirit given to those who are anointed with chrism—and imparting to them the twofold covenantal belonging to the communities of the Triune God and his people—will become more accessible and tangible to those who witness and experience these sacramental events. My goal was to unveil the mystery of chrismation and reveal it as a powerful sacrament of belonging capacitating the Christian to assume a holy identity in Christ in service in, to, and for the life of the world. I will let the reader decide.

Index

ablution, rite of, 43, 98, 100, 112
adolescence, xxxviii, 159, 171, 172, 194, 200
adolescent confirmation, xxxviii, 159–61, 166, 172, 177, 179, 191, 199, 200
Afanasiev, Nicholas, xxiv, xxxv, 90, 91, 96–102, 106–7, 112–14, 118, 124, 132, 138, 171, 183, 190, 195
affusion, 47
Ambrose of Milan, xxxi, 141, 142
anabathmoi, 114
anamnesis, 10–12, 32, 115, 123, 124, 125, 133, 199
anaphora, 6, 8, 22, 34, 103, 106, 174
Anastasis Typikon, 3
angels, xii, xviii, 7, 11, 13
anointing the sick, 124, 133, 167, 170, 199
anointing, postbaptismal, ix, xxi, xxiv, xxvi, xxx–xxxv, xxxvii, 2, 15, 24, 26–32, 34, 36, 39, 47, 50, 68–70, 87–88, 104–5, 116, 124, 133, 138, 140–43, 147–48, 150–54, 178, 189
anointing, prebaptismal, xxx, 16, 104, 108, 115–16, 137
anointing, presbyteral, 140–44, 147–48, 150, 152–53, 155, 178
anthropological maximalism, 103, 135
Antioch, xxx, xxxi, 3, 54, 115, 118, 136
Antiochian Archdiocese, 78–80, 99
Aphraat, 133, 199
Apostolic Constitution on the Sacrament of Confirmation, 145, 155
Apostolic Tradition, 79, 85, 97–98, 100, 124, 133, 141–42, 150, 155, 165, 199
Apostolicam Actuasitatem, 130–31

archangels, xii, 7, 11, 13
Arians, 42–44, 46, 65
Armenians, xxxi, 2, 5, 51, 52, 100, 183
Arranz, Miguel, xxiii, xxxi, 6–8, 10, 15–20, 23, 25–27, 29–30, 32, 37, 41, 43–44, 63
Austin, Gerard, xxxv, 158, 159, 179, 180, 187
azymes, 47

B'nai Mitzvah, 200
baptized Christians, ix, xxi, xxii, xxiv, 14, 17, 18, 23, 36, 37, 51, 52, 70, 73, 129, 134, 148, 149, 167, 169, 170
Barberini 336 (BAR), ix, xv, 2, 5, 6, 9, 11, 14–20, 23, 25–28, 30, 44–45, 47, 68
Basil the Great, xxvii, 22, 103, 106, 174
Belcher, Kimberly, 182
belonging, xii, xxvii, xxviii, xxxiv, xxxvi, 24, 32, 70, 74–76, 84, 86, 88, 89, 98, 106, 129, 134, 136, 148, 157, 169, 172, 182, 184, 185, 186, 190, 192, 194, 201–2
Bobrinskoy, Boris, iv, xxxiv, 36, 67, 90–92, 107–11, 114–18, 133, 138, 174, 190, 197
Body of Christ, xxvii, xxviii, xxxvi, xxxvii, 20, 33, 37, 54, 55, 67, 69, 70, 105, 108, 109, 111, 127, 129, 130, 131, 132, 135, 137, 157, 161, 163, 167, 169, 170, 171, 175
bowing (of heads), 9, 16, 62, 63, 65
Byzantine Catholics, 148
Byzantine Empire, 43
Byzantine Rite, vii, xi–xiii, xix, xxii, xxiii, xxvi, xxx, 1–2, 15, 19, 21, 30, 40, 41, 48, 63, 65, 91, 98, 109, 115,

203

123, 132, 150, 165, 166, 172–74, 177–79, 183, 185, 186, 189, 195

Cabasilas, Nicholas, iv, xxxiv, 36–37, 72–75, 87, 90–96, 113, 114, 116, 117, 133–35, 138, 186, 190, 197
Calivas, Alkiviadis, xxii, xxxii, 41–44, 47, 48, 50, 51, 54, 58, 87–89
Calvin, John, 126
Campus Crusade for Christ, 78
candidate, xxvii–xxix, xxxiv, 51, 53–58, 62, 68, 89, 149, 152, 158, 163, 164, 168, 169, 186, 187, 194
catechesis, 37, 39, 44, 70, 84, 89, 90, 141, 144, 148, 152, 160, 176, 177, 186, 188
catechumenate, xxxiv, 83, 85, 89
chrism Mass, ix, xxv, 125, 132, 140, 150, 157, 166, 167, 169, 170, 184, 188, 191, 192, 199
chrism, consecration of , ix, xxxi–xxxiii, 2–6, 8–11, 13–15, 21, 30–35, 38–39, 68, 109, 112, 113, 117, 123, 125, 132, 157, 165–67, 170, 181, 189, 192, 196
Christ-bearers, 136, 196
Christology, xxix, 43, 66, 67, 85, 108
citizens, 6, 11, 12, 31, 36, 38, 86, 89, 105, 119, 120, 122
cognitive dimension, xxxiv, 58, 83, 84, 87, 161, 190, 199
coinheritors, 119, 120, 122
Communion de Sainte-Esprit, 107–10
communion of saints, 55, 129, 139
communion of the Holy Spirit, xxvii, 22, 35, 117, 174, 188, 201
confession, xxi, xxvii, 16, 44, 46, 55, 57, 64, 67, 69, 85, 87–89, 121, 122
confession of faith, xxxiii, 54–57, 75, 76, 120, 145
confirmation, vii, ix, xx, xxiv–xxx, xxxv–xxxvi, 1, 2, 23, 24, 31, 32, 46, 47, 50, 56, 88, 128–31, 140–73, 176–85, 187–88, 191, 194, 195, 199, 200, 201
confirmation, of infants, 160–61, 178–79, 183, 188, 199
confirmation, reconfiguration of, xxxvi, 166, 171, 172, 184, 188
Congar, Yves, xxv, 67, 126–32, 138, 160, 163, 195, 202
Connell, Martin, 71–72
Constantinople, xxiii, 3–5, 27, 43, 44, 79
Constantinople, Council of, 23, 43
converts, vii, ix, xi, xxxii–xxxiv, 1, 23, 24, 33, 35, 36, 40–52, 54, 57–69, 72–78, 81–90, 171, 193, 194
converts, anointing of, 45, 55
converts, reception of, vii, ix, xi, xxxii–xxxiii, 1, 23, 33, 40–42, 44–46, 48, 50–52, 54, 57–65, 68, 69, 73, 74, 76, 82, 87, 88, 90
cosmology, 127, 131
cosmos, sanctification of, 109, 110, 130
covenant, xxix, 36, 39, 56–58, 63, 68–70, 72–76, 79, 84–89, 120, 121, 184, 190, 192, 197, 200–202
cross, xxi, 8, 23, 55–57, 104, 105, 121
Cyprian, 42
Cyril of Jerusalem, xxxi, 27, 37–39, 70–73, 75, 88, 90, 91, 136, 137, 185, 196, 199

Decentius of Gubbio, 141
deification, 22, 74, 103, 154
diskos, 6, 9
Divine Liturgy, xix, xxxii, 8, 9, 19, 22, 35, 64, 91, 174

ears, xvii, xxi, 23, 26, 52, 53, 62
Easter, 77, 163, 164, 172
Easter Vigil, xxii, 3, 166, 186, 191
Eastern Catholics, 46, 66
ecclesiology, xxv, 14, 66, 86, 90, 91, 96, 126, 127, 171, 182–84, 188, 201, 202
ecumenical, xxix–xxxi, xxxv, 48, 54, 55, 58, 75, 76, 85, 111, 118, 124, 126,

132, 138, 139, 144, 149, 166, 186–88, 191, 193–95, 199, 201, 202
Ecumenical Patriarchate, 4, 5, 79
ektene, 63, 65
epiclesis, 10–13, 31, 38, 70, 123
Erickson, John, xxxii, 23, 41–43, 46–48, 50, 67
Eucharist, ix, xvii–xix, xxii, xxvi–xxix, xxxi–xxxiii, xxxv–xxxvi, xxxviii, 1, 6, 9, 10, 17, 19, 21–23, 33–37, 44, 47–49, 54, 64, 66, 67, 70, 79, 88, 104, 107–9, 111, 114, 116, 117, 131, 136, 139, 140, 147, 150–54, 156–58, 161, 168, 169, 173, 175, 176, 178, 180, 188, 189, 191, 193, 194, 197, 201
eucharistic ecclesiology, 96, 171
Eucharistic Liturgy, xxi, xxii, xxiv, xxvi, 1–3, 5, 9, 16, 18, 19, 22, 30, 32, 34, 37, 43, 87, 151, 173–75, 178, 179, 192
euchologion, xv, xxi, 1, 3, 5, 6, 15, 16, 18, 20, 25, 26, 30, 63, 178
Evangelical Orthodox Church, xv, 78
Evdokimov, Paul, xxxiv, xxxv, 91, 111–14, 116, 118, 122, 124, 131, 132, 138, 190, 195
eyes, 23, 26, 52, 53, 62, 82, 117, 120, 121

feet, xvii, xxi, 26–28, 62
filioque, 47, 67, 85
First Communion, xxvii, 144, 147, 151, 153, 156, 178
first confession, xxvii, 54
Florence, Council of, 6, 47
forehead, xx, 23, 26, 27, 30, 50, 62
Fourth Crusade, 4
funerals, xi, 194

Galadza, Peter, xxiii, 27–28, 102, 114–16, 190
Gelasian sacramentary, 125, 132, 144, 162
Galatians 3:27, 18, 19, 23, 37
Gillquist, Peter, 77–82, 85

Gospel, xix, xxi, 8, 55–57, 112, 113, 130
graduation, xvii, 162, 194, 200
Great Book of Needs (GBN), iv, xv, xxxiii, 51, 52, 55, 57, 58, 62, 64, 67

Hagia Sophia, 3, 20
handlaying, ix, xxv, xxvi, xxvii, 52, 79, 97–101, 122, 140–43, 150–55, 157, 165, 168, 169, 183, 184, 188
handlaying, episcopal, 98, 144, 143, 146, 150, 154, 155, 165, 183, 184, 188
hands, ix, xxi, xxv, xxvii, 26–28, 52, 53, 62, 79, 97, 99, 100, 109, 122, 146, 152, 153, 155, 157, 168, 183
Hanks, Tom, 78
Hawk-Reinhard, Donna, xiii, xxx, xxxi, 70, 136
Herbel, Oliver, xxxiv, 78, 79, 81, 82, 84
Heretic, 23, 41, 42, 44, 89, 193
hierarchical liturgy, 114
Hilarion Alfayev, 135
Hippolytus of Rome, 97, 141
Holy Communion, xviii, xxvi–xxvii, 9, 22, 43, 45, 46, 66, 74, 122, 133, 138, 151, 161, 173, 175, 178, 197
Holy Spirit, communion of, xxvii, 22, 35, 117, 174, 188, 201
Holy Spirit, gift of, xxi, xxv, xxviii, xxxvi–xxxvii, 17, 23–29, 45, 62, 68, 89, 96, 100, 102, 103, 105, 108–10, 115, 135, 145, 146, 149, 150, 151, 160–65, 171–73, 180, 191, 195, 202
Holy Spirit, seal of, 24, 195
Holy Thursday, xiii, xxiv–xxvii, 2–9, 14, 30, 35, 157, 166, 167, 170, 184, 189, 192
Holy Trinity, xxi, 12–14, 43, 44, 56, 57, 67–69, 73, 108–10, 137, 145, 162, 174, 198

iconostasis, xix
identity formation, xxxi, xxxv, 70, 120, 122, 132, 136, 139, 195, 196, 197

205

infants, xxii, xxvi–xxviii, xxxvi, 64, 95, 135, 147, 148, 155, 164, 168, 176–82, 184, 191
inheritors, 119, 120, 122, 196
initiation, vii, ix, xiii, xxvi, xxvii, xxix–xxxi, xxxvi–xxxvii, 1–3, 5, 15, 17–19, 22, 24, 32–34, 37, 38, 40, 42, 45, 46, 56, 60–64, 69, 71–73, 88, 90–91, 93, 95, 98–108, 110, 111, 117, 118, 122, 124, 128, 130–32, 134–45, 151–61, 165–67, 169, 171, 173, 175, 176, 178, 181, 182, 188, 189, 194, 196, 198, 201
interiorized monasticism, 111–13
intermarriage of converts, 83, 86
Irenaeus of Lyons, 109, 181
Irwin, Kevin, 175, 197

Jerusalem, xxxi, 2, 3, 5, 27, 37–39, 54, 70, 75, 88, 90, 91, 100, 136, 185, 196, 199
Johannine community, 71
John Chrysostom, xxvii, xxxi, 22, 91, 115, 118–22, 136, 137, 174, 190, 196
John of Damascus, xxii
Johnson, Maxwell, xxx, xxxi, xxxv, 42, 90, 91, 100, 124, 125, 141–44, 148, 151, 155, 156, 158, 162, 165, 166, 187

Kavanagh, Aidan, xxxv, 90, 141, 147, 153, 187
king, xxv, xxix, xxxv, 6, 7, 11, 12, 20, 59, 61, 65, 72, 91, 96, 98–100, 102–7, 112–16, 118, 119, 121–33, 135–39, 154, 181, 191, 195, 196, 199
Kingdom of God, 28, 29, 103, 105, 109, 113, 130
Klentos, John, xxxii, 41–46, 48
Kyiv, 46
Kyivan Patriarchate, xv, 49

L'Huillier, Peter, xxxii, 41, 47
Laics, 97–101, 107

Lampe, G., 23, 24
Laodicea, Council of, 3
lay apostolate, xxxv, 130, 131, 163
libellus, 43, 44, 88
litanic biddings, 16, 17, 20
Lumen Gentium, 129, 130, 162, 163
Lutherans, 55, 66

Macarius of Egypt, 112, 118
Macarius of Jerusalem, xxxi, 2, 5, 100, 183
Macedonians, 43, 44, 65
martyrs, 124, 125, 181
Mass, ix, xxv, 79, 125, 140, 145, 150, 157, 166, 167, 169, 170, 173, 175, 176, 184, 188, 191, 192, 199
Mateos, Juan, xv, xxiii, 4, 20
maturity, xxviii, xxxvi, 95, 144, 158–61, 177, 179
maturity, sacrament of, xxviii, 144, 148
Menevisoglou, Pavlos, 4
Methodists, 66
Metropolitan Phillip, 79–81
Meyendorff, Paul, 62, 67–69, 133, 171
Michel, Virgil, 128
middle age, 194
Miles, Sara, 76–77
Missiology, 184
Mohyla, Peter, 46, 47, 60, 62
molieben, 172, 194
moment of consecration, 115, 165, 172
monasticism, 111–13
Monophysites, 43, 46, 66
Morozowich, Mark, xiii, xxxi, 3, 4, 6, 7, 178
Moscow Patriarchate, 46, 49, 50, 193
Moses, 6, 11, 12, 31
mouth, 23
Myron, 2, 6, 7, 11, 12, 13, 44, 45, 70, 71
Mystagogical Catecheses, 27, 136, 185

neophyte, xx–xxv, 12–14, 16–19, 21, 22, 28, 31–33, 35–39, 63, 70–72, 92–95, 97–99, 102–5, 116–19, 122–25,

128, 131, 136, 138, 140, 151–54, 157, 158, 165, 168, 175, 176, 190, 195, 196, 197, 199, 200
Nestorians, 43, 46, 65
New Covenant Apostolic Order, 79
New Testament, 6, 11, 14, 23, 24, 72, 78, 79, 132, 145, 146, 157
Newman, John Henry, 126, 132
Nicene-Constantinopolitan Creed, 54, 57, 67, 175
Nikodemus the Hagiorite, 42
North American Academy of Liturgy, xiii, xv, 176
nose, xx, 23, 27

Of Water and the Spirit, xxv, 101, 102, 118, 193
oil, ix, xxv, xxxv, 2, 3, 6, 8–12, 14, 16, 33, 38, 68, 69, 70, 74, 98, 100, 104, 106, 108, 110, 121, 124, 125, 132, 133, 140, 150, 157, 167–72, 177, 188, 191, 192, 197, 198, 199
oil of holiness, 2, 100
ordained priesthood, 126, 130, 168
ordination, 50, 78–80, 97–101, 107, 112, 118, 138, 157, 167, 168, 170
Origen, 112
original sin, 178
Orthodox Church, xi, xii, xv, xxi, xxii, xxv, xxxii, xxxiii, xxxiv, xxxvi, 1, 5, 8, 40–42, 46, 47, 49–55, 58, 60, 64–66, 68–69, 74–76, 78–89, 112, 113, 135, 183, 186, 187, 190, 192, 193, 194, 202
Orthodoxy, xxi, xxii, xxix, xxxii, xxxiii, 35, 41, 46–50, 65–67, 69, 74, 77, 78, 80, 82–86, 101, 135, 171, 184, 190, 193
Orthros, 173

pageantry, 7, 8, 30, 34
papal infallibility, 58
Pascha (feast of), xxiv
Paschal Vigil, xxii, 2, 14, 19, 20, 70, 193

Patriarch Cyril V, 42
Patriarch Filaret, 49
Pelikan, Jaroslav, xii, 78
penance, 147, 153, 172, 178
Pentecost, 59, 93, 100, 102, 114, 145, 146, 162–64, 172, 173, 175, 195
photizomenoi, 136
pneumatology, xxix, 33, 108, 114, 140, 145, 146, 162, 172, 175, 176, 181, 188, 191, 198, 201, 202
Polamalu, Troy, 78
pope, 67, 145
Pope Innocent, 141
Pope Paul VI, 145
Pope Pius X, 156
priest, xxv, xxix, xxxv, 1, 3, 6–8, 11–14, 17, 23, 31, 35, 47, 50, 62, 72, 80, 91, 96–103, 105–7, 111–16, 118–20, 122–33, 135–39, 152–54, 157, 168–70, 181, 191–93, 195, 196
priesthood, universal, xxxv, 111, 113, 116, 118, 131, 138, 195
prokeimenon, 19
prophet, xxv, xxix, xxxv, 6, 11, 12, 91, 102, 103, 106, 107, 112, 113, 115, 116, 118, 119, 122–33, 135–39, 154, 181, 191, 195, 196, 199
Protestants, 46, 112, 144
Psalm 31, xxi, 16–19, 21, 38, 56
Psalm 66, 55, 56, 57
Purgatory, 55
Purves, James, 181

Quam Singulari, 151
quinceanera, 194, 200
Quinn, Frank, 141, 142, 151

Rahner, Karl, 160
RCIA, 148, 152, 170, 180, 185
rebaptism, 42, 43, 44, 47, 49, 50, 68, 88
reconciliation, 47, 69, 172
Reformed Christians, 55, 67
Religious education, 150, 170, 172, 178, 179, 180, 185

207

renunciation, xxi, xxxiii, 16, 44, 48, 51, 53–55, 57, 58, 65, 67, 69, 85, 87, 89, 121, 122, 145, 194
ressourcement, xxiii, xxv, 90, 124, 127, 129, 131, 132, 138, 195, 200
retirement, 194, 200
righteous, 119, 120, 122, 136, 196
Riley, Hugh, xxx, xxxi
rite of passage, xxviii, 34, 144, 148, 156, 161, 166, 170, 171, 172, 194, 200
ritualization, 89
Roman Empire, 157
Roman Rituale, 144
Romans 6:3-11, xxi
Rome, Bishop of, 54, 67
royal priesthood, 7, 11, 13, 14, 31, 98, 123, 126, 130

Sabellians, 42
Sacred Congregation for the Sacraments, 151
Sacrosanctum Concilium, 145
Samuel, 6, 11, 12, 31
sanctification, 4, 6, 7, 11–14, 19, 20, 28–31, 61, 69, 109, 110, 123, 130, 190
Schaeffer, Frankie, 78
schismatic, 49, 89, 193
Schmemann, Alexander, xxiii, xxv, xxxiv, 22, 73–75, 87, 90, 91, 96, 98, 101–7, 111, 112, 114, 116–19, 122, 124, 131–33, 135, 138, 173, 190, 193, 195, 197
SCOBA, xv, 48, 49
seal (of the gift of the Holy Spirit), xxi, 1, 17, 20, 21, 23–27, 45, 61, 62, 68, 109, 146, 162, 195
Searle Mark, 181, 182
Seasoltz, Kevin, 161
Serra, Dominic, xiii, 142, 143, 154, 156
Slagle, Amy, xxxiv, 81–85
sola scriptura, 58
spiritual combat, 158
spiritual marketplace, xxxiv, 81–83, 85

St. Sergius Theological Institute in Paris, 96
synapte, 16, 17, 18, 174
synodality, 35, 184, 192

Taft, Robert, 27, 91, 166, 174
Tavener, John, 78
teaching, xvii, xxxv, 37, 53, 54, 57, 58, 70, 71, 72, 80, 87, 88, 89, 97, 106, 128, 130, 131, 148, 162, 163, 196
temples, of Christ, 122, 196
temples, of the Spirit, 74, 122, 196
Terian, Abraham, xxxi, 2, 5, 100
textualization, 25, 27, 30
The Life in Christ, iv, 36, 37, 72, 91, 92, 135, 186
theological anthropology, xxv, 14, 92, 103–7, 111, 113, 131, 132, 135, 138, 199
theosis, xxix, xxxvi, 14, 22, 36–38, 73, 74, 91, 93, 103, 105, 116, 128, 154, 185, 191, 195, 197, 198, 201
threshold rites, 194
tonsure, 63, 99, 112
trilogy, xxxv, 126, 132, 133, 195, 196, 201
Trisagion, xvii, 18
Triune God, xxvii–xxix, xxxv, 14, 22, 33, 34, 36–39, 87, 89, 91, 103, 116, 117, 122, 128, 129, 138, 166, 181, 182, 189, 190, 191, 197, 198, 201, 202
Trullo, Council of, 68
Turner, Paul, xxiv, xxvi, xxxv, xxxvi, 2, 141, 147–149, 150, 159, 160, 168, 172, 173, 186, 187, 200
Typikon of the Great Church, xv, 3, 20

Ukrainian Orthodox, xv, xvii, 49

Vatican II, 130, 145, 151–53, 155, 162, 163, 195
Vesperal Liturgy of Holy Saturday, xxii, xxiii

Vespers, 173

Walsh, Liam, xxxvi, 151, 155, 156, 173
Ward, Graham, xxix
water immersion, xx, 18, 43, 47, 56, 108, 109, 110, 116, 122, 133, 137, 197
Webber, Meletios, 74, 75, 88
wedding anniversaries, 172, 194
Winkler, Gabriele, xxx, 27

Woodcock, Eldon, 24
World, xxi, xxxi, xxxiii, xxxv–xxxvii, 7, 18, 41–43, 47, 49, 63, 75, 82, 98, 101–4, 106, 109–14, 117, 118, 121, 127–32, 134, 136, 138, 139, 163, 172, 173, 175, 185, 190, 191, 193, 195–98, 200–202

Zapivka, xviii
Zeon, 174